SPACE PLANNING

BASICS

SPACE PLANNING BASICS

Mark Karlen

Illustrations by Kate Ruggeri and Mark Karlen

Building shell drawings CAD generated by Peter Hahn

JOHN WILEY & SONS, INC.

New York Chichester Weinheim Brisbane Singapore Toronto

98   99   10   9   8   7

Library of Congress Cataloging-in-Publication Data

Karlen, Mark.
    Space planning basics / by Mark Karlen.
        p.   cm.
    Includes bibliographical references and index.
    ISBN 0-471-28459-9
    1. Interior architecture.   2. Space (Architecture).   I. Title.
    NA2765.K37   1992
    729—dc20   92-14425
                                                                              CIP

CONTENTS

Preface

Over the past dozen years of consistent involvement in delivering ASID's S.T.E.P. Workshops in the mid-west and on the east coast, I have worked with many hundreds of interior designers preparing to take the NCIDQ exam. In this process, I have been regularly made aware of the relative lack of space planning skills which so many of those younger designers bring to the practicum portions of the exam. Not only was skill lacking, but an organized approach or methodology was equally absent. The participants in those workshops have come from every region of the country, and although I've never made an accurate survey of the demographics, my observations concerning space planning skills seem to have no geographic limits.

My own classroom teaching experiences over the past twenty-plus years have given me some understanding of the complexities in successfully imparting the knowledge and skills required for the practical and aesthetic manipulation of a building's interior space. It certainly requires more than a few lectures coupled with a few exercises. And to this date, an adequate textbook to aid in the process has not been available.

This writing task had its origins about four years ago when Diana Gabriel, then ASID's Director of Education, suggested that I work with the MGI Management Institute in preparing an at-home study course in space planning specifically geared to helping young designers prepare for the NCIDQ exam. With the encouragement and editing expertise of Dr. Henry Oppenheimer, MGI's president, that course was published in 1989, and has since been taken by many hundreds of designers.

The challenge to produce a valuable aid for teaching space planning in the classroom became obvious after an extensive survey of existing written material was made during the development of the MGI course. Despite all of the traditional traumas involved in writing any book, the process in producing this volume has been satisfying and rewarding. The help of many others has been invaluable. The anonymous reviewers (whoever you are), brought to their task by the publisher, have my deep appreciation for their insights, both general and specific. Professor Wendy Beckwith at LaRoche College has brought an essential ingredient to the process with a known and experienced educator's perspective. Kate Ruggeri's skill and patience in producing many of the book's illustrations demand special appreciation. Peter Hahn's expertise in CADD was essential in producing the building shell drawings for the book's space planning exercises. Robin Tama and Ladonna Motyka generously provided their skills in preparing floor plans to demonstrate presentation techniques. The advice of many professionals was sought throughout the process, with particular concern for the programming process; in this regard, Richard Henkels and Robin Tama of Diversified Interior Design and Irene Pujol of Ewing Cole Cherry Parsky brought this specific expertise. A special thanks goes to Cookie and Ed Kelly for the use of their Arden, Delaware home and garden, where most of this volume was written. Amanda Miller, Van Nostrand Reinhold's editor for this project, was the antithesis of the traditional demanding ogre, and is the recipient of my deepest appreciation for making this such a pleasurable process. Finally, and mostly, to my wife Carmela, love and appreciation for unending support and patience throughout the entire experience.

To the degree that this book is of help to students and teachers involved in the development of space planning knowledge and skills, the reward for my efforts will be realized.

Mark Karlen

Introduction

This book is an instructional tool designed to develop interior space planning skills for typical building uses in spaces up to 4,000 square feet in size. Although this book may be used by an individual learner, it is geared for use in a conventional studio classroom setting. Its contents are three-fold:

1. explanatory text
2. descriptive graphic examples
3. recommended practice exercises

Space planning is an inherently complex process. For this reason, a series of planning exercises, starting with very small spaces and building to larger spaces with more complex program requirements, are provided as the primary technique in the development of space planning skills. In addition, basic information about space planning, the use of planning rules-of-thumb, guidelines for appropriate drawing techniques, and recommended reading and reference sources are included.

As an introduction to space planning, this book is primarily directed to intermediate level (sophomore and junior levels in a baccalaureate or first-professional-degree program) interior design students. To be more specific, it is assumed that its users possess adequate drafting skills (defined here as basic experience with drafting tools and architectural scales) and ease in understanding and preparing orthographic projections (plans and elevations). In addition, users are expected to be competent in planning conventional furniture arrangements within fixed rooms, not including large scale arrangements of office systems furniture, a basic space planning process in itself. Ideally, some background in design program development has been previously gained, but that is not necessary for a successful learning experience. Background in the planning of undivided or ''raw'' space is not required. Although specific direction to prepare for the National Council for Interior Design Qualification (NCIDQ) examination is not an intended purpose here, the basic space planning skills learned are applicable to the practicum portions of that exam.

Space planning is not a simple process involving a single category of information; rather, it is a complex dovetailing of several processes involving knowledge in many categories of information related to the organization and construction of buildings. Such processes range from program analysis and use of building code principles to environmental control techniques and the development of desired spatial qualities. Even with space planning problems of relatively small size (a few thousand square feet) and relatively simple programmatic requirements, it is impossible to completely avoid these complexities of process and information. For this reason, these complexities will be dealt with in enough depth to provide a realistic context for design problems, while maintaining focus on the central issues of space planning. Over a long time, the experienced space planner will gain an in-depth knowledge of all these complexities, but it would be counterproductive to attempt to deal with them here except in the simplest manner.

The great majority of professional space planning work lies within existing structures, rather than in the interior planning of new buildings still on the drawing board. For this reason, the great emphasis in this book is on spaces within existing structures. Interior space planning for buildings still on the drawing board is an endeavor that requires some experience in the design of structures and building shells, and therefore requires additional knowledge and skill on the part of the space planner. Those additional areas of professional involvement lie beyond the intent of this text and will be discussed in a general manner in Chapter Eight.

Finally, this textbook is meant not only to be read, but also to be worked with as a hands-on guide in the development of a creative skill. Space planning skills grow from consistently repeated practice and experience; consequently, learners are encouraged to apply sufficient hours of concentrated effort at the drawing board to gain professional quality technique. The quality of space planning solutions, particularly at the beginning of one's experience, are difficult to assess. Unlike some other forms of problem solving, space planning problems usually have many "right" answers. Rarely are there "perfect" answers. Space planning solutions involve satisfying program criteria on a priority basis where the issues at the top of the list must be solved, but where some of the issues near the bottom might only be partially solved, if at all. In its simplest terms, space planning almost always involves compromises, when one looks for "good" and "workable" solutions rather than "correct" or "perfect" solutions. Identifying and satisfying high priority or major planning criteria are part of the learning experience presented here; but the best tools to assess quality in space planning solutions are personal exchange and critique with others. Classroom discussions, both formal and informal, are of great value. Seeking out the opinion of fellow students, as well as offering criticism of others' work, will help immeasurably to develop strong critical skills. Taking advantage of classroom "pin-ups" and critiques, particularly with the expert view of the classroom teacher available (and possibly those of a guest critic), is essential in this growth process. In time, as consistent evaluation of one's own work and the work of others continues, skills in criticism improve, and one becomes a better judge of his/her own work. Despite this, at every level of professional growth, value exists in seeing another approach and in hearing objective criticism.

The step-by-step process of space planning described in this text is deliberately geared to the learning of a complex skill. It should be understood that many worthwhile and productive planning processes are used by professionals in the field; one process is not superior to the others. This is true because of the creative element involved in space planning. As one's skills grow beyond the learner's level, it is assumed that each designer will develop variations in the planning process geared to their individual thinking patterns, and they will ultimately create a complete and personalized design methodology.

Note should be made of the issue of terminology. This text contains many words and phrases that must be considered as professional jargon; they are unavoidable. They are also not universal in their use. Words and phrases such as "criteria matrix," "prototypical plan sketches," "relationship diagram," "bubble diagram," "block plan," "barrier-free," "suite," "rough floor plan," "speculative office building," etc., are used by some professionals and not by others. The use of the same word or phrase may convey varying connotations. Do not allow this lack of universality in terminology to become a stumbling block in the learning process presented here.

As your space planning skills grow and achieve professional quality, you will probably find that these new elements in your repertoire also sensitize and sharpen other related design skills and bring you several steps closer to the status of the "compleat" professional.

Recommended Reading

The bibliography at the end of this book is kept brief. It is worth taking a few minutes to read the introductory paragraphs to that list of books. The Recommended Reading that relates to this introduction has been selected for its introductory qualities. The following numbers refer to books listed in the bibliography.

6*, 7*, 12*, 14*, 22*, 27, 31

Books noted with an asterisk are also included in the Recommended Reading of other chapters.

SPACE PLANNING
BASICS

Chapter 1 PLANNING METHODOLOGY

The space planning process begins when a person, or group of people, decide to put a building, or a portion of a building, to a new and practical use, running the gamut from small residential or work spaces to vast, complex business and institutional facilities. Except in the simplest space, a small apartment or office, making efficient and functionally satisfying use of space is a complex task that is far beyond the capabilities of most building users; this is when and why the space planning specialist, interior designer or architect, is called in to solve the problem.

Space planners are presented with their task in a great variety of ways. Most users or clients are inexperienced in working with planning professionals and present their space planning problems without significantly prepared data. It is not uncommon for a business owner or manager to come to an interior designer and say, in effect: ''Our staff has grown by 60 percent over the past few years; our space is terribly overcrowded; we are still growing at a very fast rate; what should we do?'' In cases of

this kind, the designer must begin with the basic tasks of charting organizational structure; identifying personnel, their tasks, and necessary equipment; analyzing the operational process; and gaining an understanding of the human and cultural qualities of the organization. In effect, the planning professional must take on the full responsibility for organizing, analyzing, and interpreting the problem at hand.

At the other extreme, with clients who have had considerable experience in planning their spaces and may have an in-house facilities manager or staff, the designer or architect may be presented with a bound volume of extensive data on the number and types of personnel (including their equipment and square footage needs), required spatial adjacency studies, and the desired human and esthetic qualities of the completed project— in effect, a complete space planning program. In such cases, the planning professional is relieved of the responsibility of data gathering and organizing and analyzing it. Obviously, the design problem or program that is presented must be fully absorbed and understood by the designer, and some tasks of program interpretation may need to be performed. These issues will be discussed later in this chapter.

A full range of client/program situations between the two extremes has been presented above. Most clients have given some thoughtful consideration and analysis to their spatial needs before engaging professional services, but do not have the in-house expertise to make a complete analysis of their problem and present it in terms easily translated into a planning solution. It is this middle ground into which most professionals step when presented with a space planning problem.

Regardless of the experience in working with planning professionals that a client brings to the relationship, the issues of design sensitivity and insight play a major role in their discussions. Some space planning programs that are prepared by in-house facilities management personnel deal only with hard data and are of little use in understanding the subtleties of organizational dynamics or the detailed requirements of lighting or acoustics. What at first glance may appear to be a complete and professional program may still require a great deal of organization, analysis, and interpretation on the part of the designer. Conversely, some clients who are completely inexperienced in space planning matters will bring invaluable design sensitivity and insight to the project, despite their lack of categorized data.

It is very difficult to simulate real client/program situations in the classroom. Typically, students are presented a written program that defines all of the detailed requirements of a project, along with floor plans (and possibly additional drawings) of a real or imagined space. A space planning solution is drawn from this data. Though good and useful for the student's learning process, these exercises lack the dynamics of personal interchange with a client, ignoring as well such real problems as internal conflicts in the client's organization, changes in management personnel, budget constraints, dealings with building code administrators—all of which exist in actual practice situations. Bringing real or role-playing clients to classroom assignments can be helpful, just as planning within actual spaces students can walk into and survey has value in making the space planning problem realistic. Despite these devices that simulate reality, students should be aware that the idiosyncrasies created when dealing with a broad variety of personalities, unusual time frames (from projects with tight deadlines to those that extend over years), and stringent budget requirements will create added and challenging elements to the space planning process when they move from the classroom to the professional setting.

DEFINING TERMS AND INTENT

The title of this chapter, "Planning Methodology," is a phrase used throughout this text to describe the phase of the space planning process that begins when the planning problem is presented to the planner (with or without a program) and ends when physical planning commences, usually with bubble diagrams or block plans. In some professional circles, this is called the pre-design process—meaning all of those necessary steps of data gathering, research, analysis, and interpretation before actual planning. For many in the design fields, "planning methodology" and "programming" are synonymous, although some would argue that the charting and diagramming described here as part of planning methodology fall outside the bounds of programming.

A great deal has been written about the general area of planning methodology. Books and articles are available about the interview process, questionnaires, observation techniques, idea generation, spatial analysis and theory, programming, design methods, problem solving, graphic thinking, etc. As noted in the Introduction, a unified terminology universally used or accepted by professionals in the field does not exist. Despite this lack, if one will read comprehensively in this subject area, a body of knowledge exists that provides a broad variety of useful approaches to the pre-design process.

Very little has been written about space planning techniques, particularly from an instructional viewpoint. Space planning skills have generally been learned in a mentorship mode, at the drawing board, in the studio classroom and/or the professional office drafting room. The primary intent of this book is to provide a written foundation for the space planning process. Although a planning methodology is described and recommended here, it is dealt with in a concise manner, to give full attention to the more allusive, drawing-board-related parts of the process. This should not be construed as a decrease in the value of the pre-design process; to the contrary, good space planning cannot be accomplished without the professionally thorough pre-design analysis generally defined here. A simple and workable method will be concisely described and recommended in order to move on quickly to the physical planning phase. Students are strongly encouraged to read about and acquire skills in a broad range of pre-design techniques, both verbal and graphic, in order to gain many analytical tools to apply to the problem solving challenges they will ultimately face as professionals. The recommended reading at the end of this chapter provides direction for expanding that knowledge and those skills.

Another brief note on terminology. Several steps in the space planning process described and recommended throughout the text are identified by words or phrases unique to the text, such as *Criteria Matrix* and *Relationship Diagram*. In each case, these words or phrases will be described and defined thoroughly, and potential conflicts with other terminology common to the field will be identified.

THE SYNTHESIS GAP

Among professionals working in the field, a generally accepted process or sequence of tasks occurs from the point at which the planner begins to work on a project, to the point at which project analysis is complete and the physical planning process begins. Despite many variations in technique or terminology that planners may apply, that basic process consists of the following steps:

1. Interviews
a. executive level (organizational overview)
b. managerial level (departmental function)
c. operational level (process and equipment detail)

2. Observation (of existing or similar facilities)
a. assisted observation
b. unobtrusive observation
c. inventory of existing furniture and equipment
   (when it is to be reused)

3. Establish architectural parameters
a. acquire complete base plan data
   (including mechanical and electrical services)
b. compile contextual data
   (architectural, historic, social)
c. research code constraints

4. Organize collected data (the *First Phase Program*)
a. place data in sequential format most useful for planning
b. summarize confirmed quantitative factors
   (square footage, FF + E count, equipment sizes, etc.)
c. record first thoughts on conceptual planning approach

5. Research the unknowns
a. gather detailed information on process and equipment
b. gather "case study" information on similar facilities
c. integrate researched data with First Phase program

6. Analyze the data
a. discover planning affinities (working interrelationships, public/private zoning, special acoustic needs, etc.)
b. discover scheduling affinities (maximize use of space)
c. identify planning/architectural relationships
   (site, structural, mechanical, and electrical conditions)

7. Interpret and diagram the data (the *Complete Program*)
a. define the functional problems in planning terms
b. establish a basic conceptual approach
   (in terms of human/social and image/esthetics objectives)
c. prepare relationship or adjacency diagrams
   (for client and designer visualization)

8. Summarize the data (the *Finished Document*)
a. finalize project concepts—STATE THE PROBLEM
b. outline and tally basic budget issues
c. prepare a package for client approval *and* to serve as the designer's manual for space planning

The analytical process described above will never produce a space planning solution. Regardless of how thorough the process may be, analysis must be put aside, and a synthesis process begun, to create a physical solution. That synthesis requires a creative understanding of all elements of the analysis, to place the programmatic elements in a physical juxtaposition that will satisfy the users' needs. The word "creative," in this context, must be seen in its broadest sense, in which functional, esthetic, and technical issues must be addressed and resolved. The heart of the problem solving task in space planning occurs in making the transition from the analytical, pre-design phase of the project to the creative, design solution phase.

The entire design process is one of synthesis, in which many disparate factors are integrated into a useful whole; but the initial mental or creative "leap" from the analytical phase to recording or drawing on paper the first physical solution is the most difficult single step in the process. If the pre-design process is very thorough, it may bring the planner several steps closer to a physical solution, or may make the creative "leap" a shorter, easier one. For the purposes of this text, the void between the completed design program and the planning solution will be referred to as the "*Synthesis Gap*," and it might best be visualized graphically:

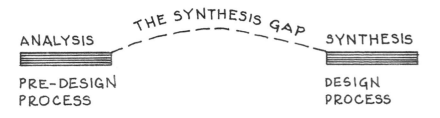

If the pre-design process has been skimpy or inadequate, the Synthesis Gap will be wider and more difficult to manage:

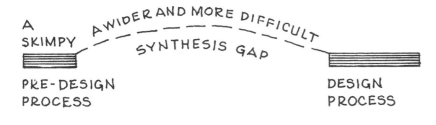

If the pre-design process has been thorough and insightful, the Synthesis Gap will be narrower and easier to manage:

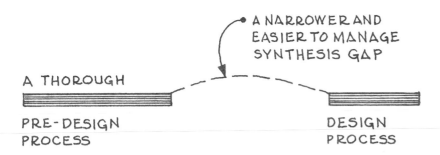

From a practical, professional setting viewpoint, the planner needs an efficient and reliable process to turn to each time a space planning project is encountered. Gathering a few basic facts and then staring at a blank floor plan waiting for inspiration to strike is an utterly impractical approach. A well-established design methodology is needed to meet the typical time pressures of the profession and to solve space planning problems in a manner that fully satisfies the needs of the client and user.

When space planning problems become both large in scale and complex in function, solutions become illusive or less obvious and the problem solving process can feel intimidating. A basic principle, fundamental to all design methodologies and helpful to remember when projects loom too large and difficult, is: Break down problems to their smallest and most manageable elements. Rather than be confronted by a maze of complex and seemingly unrelated factors, take the problem apart and reassemble it. View the elements as smaller, more controllable components, and then reorganize them in a sequence or in groupings that relate to the space planning problem. This is all part of the process to narrow the Synthesis Gap.

THE DESIGN PROGRAM

In space planning terms, design programs are written documents that qualify and quantify the client / user needs for a given project. In addition, most programs are accompanied by adjacency or relationship diagrams that often express physical planning relationships more articulately than verbal descriptions. While the basic skills required to prepare a program are not unusual or complex, do not expect to be able to prepare a professional quality program in the first attempts. After repeated experience, the skills required for interviewing, observation, research, analysis, and documentation become well honed, and one is then prepared to accomplish the real goal of programming—setting the stage for the planning and design process.

Interviews
When planning projects are small and groups are tightly managed, it may only be necessary to interview one person: a proprietor, manager, or director. As projects increase in size and/or complexity, the number of people who must be interviewed increases correspondingly. Size and complexity are quite different issues. Even though projects may be small in size, it would be unusual to plan a typical residential renovation without

interviewing both wife and husband, or both partners of a small law firm when planning new office facilities for the firm. When size or complexity demand interviewing several people, selecting the most appropriate people for those interviews is a skill unto itself. That selection is often dictated by the client and not left up to the designer's discretion.

It is essential that the interviewer be prepared with an organized and consistent set of questions—"winging it" just doesn't work. Generally, it is advisable to give the set of questions to the interviewees in advance of the interview, to better prepare them to respond in an organized manner, and (when employees are involved) to lessen their chance of approaching the interview session with apprehension or anxiety. Rather than use a recording device, most experienced planners take interview notes, because tape recorders can be an intimidating intrusion on the easy rapport desired between programmer and interviewee. Except to gather dimensional and other quantitative data, questionnaires are not in widespread use; personal exchange is necessary to get beyond the superficial issues and to uncover the subtleties of space planning requirements. A great deal of informational and instructional literature exists concerning the acquiring and developing of interview skills valuable in approaching the interviewing task from a knowledgeable and professional perspective.

Observation
Observing existing facilities to see and understand operational and/or equipment related processes is often an integral part of the interview process. Typically, a manager, senior partner, or department head will take the interviewer on a tour of the entire facility, or a portion of the facility for which they are responsible. In many cases, this kind of guided walk-through is adequate to the situation. But particularly when complex interpersonal relationships are involved, a walk-through may not be adequate. The fact that people act differently from the norm when they know that they are being observed is well known. Some special situations warrant the use of unobtrusive observation, in which the observer is not seen, or at least not noticed—the proverbial "fly on the wall." While the instructive literature concerning this observational technique is limited, enough exists to direct the learner in acquiring appropriate skills.

It is not unusual to plan a project in which a facility or operation for observation does not exist. In this case, it is advisable to visit and observe facilities having similar functions or operations. Even if the facility being planned does not involve unusual processes, as might be the case in a conventional business or legal firm, unless one is especially knowledge-

able about the day-to-day functions, observing similar facilities is time well spent. This observation falls into the category of "case studies" and will be discussed further in "Research the unknowns," later in this chapter.

Many space planning projects require the reuse of existing furniture and equipment. Inventorying and dimensioning great quantities of existing furniture and equipment is usually a tedious, but necessary, procedure.

Establish architectural parameters
Ideally, the basic architectural constraints and parameters of a given project should be established during the programming phase, so that the relationships between client needs and the qualities of physical space can be considered from the outset. Highly detailed information about the physical setting is not necessary at this early phase of project involvement; too much detail might even get in the way at this point. The basics here are:

1. a base floor plan(s), at a scale large enough to be useful, and accompanied by enough data about mechanical and electrical services so that plumbing constraints, HVAC delivery systems, and primary electrical access points are known;
2. contextual data concerning the basics of architectural, historical, and social factors;
3. building and zoning code requirements in enough detail to avoid basic code violations in general space allocations.

Most of the detailed architectural data is not needed until the physical planning and design phases of the project have begun. In some cases, the contextual factors, particularly those related to the human and social environment, will play a major role in determining the conceptual approach to a project. In these instances, significant data gathering and research of the critical contextual factors should become part of the programming process.

Organize collected data (the First Phase Program)
After the interviewing and observation tasks have been completed, and the basic physical setting information has been acquired, it is time to organize all of the data accumulated to date. Although it is unlikely that all the necessary project information is known, great value exists in organizing a first phase program at this point, in which the collected data is put into a useful sequential format, and quantitative factors, such as square footage and furniture/fixture tabulations, can be easily seen and extracted. This organizational process requires a basic analysis of the client's

organizational structure and the project's planning needs. Most importantly, it should identify what is still lacking. What critical information not obtained in the interview process will require additional interview time and / or research? What conflicts in the given data require investigation? What subtleties in interrelationships have been hinted at, but not really defined? What technical equipment and processes need to be researched and more fully understood to space plan with them intelligently? These and other questions will arise requiring investigation and research. Techniques to organize the collected data will be discussed in "Analyze the data," and again later in this chapter.

Research the unknowns

From planning nuance to hard dimensional information, the kinds of gaps in program data described previously should be sought out at this point in the process. As with architectural parameters, too much detail is unnecessary, and can even be a hindrance; a lot of dimensional and process data is more appropriate to research later, during the design process. The programmer must draw the line between what is needed to analyze the project and what will be needed later to design the project. Some case study research is often valuable at this stage. Again, complete case study data is unnecessary, but some basic factors on spatial organization, corporate or institutional space standards, circulation percentages, and the like, for facilities of similar size and function, can provide realistic comparison and guidelines for the project at hand. Enough common factors exist among law offices, medical clinics, or day-care centers to make such information useful. Case study research is probably more useful during the planning and design phases of the project, but its value during the pre-design phase should not be overlooked.

Analyze the data

With all of the informational material now at hand, a comprehensive analysis of all the project's planning factors must be made. When a project is large enough to require it, the analysis process might begin with making or adjusting an existing traditional organizational chart, identifying lines of authority, and grouping of functions. Beyond this traditional technique, many other analyses should be made:

1. Spatial adjacencies need to be articulated.
2. Working relationships, both inter and intradepartmental, require identification, including traffic flow of personnel, visitors, and materials.
3. Public and private functions and zones should be identified.
4. Special acoustic requirements should be defined.

5. Need for natural light, air, and view (more simply, windows) should be evaluated for each function and area.
6. Groupings of facilities requiring plumbing connections should be identified.

These, and any other factors that will bear on the space planning process, should be understood fully and seen in proper perspective to the whole of the problem.

One planning factor that warrants separate analysis and is too often overlooked, is scheduling the use of facilities because it is a factor of time, rather than space. An analysis of how space is scheduled for use, coupled with knowledge of moveable partition construction techniques (sliding, folding, coiling, etc.), can result in significantly more efficient and economical use of space.

To this point, no mention has been made of computers in the programming process. It should be obvious that computerization can play a major role in programming analysis and documentation—from spread sheet formats to data tabulation and summaries. Although many planners utilize computer techniques in the programming process, a commercially available software package for this purpose has not yet begun to dominate this area of professional practice.

Interpret and diagram the data (the Complete Program)

As they relate to programming, a fine line often exists between analysis and interpretation. Despite the similarities in their meaning, value is derived in making a distinction between them. "Analysis" here refers to creating an understanding of the problem that is directly deduced from the gathered data; while "interpretation" here refers to insights about the problem that have been gained through the unique perspective of the trained designer. Designers often have the opportunity to get to know their clients' needs in great detail and are subsequently able to make penetrating and ingenious interpretations of the programmatic information. Those interpretations are often among the most creative contributions a designer has to offer within the problem solving process. The nature of the insights gained can range from a relatively small and internal process to a major shift in the client's organizational structure. Although significant new perspectives cannot be guaranteed, they are not uncommon, since the designer comes to the problem from a fresh, outsider's point of view, unfettered by the "history" of the client's circumstances, and is asked to "see" the organization as a whole. From this unique vantage point, the designer can make evaluations and recommendations that are invaluable, since no one else is in a position to gain that special perspective.

Another form of interpretation that occurs during the programming process is in the translation of the verbal program content into diagrams. The use of this diagramming technique is well established and is a part of many design programs. A wide range of graphic styles are used, and a great deal of verbal terms identify them, from "adjacency diagrams" and "bubble diagrams" to "space adjacency studies" and "program analysis studies." Despite the drawn and graphic quality of these diagrams, they are still clearly part of the pre-design process since they are a graphic abstraction of the written program and not an attempt to realistically solve the problem. Particularly with larger scale projects, diagrams are often drawn of both the entire organizational structure and various segments or departments within the organization. Often, a series of diagrams will accompany the written program to provide a comprehensive graphic translation of the verbal document. As every designer knows, the graphic view can say precisely what words may still leave unclear. Later in this chapter, a graphic technique, a "relationship diagram," will be described and recommended as an integral part of the pre-design process.

Summarize the data (the Finished Document)

The programming effort must be summarized and documented before moving on to the design phase of the project. In some cases, the program material is recorded in an informal manner and is used only by the designer as an internal design tool and is not seen or used by others. In most cases however, particularly in a formal designer/client relationship, the program is finished in a bound document presented for client approval before the beginning of the design phase of the project. Regardless of format or designer/client relationship, it is necessary to bring the programming process to an appropriate close.

If the programming process has been thorough, the programmer has become completely immersed in or surrounded by the problem and is now able to make an overview statement about the problem as a whole. Whether this is referred to as a "concept statement" or "statement of the problem," significant value exists in crystalizing one's thoughts in a comprehensive verbal perspective of the problem that will precede the detailed program data. This statement should deal with the spirit of the problem and not its details and represent the broad human, social, aesthetic, and philosophic aspects of the programmer's thoughts concerning the project.

In its final form, the program should be a well integrated package containing:

1. an overview statement;
2. a detailed, function by function, written program describing all project needs and concerns;
3. diagrams that translate the planning relationships into visual terms;
4. numerical summaries of spatial and furniture/equipment needs as a first indication of project budget factors.

When the entire programming process is complete, a great deal has been accomplished. Most importantly, the designer has a complete and documented understanding of the problem. The program document is the ideal tool to communicate both broad conceptual issues and the detailed planning concerns of the project with the client. And once the design process has begun, the program should be used first as a planning guide, and later as the evaluation tool to measure the "success" of the design solution. In other words, has the design met the carefully programmed needs of the problem?

CRITERIA MATRIX

Whether the designer has personally compiled the program or has it presented by the client in a completed form, it is typically a multipaged document in a format which is far from ideal for space planning purposes. This is usually true in the classroom also, where students are given a lengthy verbal description of a space planning problem that is difficult to immediately translate into space planning terms. The designer needs a concise and abbreviated format, with program elements organized in a practical sequence, to find information without flipping constantly through many pages of data, and where spaces, rooms, or functions are categorized and grouped in relation to the project's adjacency requirements.

The Criteria Matrix, described in the following paragraphs, is a useful technique to condense and organize the conventional written design program. It is applicable to both small and large projects and is adaptable to both tight and open time frames or deadlines. When time permits, the matrix can include all the project's design criteria; when time is tight, the format can be condensed to identify only the most critical planning considerations.

In this context, the word "criteria" refers to the program requirements, and the word "matrix" is best described as a "rectangular arrangement of elements into rows and columns'' *(Webster's New Collegiate Dictionary)*. The criteria matrix attempts to verbally and visually organize design program requirements in as concise a form as possible, achieving an overview of the problem in an ''at-a-glance'' format. In its most basic form, it is a rectangular grid of notation spaces with names of rooms or spaces (or functions) listed in the vertical column to the left, and columns for verbal and/or numerical indications of program requirements in the succeeding columns to the right. A basic blank matrix for Design Program 2S (see Appendix, page 128) is shown in Illustration 1–1, indicating notation columns for the most critical space planning factors: 1) square footage need, 2) adjacency requirements, 3) public access, 4) daylight and/or view, 5) privacy needs, 6) plumbing access, 7) special equipment, and 8) special considerations. A format as abbreviated as this can be of great value in making the planning process more efficient, while avoiding the potential for overlooking critical factors.

BLANK CRITERIA MATRIX   ILLUS. 1-1

CRITERIA MATRIX FOR: UNIVERSITY CAREER COUNSELING CENTER	SQ FOOTAGE NEEDS	ADJACENCIES	PUBLIC ACCESS	DAYLIGHT AND/OR VIEW	PRIVACY	PLUMBING	SPECIAL EQUIPMENT	SPECIAL CONSIDERATIONS
① RECEPTION								
② INTERVIEW STA.(4)								
③ DIRECTOR								
④ STAFF								
⑤ SEMINAR RM								
⑥ REST ROOM (2)								
⑦ WORK AREA								
⑧ COFFEE STATION								
⑨ GUEST APARTMENT								

When time and the designer's interest permit, the criteria matrix can be expanded to include a broader range of factors, including furnishings, HVAC requirements, lighting design, color, materials and finishes, and future planning needs. When project size requires it, rooms or spaces (or functions) can be grouped or clustered in departments or divisions. For the sake of demonstrating a fuller potential of the criteria matrix as a pre-design tool, the first 2 sheets (of a total of 5) for a 20,000 square foot, one-story suburban office building are shown in the reduced Illustrations 1–2A and 1–2B. It should be noted that the full 5 sheet matrix is the result of more than 100 hours of professional time extended over several weeks.

The degree of complexity or completeness of the criteria matrix can be adjusted to meet the needs of the size and scope of the project, as well as the amount of time available. Even when time constraints are unusually tight, the matrix approach can be used as a rapid organizer of basic planning data. To be more specific, if the designer will come to reasonably quick decisions, a completed criteria matrix for Design Program 2S could be accomplished within a half-hour, particularly if the designer develops a legend of letters and/or symbols, as shown in Illustration 1–3. It must be noted that the square footage column has been left blank.

The one aspect of the matrix that involves more than fundamental intellectual analysis is the development of square footage figures. The process for assigning figures to that column is a skill unto itself. Before attempting any of the suggested criteria matrix exercises, it is necessary to understand the critical importance of square footage figures and how they can be quickly approximated.

PROTOTYPICAL PLAN SKETCHES

As one gets further into the space planning process, it will become more obvious why it is important to have reasonably accurate square footage approximations for each room or space *before* the physical planning process begins. Without explaining any of the details here, almost all space planning projects have strict budget limitations; consequently, square footage figures have a direct relationship to interior construction and furnishings costs. At this point, let us simply note that if the space-by-space square footage requirements total more than the square footage contained in the building shell, the spaces will not fit within the exterior and/or demising walls. Conversely, if the space-by-space total is significantly less than the square footage contained in the building shell, the building will be underutilized and is likely also to have awkward and oversized circulation spaces.

For certain kinds of spaces, the square footage column may be filled in with relative ease and speed. For example, if one has considerable experience in office planning, it may be possible to quickly respond to the program description of an executive office, counseling room, or conference room with an estimate of square footage needs. And the same may be true of almost any kind of typical space, such as a reception room, kitchen, or public restroom. Generally speaking, accomplished designers can make quick (without sketches or calculations) approximations of square footage needs by using their personal store of past project experiences of a great variety of rooms and functions. But spaces with unique requirements will have to be dealt with, when past experience will not help in making quick approximations. And for less experienced designers, particularly at the student level, approximations for many typical rooms or spaces may be difficult.

When past experience will not help, the use of prototypical plan sketches will usually provide the needed information. The word "prototypical is synonymous with "generalized" or "abstracted," and "sketch" is defined as quick and for informational purposes only. For example, a design program may call for a "Director's Office" with a 36″ × 72″ desk, a matching credenza, a desk chair, two guest pull-up chairs, lounge seating for four people, and 35 linear feet of book shelves. Unless one's professional experience provides a quick and assured square footage figure for this room, it is best to take a few minutes to quickly sketch one or more floor plans of such a room to establish approximate size needs, as shown in Illustration 1–4.

Almost any kind of paper and drawing tool are acceptable for this purpose (probably a roll of sketch tracing paper and a medium weight pencil are best), and drawing quality is not an issue. Some designers find that working over a $1/8″$ or $1/4″$ grid paper background (or directly on grid paper) is helpful to keep the plan sketches quick and reasonably proportional. But don't be too careful in making these sketches since their use is limited; it is even unnecessary to work in a particular scale, as long as one keeps track of the dimensional factors.

It should be obvious that a basic knowledge of typical furniture sizes, arrangements, and dimensional relationships between individual pieces of furniture is essential here; otherwise, one cannot work with appropriate speed. Many interior designers tend to work in only one aspect of the field (residential, hospitality, offices, health care, etc.); if a designer finds him or herself working outside of his / her accustomed area of expertise, familiarization with a new set of furniture standards may be necessary. Certainly for students, whose knowledge base is less complete, regular referral to standard reference sources and / or furniture catalogs will be required. To expand one's knowledge and experience in these areas, specific exercises given in Chapter Six are designed to bolster those skills.

To demonstrate the use of the prototypical plan sketch technique, Illustrations 1–5A and 1–5B, each drawn by a different designer, provide several examples. These sketches are for rooms and spaces described in Design Program 2S, and have been reduced from their original size so that more examples could be shown.

An additional advantage is derived in producing prototypical plan sketches during the pre-design phase of a project, *beyond* the value of approximating square footage needs. An intuitive sense of the specific needs of each space is developed in the process, providing a "feel" for better room proportions (square, or a long and narrow rectangle), window locations, door access points, and internal furniture and equipment relationships within each space.

To work quickly and efficiently with this pre-design technique takes considerable practice. Under conventional professional conditions, prototypical plan sketches are accomplished with dispatch, since they are generally left as an unfinished product developed for informational purposes only. On some occasions sketches may be refined and then serve as corporate or institutional standards for a particular organization, but studies of that kind are usually full-blown projects of their own.

COMPLETING THE CRITERIA MATRIX

With the prototypical plan sketches completed, it is now time to go back to the Criteria Matrix and fill in the "Square Footage" column for those spaces for which one was unable to estimate size based on previous planning and design experience. But even with this accomplished, an element is still missing in the square footage figures—the space needed for circulation (halls, corridors, vestibules, etc.) and partition thickness.

COMPLEX CRITERIA MATRIX

BUILDING & DESIGN

Area or Department	Space or Function	Description of Function	Size	Proxemics	Equipment and/or Furnishing
EXTERIOR	STREET ENTRANCE	Vehicular entrance to site from Hornig Rd.	2-14' Lanes w/splayed sides for easy turns.	On Hornig Rd/easy access to both office and warehouse.	Signage - easy to read for approaching veh'les.
	PARKING	For Employees and Visitors.	Now - 128 Empl. 10 Vis. / Later 214 Empl. 20 Vis.	Conv. to Hornig St. entry, office, Recpt'n Area, and Pedesteian Warehouse entr.	Directional signage.
	BUILDING EXTERIOR	Creates corporate image to Emp.,Vis. and Passer-by Public.		Visual outreach to Roosevelt Blvd and Woodhaven Rd. is of secd'ry importance.	
	PEDESTRIAN ENTRANCE	Primary - for office empl. and visitors. Sec'd'ry- for wareh'se empl.		Primary - adjacent to main Reception Room. Second'y- direct access to warehouse employ. Locker Rm.	Exterior seating, such as benches, sitt'g walls, etc, for small park-like sett'g.
	LOADING AREAS	Daily + frequent loading + unloading. PEI/Gen. + LR could share same ext. area, if specific dock and door areas are seperated.	PEI/Gen needs 4 truck bays of vary'g sizes LR needs 3 truck bays of vary'g sizes.	Immediately adjacent to staging areas + shipping tables within both PEI/Gen. + LR warehouses.	PEI/Gen- both med. spaces to have dock levelers. LR - med. to have wedge on ramp.
	RECREATION	Break, lunch and other non-work time exterior rest + leisure activities.	Accomm. one-third of total staff in passive activities (conver., chess/ch-eckers, sunn'g,etc.)	Immediately adjacent to large grp. funct'ns (lunch, mtg, train'g) could be next to main pedes-tr'n entrance. Could be a major view space from office areas.	Seating (benches, walls), t'bls (din'g, games) tbl umbrellas (semiprotection, decor'tve), moderate exercise
RECEPTION PEI/Gen + LR	The main entrance point for all office employees + all visitors. The hub of all internal office circulation.				
	VESTIBULE	Wind + temperature break between inter. + exter.	50 sf. to 100 sf.	Transition area between exterior pedestrian entrance and the receptionist's desk.	
	RECEPTION STATION	Greet'g point for visitors. Check-in/check-out point for staff. Basic security check-point.	250 sf. to 350 sf.	Immed. adj. to + direct visual contact w/Vest. drs. Adj. to wait'g area. Hub of internal office circulat'n. Easy-to-understand paths to entire bldg	Two work stations, both visible, or one screened. Parcel ledge to seperate visitors from reception't.
	WAITING	Visitor Waiting	6 to 8 guests, approx. 200 sf. to 300 sf.	Adjacent to reception station gallery and circulation paths to major office departments.	Upholstered lounge seating (not too low or too comfor-table) - use system for easy change or additions.
	POWDER ROOM	Toilet facility for guests.	25 sf. to 35 sf.	Immed. adj to waiting area. Visual supervis'n by receptionist.	Toilet. Sink in vanity.
	GALLERY	A small space for exhibit-ing fine art work in a tr-ditional gallery setting.	300 sf. to 400 sf.	Immed. adj. to waiting Area. Access from Vest. w/out walking thru Waiting Area. visual access from Recept'n for basic se-curity against theft/vandalism.	Picture hanging system for walls. Pedestal system for sculpture. Free-standing exhibit system for addit-ional 2D display.
CORPORATE MANAGEMEMT	An executive suite which is conveniently located, but a little removed from other office functions and departments. As a group, it should be immediately adjacent to the other corporate funct-ions (Accounting, Computer, Marketing and Presonnel)				
	STEVE FISHER	Executive office with conversation area.	300 sf. to 350 sf.	In a central operating position within the management team. Adj-cent to a secretary shared with Murray Fisher. Adj. to a small co-nference room for exclusive cor-porate management use.	Desk, credenza, desk chair, 2 guest chairs, lounge seat. for 6 (personal choice in furniture selections).
	6 CORPORATE OFFICES	Executive offices for very active and busy people.	200 sf. to 225 sf.	No prioritization of placement all 6 executives work together. Each should have easy contact w/their immediate staff.	Desk, credenza, desk chair 2 guest chairs, and (A) con-versation seat'g for 3 or 4 or (B) conf. table for 4.
	SUPPORT STAFF	Administrative assitance and secretarial duties di-rectly related to the corp. management group.	2 lg.stations now @100 sf. 3 med. stations later @ 75 sf.	One station between Steve + Murray. One station adj. to Joe. 3 future stations adj. to Adam and Roger.	Systems furniture (includ'g wall panels when required) and operational seating. Immed. use files adj. when and if required.
	CONFERENCE ROOMS	To serve corporate mgt. con-erence needs of 5 or more people.	Small - 8 to 10 people 225 sf.± Large - 20 people 575 sf.±	Small is best placed between Steve + Mary. Large should be convenient for all executive offices and outside visitors.	Pedestal leg conf. table. Uphol. swivel chairs w/ ped. base. Proj. wall + marker surfaces. Bev. counter. Misc. storage.

PROGRAM

Date:	
Revised	

Thermal Comfort	Acoustics	Lighting	Color	Materials	Enviromental Qualities and Special Comments	Future Factors
		Low level lighting, 2' above grade.			Welcoming/use plants to identify.	None.
		Mid Level Ltg. 8' to 10' above gr.			Aviod "sea of cars" Appearance - use earth Berms and plants to Humanize.	Future park'g could be on upper deck.
		Not Required.	Colourful and warm.	Use a variety of mater'ls - nat'r'l and man/made.	Present an image of "prof'n'sm + hum'n'sm" - aviod monumentality.	Future add'ns to maintain orig. image.
		Well lighted w/low + med. level fixt's - incorp. walls, plant-ing, sculp., fount'ns +/or walls murals.	Concentrated use of col. - potent'lly in both bldg mater'ls + fine art works (sculp. gl-azed murals walls etc.	Most personal contact w/bldg ext.- special att'n to scale and texture of bldg mat-erial.	Major focal point - use sc-ulpture and/or fountains ~ an extension of Recept'n Rm.	Orig. image could be expanded.
Deep overhang protect'n for load'g docks, plus radiant heaters.		General driveway area lighting + general li-ghting of dock areas.	Light, reflective surfaces.	Wall mater'l able to take regular major abuse. Dock flr. mat-er'l tough + smooth.	Paved areas must drain off easily. Snow removal must be efficient, consider use of elect'lly. heated paved areas.	Loading areas will grow pr-oport'n'lly w/their resp-'t've wareh'-se areas.
		Decorative lighting of foliage.	Opport'nty for lots of color in furn'h'gs, plant mater'l, pav'g adjacent wall surf's, window awing, etc.	Fast drying, easily maintained.	Create a park-like sett'g. Utilize water + fountains; lunch, business meet'gs + train'g sessions could move out to this area.	Must accomm. one third of ultimate work force.
Air surge for slightly exaggerated temp. change.		Ambient. An integral part of planned ltg. for main reception spaces.	Subordinate to main reception spaces.	Very durable. Glass in doors for safety; floor to absorb water + snow.	An integral part of the planned reception area.	None.
Tc-1. Avoid entrance door drafts.	A-1.	Special ltg. req. for sculptural qulities of the recept'n area. Not overly dramatic. Task ltg. for desk.	Colorful. An integral element in the plan-ning of the main entr. space of the bldg.	Very durable. Appropiate luxury. Consistent for entire reception area.	Spacious, express firm's success. Use of perman-ent fine art works. Large environ't w/high ceiling.	3rd work sta-tion req'r'd; screened.
TC-1.	A-1.	Ambient. Day ltg. + view desired. Articu-late sculp'l quality of space.				More people in future.
TC-1 - High ventilation.		Ambient.	C-2.	Durable and water resistant.		
TC-1	A-1.	Ambient, plus track system for exhibit light. Control nat-ural light.	Neutral colors to avoid conflict with exhibited works.	Tackable wall surfaces desireable.	A special space, inviting, to bring pleasure and enlightenment to employees and visitors.	Could expand. if successful.
TC-1.	A-2	Task/ambient plus accent.	Personal choice.	Personal choice.	Exemplify the corporate image of professionalism and humanism. Clearly a customized interior. Personal art selections. Personal coat closet	None
TC-1.	A-2.	Task/ambient plus accent.	Personal choice or corporate selection could be made.		Environ't to express dyna-mism, not pomp. Some opportunity for personali-zation.Personal coat closet.	2 to 3 more offices.
TC-1.	A-1.	Task/ambient.	C-1 plus decorative accents of corp. mgt. group.	M-1.	Efficient, open, dynamic prof'l.This area important to interior corp. image.	None.
TC-1 plus high level air change.	A-2 - at least a 50 db STL enclosure.	Task ltg. for table. Sep. switch wall was-hers for tack. + mark-er surfaces. Dim. for projection.	Med. level contrast, med. + lt. tones (av-iod deep tones except on floor).	M-1. Highly customiz-ed for important ima-ge space.	Important to convey corpor. image of professionalism + humanism. These spaces shou-ld also be distinctive + sop-histicated; clearly customized	None.

COMPLEX CRITERIA MATRIX

	FILE + WORK ROOM	Files for corp. mgt. only also - coats, small copier, gen. work space.	100 sf. to 120 sf.	Primarily accessable by support staff.	Ptd. stl. cabinets. Small copier.
	POWDER ROOM	Corpt. Mgt. group visitors only.	25 sf. to 35 sf.	Conv. for Corp. Mgt. group visitors.	Toilet. sink in vanity.
ACCOUNTING	A corporate function, generally adjacent to Corporate Management and specifically adjacent to Joe Leirer,s office. Also generally adjacent to the Computer Dept.				
	MANAGER	General supervision of the dept.	150 sf.‡	Adjacent to Controller's Office. Positioned to supervise the dept.	Desk, credenza, desk chair 2 guest chairs, shelves 10 file drawers, EDP work space storage.
	STAFF ACCOUNTING	Concentrative and detailed work.	100sf to 110sf (status)	Adjacent to Account'g Mgr	F-4
	CREDIT DEPT	Concentrative and detailed work. A lot of telephone activity.	Mgr = 90 sf. Staff = 75 sf.	Adjacent to Assistant Controller	F-4
	BOOKKEEPING	Bookkeeping and general office functions. Accounts payable and receivable, secretary, clerical staff.	6 station @ 75 sf.	Physically central to the department	F-4
	PAYROLL	Confidential and concentrative work.	100 sf.	Easily available to acct'g. mgrs. but in a fairly remote or private location	F-4
	FILES	for exclusive dept'l use.	200 drawers 40 w/5 dr. ea. 300 sf. to 350 sf.	physically central to Acct'g Dept; closest to bookkeepers.	5 drawer, vertical type, lockable
	LIBRARY WORK RM.	Central reference and equipment room	120 sf.	Physically central to the department.	Shelving for ref. books and manuals. Storage for EDP files. Work space for common equip. e.i. faxs machines, 2 p.c.'s + sm. copier.
	HUDDLE SPACE	Casual, impromptu conference space for up to 4 or 5 people	65 sf. to 90 sf.	Physically central to the department, but positioned for minimum acoustic distraction to others, without requiring physical enclosure.	42"Dia. or 36"x60" Table, 4 pull-up chairs.
DATA PROCESSING DEPARTMENT	A corporate function, generally adjacent to corporate management and the Accounting Dept.				
	DP ASST. MANAGER	Visual supervision of the DP Dept.	150 sf.‡	Adj. to DP Mgr. Physically central to the dept.	F-10 EDP plus an extra guest chair
	PROGRAMMING STAFF	Quiet and concentrative work, central to the dept's purpose	75sf +/-	Physically central to the Dept.	F-4
	OPERATIONS SUPERVISOR	Quiet and concentrative work, central to the dept's purpose	75 sf. +/-	Physically central to the dept. Easy access to Equipm't Room.	F-4
	KEYING STAFF	Quiet work in open space	75 sf. +/-	Physically central to the dept.	F-4
	HUDDLE SPACE	SAME AS HUDDLE SPACE FOR ACCOUNTING DEPT, ABOVE			
	TAPE LIBRARY	Space for storage of manuals, books, EDP files, tapes, etc., commonly used by all dept. pers'l.	250 sf. to 350 sf. to be more specifically defined in near future.	Physically central to the dept.	Painted metal shelving and filing, reference table and chairs, small copier.
	EQUIPMENT ROOM	Room for commonly used equip (especially noisy equip.) and other common work tasks	No. and size of equipment shall determine room size. IDENTIFY	Easy access for dept. staff but off to one side.	To be identified in near future. Include work table.
	COMPUTER ROOM	Strictly for equipment	Approx. 900 sf. - "ideal layout" will be provided by WANG.	Easy access for dept. staff, but off to one side.	As specified by WANG and/or others.
OPERATIONS DEPARTMENT	A corporate function, generally adjacent to Corporate Management and specifically adjacent to Mary Lynch's office. Also generally adjacent to the Accounting Department. Frequent interaction with outside visitors.				
	MARKETING/ ADVERTISING	Quiet, confidential work	150 sf.‡	an integral part of this small dept.	F-10, plus an extra guest chair.

Sheet no: 2

		Task/minimal ambient.	Consistent with adj. spaces.			More filing needed?
TC-1. High ventilation.		Ambient.	C2.	Durable and water resitant.		
TC-1	A2	Task/Ambient.	C-1	M-1 (clg. can be nonacoustic.	Appropriate for both concentrative work and informal conferencing. Personal coat closet.	None
TC-1	A-1	Task/Ambient	C-1	M-1	EQ-1	NOW = 1 LTR = 2 to 4
TC-1	A-1	Task/Ambient	C-1	M-1	EQ-1. A little remote because of telephone activity acoustics.	Grow to 3 to 4.
TC-1	A-1	Task/Ambient	C-1	M-1	Mix of concentrative work with a lot of personal interaction within the bookkeeping group and some interaction with others.	Grow to 8 to 10.
TC-1	A-1	Task/Ambient	C-1	M-1	EQ-1 with an added degree of visual privacy.	None
		Task lighting for file search plus minimal ambient ltg.	consistent with adjoining spaces.		purely functional	Not identified.
TC-1. Add'l air flow if req'd by elec. equip.	A-1	Task/Ambient	C-1	M-1	EQ-1	Identify future needs
TC-1	A-1,	General	C-2, + strong accent color in furnishings or on ltd. wall surface or panel	M-1 + added absorb'g mat'l on walls	conducive to stimulating, verbal exchange (good place for graphic art work).	Not identified
TC-1	A-2	Task/Amb't	C-1	M-1	EQ-1, must appear to be accessible.	None
TC-1	A-1	T/A	C-1	M-1	EQ-1	Staff of 1 will grow to 3 or 4
TC-1	A-1	T/A	C-1	M-1	EQ-1, while in direct contact with keying staff.	None
TC-1	A-1	T/A	C-1	M-1	EQ-1	Staff of 2 will grow to 3 or 4
TC-1, + special for fire resistive tape rooms	A-1	T/A	C-2	M-2	EQ-1 + 2-25 sf. fire resistive rooms for tape storage.	Not identified
Gear to heavy load of printers, bursters, other equip.	A-1 and A-2	General	C-1	M-1, w/highly absorbant acoustic material on walls.	Fully enclosed, strictly functional handle heavy AVAC requirement.	Not identified. Must plan for future.
Must meet rigid temp. and humidity standards.	A-1 and A-2	General	C-1	Raised flr. system, VWC acoustic tile clg.	Strictly functional	Not identified. Must plan for future.
TC-1	A-2	T/A	C-1	M-1	Personal coat closet.	Now = 1 Future = 2

CRITERIA MATRIX

FOR:
UNIVERSITY CAREER COUNSELING CENTER

	SQ FOOTAGE NEEDS	ADJACENCIES	PUBLIC ACCESS	DAYLIGHT AND/OR VIEW	PRIVACY	PLUMBING	SPECIAL EQUIPMENT	SPECIAL CONSIDERATIONS
① RECEPTION		② ⑤	H	Y	N	N	N	TRAFFIC HUB ADJ. TO MAIN ENTRANCE
② INTERVIEW STA.(4)		① ④	M	I	L	N	N	FEEL LIKE A TEAM OF FOUR
③ DIRECTOR		④	M	Y	H	N	N	HIGHEST IMAGE ACCESS TO REAR DR FOR PRIVATE EXIT
④ STAFF		③	M	Y	M	N	N	
⑤ SEMINAR RM		① ⑥ ⑦	H	I	H	N	Y	A/V USE IMPORTANT CLOSE TO ENTRANCE
⑥ REST ROOM (2)		CENTRAL	M	N	H	Y	N	
⑦ WORK AREA		② ④ CENTRAL	L	N	M	Y	Y	
⑧ COFFEE STATION		CENTRAL	H	Y	N	Y	Y	CONVENIENT FOR EVERYONE
⑨ GUEST APARTMENT		REMOTE	L	Y	H	Y	N	RESIDENTIAL CHARACTER

LEGEND

H = HIGH
M = MEDIUM
L = LOW
Y = YES
N = NO/NONE
I = IMPORTANT BUT NOT REQUIRED

NOTE: IN "ADJACENCIES" COLUMN ⊗ - INDICATES ADJACENCY IMPORTANCE
⊗ - INDICATES MAJOR ADJACENCY IMPORTANCE

PROTOTYPICAL PLAN SKETCHES: DIRECTOR'S OFFICE ILLUS. 1-4

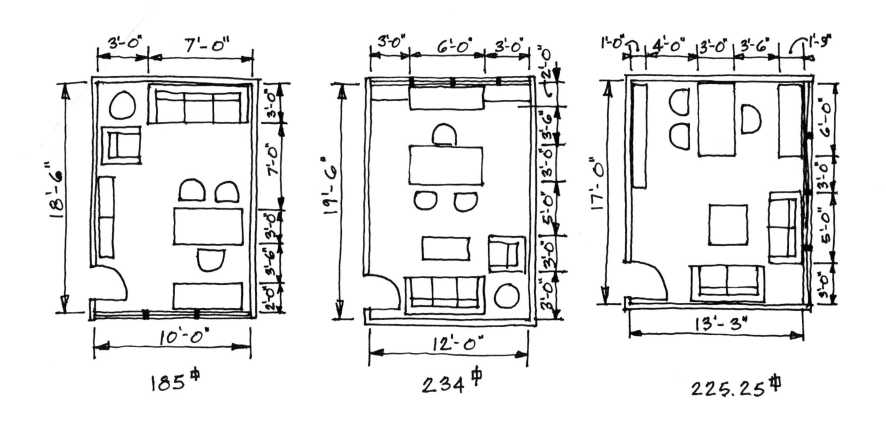

185 ◫

234 ◫

225.25 ◫

PROTOTYPICAL PLAN SKETCHES: DESIGN PROGRAM 2S

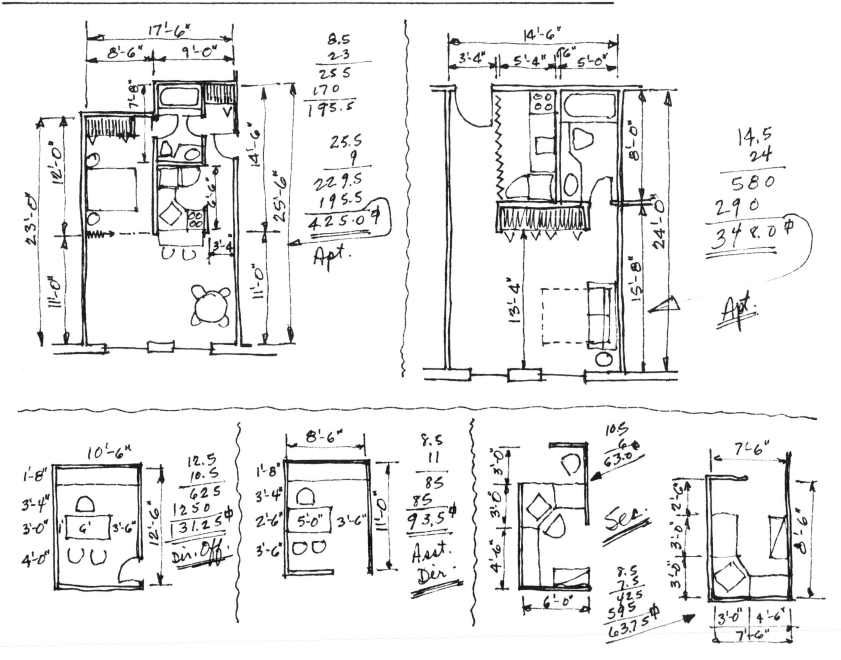

8.5
23
255
170
195.5

25.5
9
229.5
195.5
425.0 φ

Apt.

14.5
24
580
290
348.0 φ

Apt.

12.5
10.5
625
1250
131.25 φ

Dir. Off.

8.5
11
85
85
93.5 φ

Asst.
Dir.

10.5
6
63.0

Sec.

8.5
7.5
425
595
63.75 φ

16

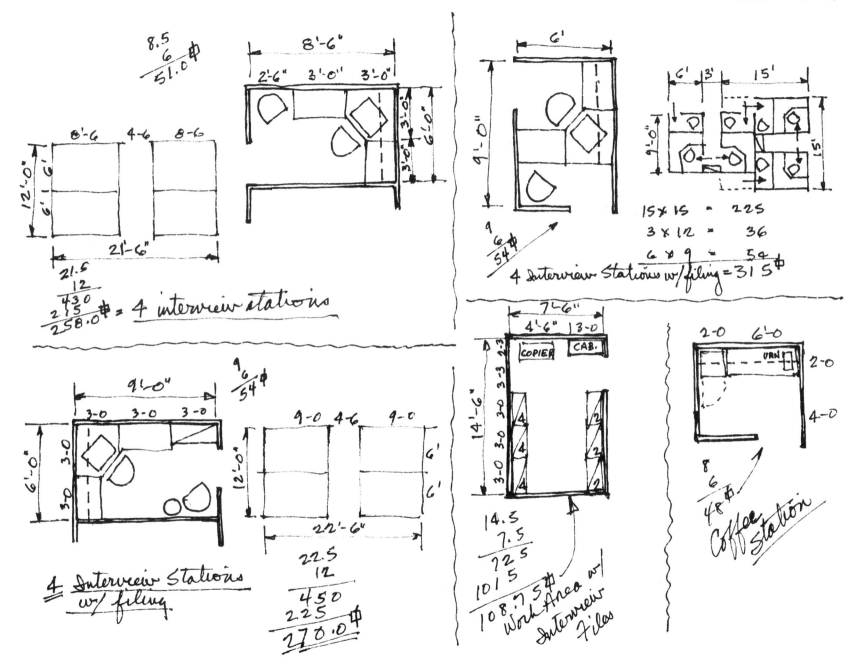

8.5
6
51.0 #

8'-6"   4-6   8-6

8'-6"   2'-6"   3'-0"   3'-0"

12'-0"   6'1"   6'-0"   3'-0"   3'-0"   3'-0"

21'-6"

21.5
12
430
215
258.0 # = 4 interview stations

6'   6'   3'   15'

9'-0"   9'-0"   15'

9
6
54#

15 × 15 = 225
3 × 12 = 36
6 × 9 = 54
4 Interview Stations w/ filing = 315 #

4 Interview Stations
w/ filing

9'-0"   9
6
54#

3-0   3-0   3-0

6'-0"   3-0

9-0   4-6   9-0

12'-0"   6'   6'

22'-6"

22.5
12
450
225
270.0 #

7'-6"
4'-6"   3-0

2-3
COPIER   CAB.

14'-6"   3-3   3-0   3-0
4   4   4   2   2   2
3-0

14.5
7.5
725
101 5
108.75 # Work Area w/
Interview Files

2-0   6-0

URN   2-0

4-0

8
6
48#
Coffee Station

17

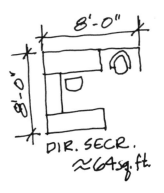

DIR. SECR.
≈ 64 sq.ft.

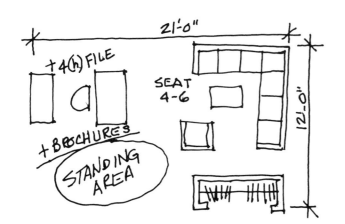

+ 4(h) FILE

SEAT
4-6

+ BROCHURES

STANDING
AREA

RECEPTION ≈ 250 sq.ft.

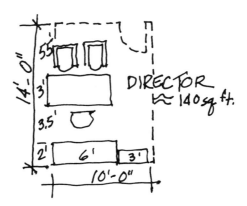

14'-0"

5.5
3'
3.5'
2'   6'   3'

10'-0"

DIRECTOR
≈ 140 sq ft.

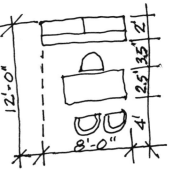

12'-0"

2' 3.5' 2.5'
4'
8'-0"

ASST. DIR.
≈ 96 sq.ft.

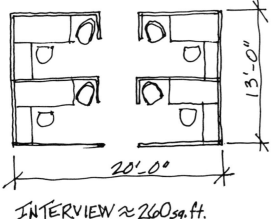

13'-0"

20'-0"

INTERVIEW ≈ 260 sq.ft.

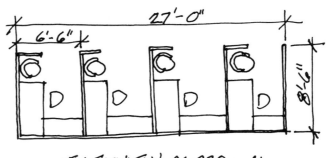

27'-0"

6'-6"

8'-6"

INTERVIEW ≈ 230 sq.ft

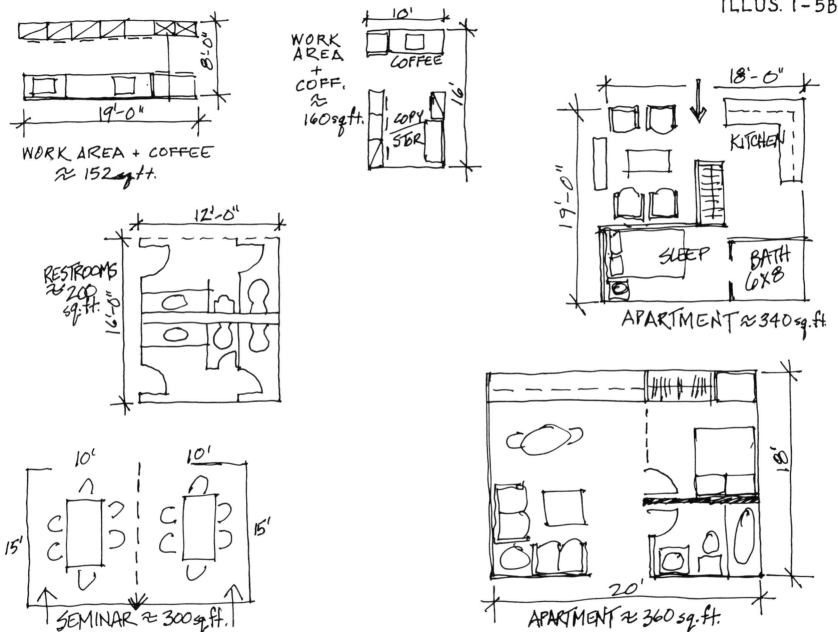

ILLUS. 1-5B

WORK AREA + COFFEE ≈ 152 sq.ft.

WORK AREA + COFF. ≈ 160 sq.ft.

COFFEE

COPY STOR

RESTROOMS ≈ 200 sq.ft.

APARTMENT ≈ 340 sq.ft.

KITCHEN

SLEEP

BATH 6X8

SEMINAR ≈ 300 sq.ft.

APARTMENT ≈ 360 sq.ft.

For most non-residential interior facilities, a factor of 25 to 33 percent of the square footage total for all required spaces will be a reasonably accurate estimate of the space needed for circulation and partitions. An absolutely reliable factor for this element does not exist; it will vary from project to project, depending on the configuration and construction of the building shell and the nature of the functions to be performed in the space. In general terms, when building or space configurations are complex, and/or structural spans are short (with interiors having closely spaced columns or bearing walls), and/or functional planning requirements demand a lot of separate spaces (such as offices, examining rooms, or lab booths), it is likely that the circulation/partition factor will be higher than normal. Only extensive experience in space planning will permit one to make an educated guess at what the factor might be for any specific user/building situation. A 25 percent factor is practical for most space planning problems because it permits one to err on the side of safety and is specifically recommended for use with the space planning exercises accompanying this text.

Until this point in the predesign process, it has not been specifically necessary to know the size of the available space; but with the criteria matrix now complete, it is time to measure and calculate the useable interior square footage available within the building shell. After the available square footage has been determined, then calculate 75 percent of the available square footage; that result should be approximately equal to the total square footage of all the spaces listed in the criteria matrix. Another approach to this calculation that will bring the same result is to divide the total square footage of all the spaces in the criteria matrix by three, and add the result to the square footage total (or 1.33 × the square footage total); this result should approximately equal the useable square footage available within the building shell. An allowance or tolerance of approximately five percent in either direction is usually workable; however, it is likely that an adjustment in the square footage column figures (up or down) will be required to attain a fairly close match between space needed and space available. One's first attempts at "juggling" the square footage numbers may seem difficult and tedious; as with all aspects of the space planning process, experience will permit this awkward trial-and-error numbers game to be accomplished easily and quickly. This is an essential part of the process, since a significant mismatch between the estimated amount of space required and the actual amount of space available will make the physical planning process very difficult. Using the square footage numbers arrived at in the prototypical plan sketches shown in Illustrations 1–5A and 1–5B, the square footage column in the criteria matrix for Design Program 2S has been completed in Illustration 1–6. With a one-third circulation factor added, the square footage total (2443 square feet) com-

pares favorably with the square footage available in Building Shell 2S (2500 square feet). The use of program/shell combination 2S for illustrative demonstrations will continue throughout the text.

An additive variation to the criteria matrix that some designers find useful can be made part of the matrix with little extra time. Probably the most widely used matrix technique among space planners is the adjacency matrix. Although limited to defining the adjacency aspects of the program data, its graphic/visual qualities have been found to be very useful. With a simple addition to the left of the criteria matrix, this graphic approach to visualize the adjacency factors of the design program can become a valuable supplement to the other factors already accounted for in the matrix. Illustration 1–7 demonstrates the ease with which this can be accomplished, using a very basic set of legend symbols to articulate the relative levels of adjacency importance.

To summarize the value of the criteria matrix as a space planning tool, four important steps in the process have been accomplished:

1. The basic program elements have been considered, evaluated, and organized for planning purposes.
2. This analysis has been put into quick reference format.
3. If referenced regularly in the planning process, the matrix ensures thoroughness and attention to detail.
4. The matrix becomes an excellent evaluation tool at the completion of the space planning process to check the finished plan solution's ability to fulfill the design program requirements.

EXERCISE 1–1

Using the design programs provided in the Appendix, develop a criteria matrix for at least one or two of the 1500 square foot and the 2500 square foot problems, including the square footage column and any prototypical plan sketches required. These matrixes should be done in an unhurried manner, so that the exercise provides a meaningful learning experience. Save the results of these exercises for use in further exercises that will be presented and recommended later in this chapter, as well as in Chapters Two, Six, and Seven.

RELATIONSHIP DIAGRAMS

The Relationship Diagram is an excellent transition between the essentially verbal analysis of program development and the completely graphic

CRITERIA MATRIX FOR: UNIVERSITY CAREER COUNSELING CENTER	SQ FOOTAGE NEEDS	ADJACENCIES	PUBLIC ACCESS	DAYLIGHT AND/OR VIEW	PRIVACY	PLUMBING	SPECIAL EQUIPMENT	SPECIAL CONSIDERATIONS
① RECEPTION	250	② ⑤	H	Y	N	N	N	TRAFFIC HUB ADJ. TO MAIN ENTRANCE
② INTERVIEW STA. (4)	220	① ④	M	I	L	N	N	FEEL LIKE A TEAM OF FOUR
③ DIRECTOR	140	④	M	Y	H	N	N	HIGHEST IMAGE ACCESS TO REAR DR FOR PRIVATE EXIT
④ STAFF	180	③	M	Y	M	N	N	
⑤ SEMINAR RM	300	① ⑥ ⑦	H	I	H	N	Y	A/V USE IMPORTANT CLOSE TO ENTRANCE
⑥ REST ROOM (2)	200	↑ CENTRAL	M	N	H	Y	N	
⑦ WORK AREA	120	② ④ ↑ CENTRAL	L	N	M	Y	Y	
⑧ COFFEE STATION	50	CENTRAL	H	Y	N	Y	Y	CONVENIENT FOR EVERYONE
⑨ GUEST APARTMENT	350	REMOTE	L	Y	H	Y	N	RESIDENTIAL CHARACTER

LEGEND
H = HIGH
M = MEDIUM
L = LOW
Y = YES
N = NO/NONE
I = IMPORTANT BUT NOT REQUIRED

TOTAL NEEDED = 1810 S.F.   TOTAL AVAILABLE = 2500 S.F.
2500 S.F - 625 SF = 1875 S.F   LESS 25% FOR CIRCULATION = 625 S.F.

NOTE: IN "ADJACENCIES" COLUMN ⊗ - INDICATES ADJACENCY IMPORTANCE
                               ⊗ - INDICATES MAJOR ADJACENCY IMPORTANCE

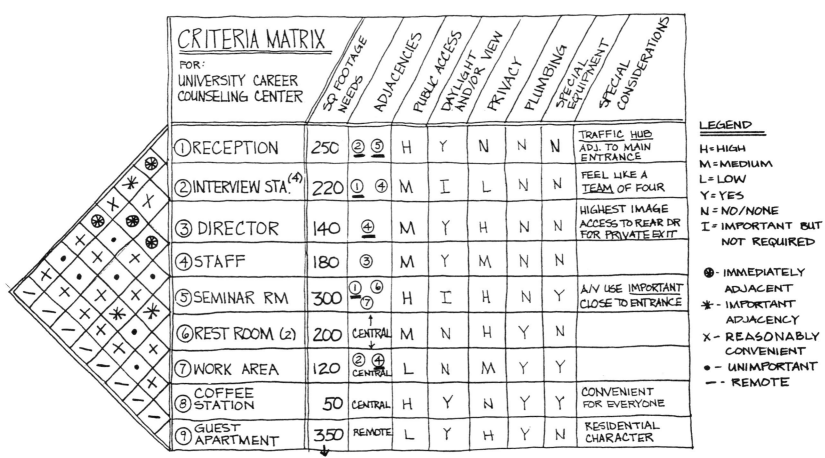

CRITERIA MATRIX FOR: UNIVERSITY CAREER COUNSELING CENTER	SQ FOOTAGE NEEDS	ADJACENCIES	PUBLIC ACCESS	DAYLIGHT AND/OR VIEW	PRIVACY	PLUMBING	SPECIAL EQUIPMENT	SPECIAL CONSIDERATIONS
① RECEPTION	250	② ⑤	H	Y	N	N	N	TRAFFIC HUB ADJ. TO MAIN ENTRANCE
② INTERVIEW STA.(4)	220	① ④	M	I	L	N	N	FEEL LIKE A TEAM OF FOUR
③ DIRECTOR	140	④	M	Y	H	N	N	HIGHEST IMAGE ACCESS TO REAR DR FOR PRIVATE EXIT
④ STAFF	180	③	M	Y	M	N	N	
⑤ SEMINAR RM	300	① ⑥ ⑦	H	I	H	N	Y	A/V USE IMPORTANT CLOSE TO ENTRANCE
⑥ REST ROOM (2)	200	↑ CENTRAL ↓	M	N	H	Y	N	
⑦ WORK AREA	120	② ④ CENTRAL	L	N	M	Y	Y	
⑧ COFFEE STATION	50	CENTRAL	H	Y	N	Y	Y	CONVENIENT FOR EVERYONE
⑨ GUEST APARTMENT	350	REMOTE	L	Y	H	Y	N	RESIDENTIAL CHARACTER

LEGEND

H = HIGH
M = MEDIUM
L = LOW
Y = YES
N = NO/NONE
I = IMPORTANT BUT NOT REQUIRED

✹ - IMMEDIATELY ADJACENT
✳ - IMPORTANT ADJACENCY
X - REASONABLY CONVENIENT
• - UNIMPORTANT
— - REMOTE

TOTAL NEEDED = 1810 S.F.
2500 S.F. - 625 S.F. = 1875 S.F

TOTAL AVAILABLE = 2500 S.F.
LESS 25% FOR CIRCULATION = 625 S.F.

NOTE: IN "ADJACENCIES" COLUMN

Ⓧ - INDICATES ADJACENCY IMPORTANCE
Ⓧ̲ - INDICATES MAJOR ADJACENCY IMPORTANCE

techniques used in physically planning a space. As described earlier in this chapter, the relationship diagram is still part of the pre-design process, because it represents a graphic abstraction or interpretation of the program information, rather than a planning solution. If handled efficiently, the essential values of the relationship diagram process can be gained over a relatively short period of time; a time expenditure that is certainly warranted for a procedure that may reveal the essence of the inter-relationships and adjacencies between and among the rooms and spaces called for in the program. As is true of all of the other steps in the pre-design process, developing relationship diagrams helps the planner become immersed in the project's requirements and relationships.

Here's how to proceed. With the criteria matrix just completed and the required rooms and spaces fresh in one's mind, draw a circle for each of the required spaces so that their position on the paper represents a correct or appropriate relationship to the other spaces. Rooms or functions that should be close to one another should be drawn close together, while those spaces that do not require closeness (or may even suffer from being placed in close proximity) should be drawn at a distance from one another. Use connecting lines between the circles to indicate travel or circulation patterns between spaces; those connections should be coded by using heavy or multiple lines for important or heavily traveled connections, and lighter connecting lines between spaces where circulation adjacency is less important or less traveled. The diagram should not be related to the building shell shape or configuration or to any architectural scale. It is a good idea to have the circles approximately proportional in size; ideally, a circle representing a 300 square foot conference room should be about three times the area of the circle representing a 100 square foot office. At least two or three diagrammatic arrangements should be attempted to explore a variety of viable sets of relationships. All of this should be done relatively quickly and intuitively. As with the prototypical plan sketches, drawing quality is not an issue here, since the diagrams are a design, not a presentation, tool. A short role of inexpensive tracing paper and a soft pencil or felt-tipped marker are fine for this purpose. Rather than bothering to erase in order to revise, it is usually more efficient to make changes by placing another layer of tracing paper over the original and redrawing it. To demonstrate one basic graphic approach to relationship diagrams, Illustration 1–8 provides a few examples of visually interpreting the requirements of Design Program 2S, for which a criteria matrix was prepared and shown in Illustration 1–6.

As one begins to develop skill in drawing relationship diagrams, graphic and/or verbal notations should be added to indicate important planning needs such as windows, segregation of public and private areas, acoustic barriers, etc., shown in Illustration 1–8. Color can be used as a coding tool to identify similar functions or planning relationships, such as privacy or adjacency. Over time, designers find that a personalized visual notation system is developed that they are able to draw upon as an efficient and expressive pre-design tool. As an alternative to the drawing process and if time is not a factor, using heavy paper (such as cover stock), cut out circular or rectangular labeled templates for each of the rooms or spaces and move them about to develop relationship diagrams. This can be a useful variation in technique, but remember that each viable relationship arrived at must be recorded in some way before moving on to the next arrangement of templates.

As mentioned earlier, relationship diagrams, after some modest graphic refinement, are made a part of the finished design program document. Although their primary purpose is to help the planner gain a first visualization of program requirements, if skillfully drawn (and with the non-professional's visualization capabilities in mind), they can often help clients and users to better understand the content of the design program. In this context, it is important to ensure that the diagrams do not resemble a floor plan, so that the non-professional will not confuse them with actual floor plans to be developed later.

EXERCISE 1–2

Using the criteria matrixes developed in the previous exercise, draw at least a few relationship diagrams for each of them. Make an attempt to begin to create a personalized diagramming and symbol language. Again, save the results for use in continuing exercises in Chapters Two, Six, and Seven.

A FINAL NOTE ON PLANNING METHODOLOGY

This concludes the discussion of programming and the pre-design process, it is time to move on to the physical planning process and the development of a floor plan, with all of its broader spatial and design implications. But it is important to note that programming and its graphic products are rarely completely developed at this point. As one begins to develop bubble diagrams and rough floor plans for the project, it is natural for new concepts, functional relationships, multiple uses of space, etc., to emerge—ideas that had not surfaced in the pre-design phase. If the new ideas are an improvement on those embodied in the program, it would be

RELATIONSHIP DIAGRAMS: DESIGN PROGRAM 2S

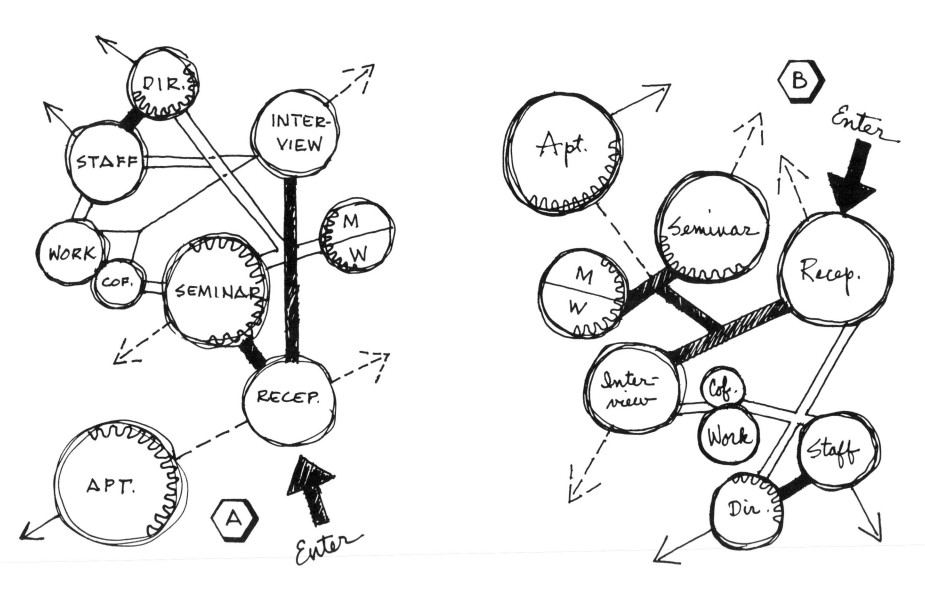

LEGEND

- ▰▰▰ = IMMEDIATELY ADJACENT
- ═══ = CLOSE + CONVENIENT
- ─── = CONVENIENT
- ----- = MINOR RELATIONSHIP
- ∿∿∿ = ACOUSTIC PRIVACY
- ⟶ = NATURAL LIGHT +/or VIEW

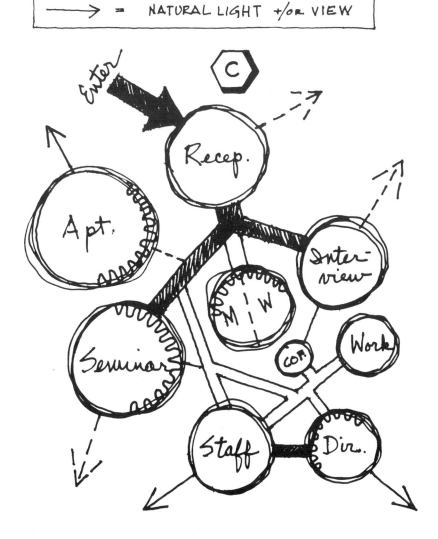

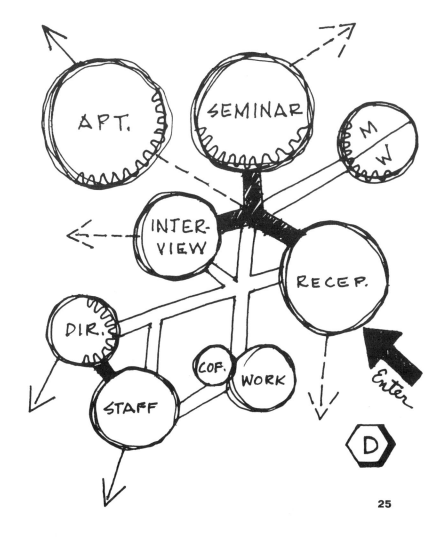

irresponsible to ignore them and not revise the original program. In the professional setting, it is common to have new planning factors introduced after the initial programming phase has been completed—factors completely outside the designer's control. For example, programmatic changes could be new management decides to change organizational structure or a lease agreement is rescinded by the client's landlord. These situations leave the designer no choice but to go back to the program and make revisions. Said in its simplest terms, design programs are rarely static documents after their original development and completion. Rather, it is common practice to revise the program as design ideas develop and outside factors evolve and change. The space planner must face the problem solving task from a position of flexibility equal to the demands of the process.

Recommended Reading

6*, 7*, 17*, 21*, 22*, 28*, 29, 30

Books noted with an asterisk are also included in the Recommended Reading of other chapters.

Chapter 2 THE FIRST PLANNING STEPS:
Bubble Diagrams and Block Plans

To this point, efforts to solve a space planning problem have been carried out through methods of data gathering, analysis of user needs, and first attempts to establish a general concept or approach to the project. Although some physical planning has taken place in drawing prototypical plan sketches of specific functions or rooms and abstract relationship diagrams of the organization as a whole, the overall plan has not yet been approached from a realistic planning viewpoint.

Taking the initial leap from these pre-design steps to the more creative development of a floor plan that solves the practical and esthetic problems of the users is the most difficult and critical element in the space planning process. Programming is essentially a process of analysis; planning (and design) is essentially a process of synthesis. Transition from the analytical mode of programming to the creative mode of planning will never be easy—a gap will always exist. Ideally, one makes the gap as small and manageable as possible. The ''synthesis gap'' will be short to the degree that one's programming results are complete and thorough.

The minimized size of the gap is the reward of good programming. But the gap will always be there, and a creative synthesis spanning it is required to bring together all the divergent elements of the space planning problem.

BUBBLE DIAGRAMMING

With the programming phase completed, one could simply begin by sketching or drafting a floor plan. However, with a problem involving more than a few spaces or functions, the likelihood of developing a ''good'' plan the first time around is slim. It's not very likely that a ''good'' plan would emerge after the first few attempts, and each of these attempts would be relatively time consuming, since floor plans involve partitions, door swings, the placement of plumbing fixtures and equipment, etc. Furthermore, when a good plan has emerged, it's difficult to know whether a significantly better plan (or plans) can be developed. Surely, a better or more efficient approach to solving the problem exists than this trial and error development of full-blown floor plans. To eliminate this time consuming approach, the technique used most by experienced space planners is the bubble diagram. Simply stated, it is a trial and error method to *quickly* explore *all* the planning options, both good and bad, of a given space planning problem. Although its purpose and results are primarily two-dimensional, some basic three-dimensional issues can also be dealt with in the process of arriving at a floor plan solution.

The tools required are simple. Obviously, a base floor plan of the building is needed. In addition, the planner needs *lots* of tracing paper, an architectural scale, and soft or flowing media with which to draw. Most typically, rolls of inexpensive yellow tracing paper are used (sometimes called "trace," or "yellow trace," or "bumwad"), although any reasonably transparent tracing paper, yellow or white, can be used. Almost any drawing media can be used, but markers or soft wax-colored pencils are among the best since they flow on the paper easily and make a bold mark without effort.

The general approach and attitude should be free and intuitive, roughly to scale, and (at least at the outset) essentially nonjudgmental. In this context, "nonjudgmental" can be defined as "uncritical" or "without evaluation." The purpose is simple: to efficiently explore and record *all* the basic planning options of the problem.

Just as the design program must be read and analyzed before one starts the planning process, the floor plan of the existing space must be "read" and analyzed before the physical planning process begins. It is important to study the existing space to understand its configuration, geometry, structural framework or elements, the location, type and quantity of windows, unique architectural elements (such as a fireplace or monumental stair), HVAC system, plumbing supply and waste lines, etc. To some degree, a full understanding of the relative importance of each factor will slowly develop as the bubble diagramming process continues. Despite this, it is time well spent to take a few minutes (exactly how many depends on the time pressures of the circumstance) before the bubble diagramming process begins in order to (with architectural scale in hand) study, analyze, and understand the nature of the space within which you are working.

First, tape down the floor plan of the building shell to the drawing board. If the reflected ceiling plan contains graphic information that might have a bearing on the planning solution (such as low ductwork, significant changes in ceiling height, skylights, etc.), it's a good idea to place this under the floor plan so that those influencing factors can also be seen. (If the floor plan is not on translucent paper, you can lightly sketch the influencing reflected ceiling plan information on the floor plan.) As shown in Illustration 2–1, roll out the tracing paper over the floor plan, hold the roll in your non-drawing hand (each diagram is drawn too quickly to bother with taping down the tracing paper), and begin to draw.

With the completed Criteria Matrix in front of you, try all the planning options that come to mind. From one viewpoint, the correct process would be to methodically try each room or function in each location where it could fit (except for fruitless possibilities such as trying to place plumbing fixtures that are too far, codewise, from a plumbing chase). However, much of the intuitive potential of bubble diagramming would be lost with so rigid a process. Conversely, if one were to be exclusively intuitive, without any planned order or approach to the process, it would be difficult to know if all the possibilities had been explored. Some middle ground between being laboriously systematic and erratically spontaneous should be found; it simply takes some experience with the process to find a personally comfortable track between these extremes.

ILLUS. 2-1

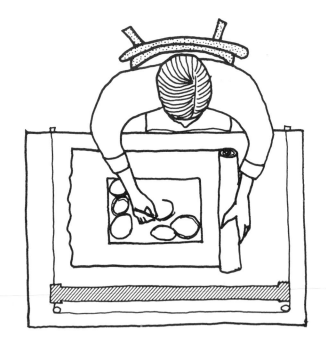

Often, one large or major space requires accommodation and will only fit well in two or three locations in the existing space; each of these locations can become the generator for more bubble diagrams. Plumbing accessibility is usually a significant planning limitation; placing rooms with plumbing fixtures (kitchens, baths, public restrooms, etc.) within the permitted distances to existing plumbing chases required by the prevailing plumbing code, presents another basic starting point from which a series of diagrams may be generated. Some rooms or functions demand immediate access to light and air (windows), while others are often better placed in the deep interior regions of the available space. Adjacency to a main exterior door or primary elevators may automatically locate an entrance or reception space. All of these factors can become the initiator for a whole series of diagrams.

Acoustic considerations, such as the segregation of quiet and noisy functions, may be a significant planning factor. Leaving space for circulation (corridors, stairs, aisles, etc.) is a must in the development of workable bubble diagrams. If these travel paths are not incorporated within the bubble diagrams, the results will be of little value when it's time to translate the diagrams into floor plans. Circulation issues are often important enough to require a series of diagrams of their own, in which travel/traffic paths and patterns are studied independently, as seen later in Illustration 6–3. It is common for space planning problems to present unique factors that demand the location of an important function in one area only—for example, the specific location of major computer equipment due to the unreasonable cost of relocating the electrical wiring throughout an entire building. The succeeding three chapters, Three, Four, and Five, will elaborate on the important influences on the space planning process.

Each bubble diagram should take only a few minutes to draw. Do not belabor any individual diagram, but rather, move on to the next variation on a fresh section of tracing paper; certainly, an eraser should not be anywhere in sight. Try all of the variations that come to mind, even if they don't appear to be particularly promising; they could generate other ideas that otherwise might not have come forth. The nonjudgmental approach is utilized here—don't be too tough or self-critical in evaluating the bubble diagram results while they are still in process. One good and basic approach to generate many possibilities is to take each of the generating conditions, such as entrance points, plumbing chases, a very large space, need for light and air, etc., and, utilizing the limited number of planning positions permitted by that condition, draw as many diagrams as are reasonable on that basis. As an example, suppose that architectural constraints and plumbing stack locations will permit only two solutions to

public restroom locations; then generate as many reasonable (and possibly, a few unreasonable) diagrams as you can, starting with each of those two placement solutions. This process can be repeated with each of the determining existing conditions. It is impossible to draw too many bubble diagrams; exhaust all of the possibilities to ensure that all planning options have been explored. Even for a relatively small space, such as the one shown in Building Shell 2-S (used throughout for demonstration purposes), it would not be unusual to generate 20 to 30 bubble diagrams.

As the bubble diagrams are in process, it's a good idea to record thoughts about many special factors. This becomes a personalized notation system in which one develops a group of graphic symbols to quickly express planning needs and ideas. As explained earlier, some indication of traffic flow and circulation spaces are important to record. Interior door and window locations, new plumbing chases (if possible), acoustic barriers, barrier-free accessibility, etc., should all become part of the "notation system." Even esthetic/spatial issues, such as notations about ceiling heights, interior vistas, and visual rhythm or sequencing are worthy of recording at this stage. Some planners like to use several colors while diagramming, to visually "color code" important factors such as public versus private spaces, acoustic and/or visual privacy, need for light, air, and view to the exterior, etc.

This process is not limited in its use to office spaces, health care facilities, or restaurants; it is relatively universal in its applications and should be thought of as a first-step space planning technique for all types and sizes of interior spaces. Despite the fact that the described process may sound like a "by-the-numbers" approach, bubble diagramming is a complex, creative process and cannot be confined to a mechanical procedure. Negotiating one's way over the "synthesis gap" is a creative leap. Each planner invariably develops a personalized method to deal with the number of variables at hand and to record their ideas. No one "correct" way to develop or draw bubble diagrams exists, nor is there an accepted professional standard for the final product of the process. The graphic results are usually a personal "notation system" the planner uses to go on to the next planning step (the development of a rough floor plan), and the diagrams are usually not seen or used by others.

To give you some ideas about what your bubble diagram results might look like, the next three double pages (Illustrations 2–2A, 2–2B and 2–2C) contain the graphic results of three experienced designers solving Design Program 2S in Building Shell 2S. (These program and shell designations are explained in the following paragraph.) It is obvious that both

BUBBLE DIAGRAMS: DESIGN PROGRAM 25

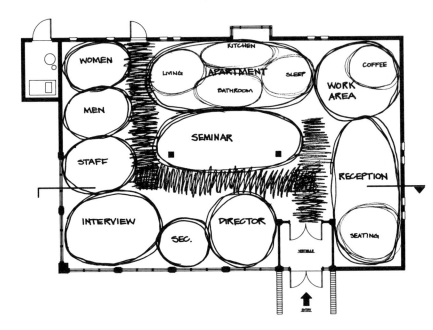

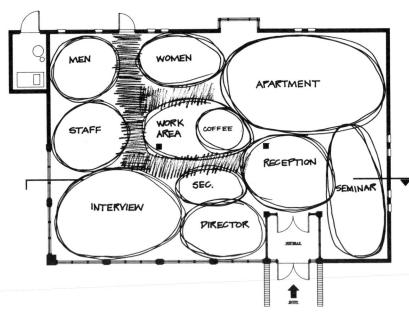

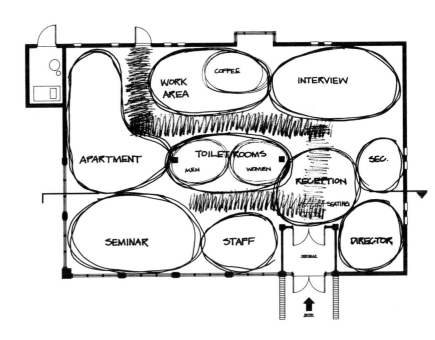

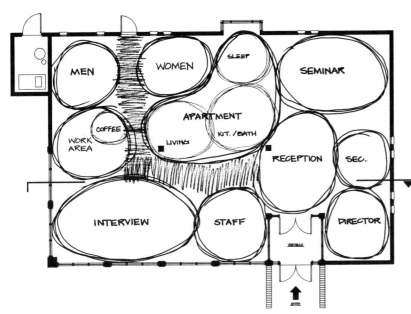

BUBBLE DIAGRAMS: DESIGN PROGRAM 25

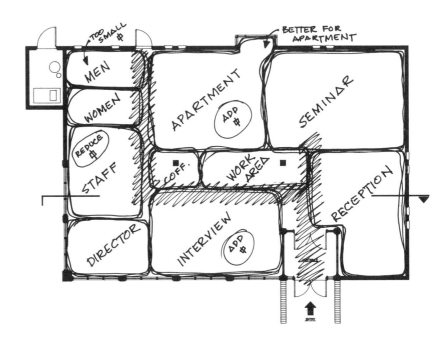

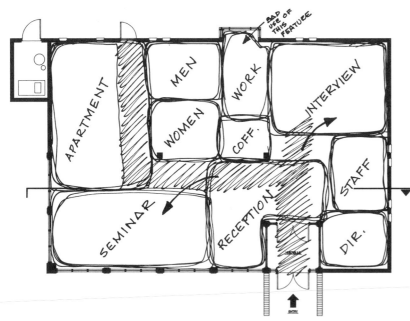

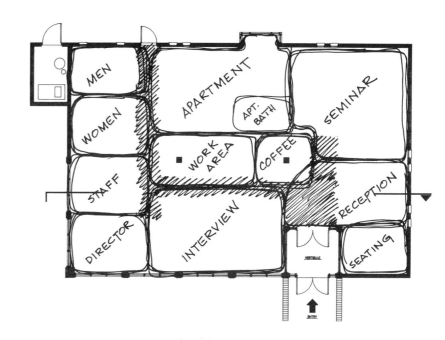

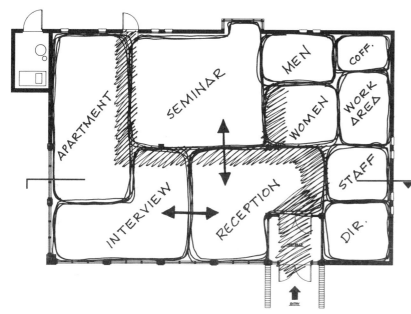

BUBBLE DIAGRAMS: DESIGN PROGRAM 25

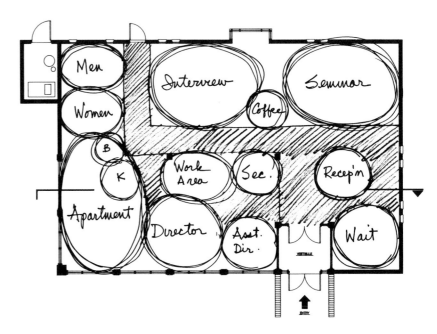

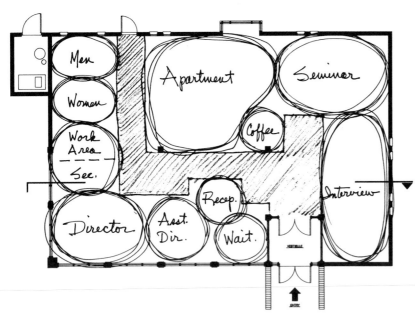

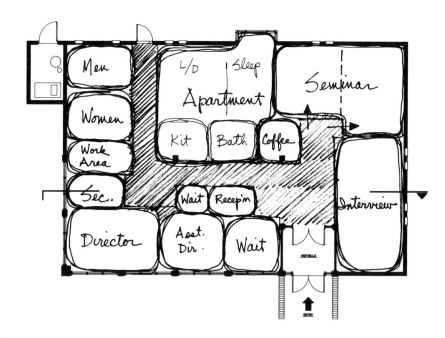

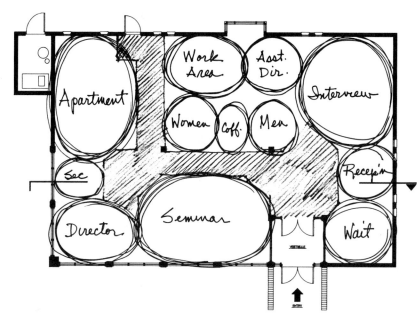

the method to solution and the graphic style of each designer is quite different, yet each has produced a workable result and is ready to move on to the development of a floor plan.

SPACE PLANNING EXERCISES

Three series of space planning exercise problems are provided in the Appendix, starting on page 117. Each series contains three design programs and three building shell floor plans, providing the potential for nine planning exercises in each series, and 27 exercises in all. The first series involves spaces of about 1,500 square feet; the second, spaces of about 2,500 square feet; the third, spaces of about 4,000 square feet. Although prepared exercises of this kind will not be helpful in the development of programming skills or in coming to terms with the detailed requirements of "real" spaces, they are helpful in quickly getting down to the specifics of the space planning process. Ideally, classroom projects will provide additional planning problems where program development and the detailed idiosyncracies of existing spaces are included in the process. Note should be made that the letter designations used to identify the programs and shell are *not* related; Program 3B can be used in planning Shells 3A and 3C, as well as with Shell 3B.

EXERCISE 2–1

At this point in your learning process, it would be very valuable to try your hand at bubble diagram solutions for at least two or three of the program shell combinations provided in the Appendix, starting with one or two in the 1500 square foot series, followed by one or two in the 2500 square foot series. It would be time efficient to use the Criteria Matrixes developed in the exercises recommended in Chapter One as the basis for the bubble diagrams developed here.

After the diagramming possibilities of a particular planning problem have been exhausted, the results should be reviewed and the two or three "best" diagrams selected from the many diagrams that have been drawn. In this context, the "best" diagrams are those having the greatest potential for further development into a good and workable floor plan. One by one, place each of these selected diagrams over the floor plan and then place a fresh section of tracing paper over the "good" diagram and revise it by modifying the shapes and sizes of the "bubbles," more clearly identifying circulation spaces and paths, more accurately locating plumbing chases, doors, or access locations, acoustic barriers, esthetic or spatial features, etc. One could have a second overlay diagram, in which the

"bubbles" evolve into round-cornered rectangles (assuming rectangular rooms and spaces). This revising process moves away from the quick and spontaneous approach of the original diagrams, and we enter into a deliberate selective, problem solving mode. Despite its amorphous graphic quality, this is the first "design" step in the space planning process. Regardless of the specific drawing and refining technique, by the time the bubble diagram process is complete, a *very rough* or abstract floor plan should emerge. Partitions, door swings, fixtures, etc., are not yet identifiable, but a roughly-to-scale allocation of floor space has been established, along with several basic design and construction determinations. The results of this refining process are shown in the extreme right examples in Illustrations 2–2B and 2–2C.

EXERCISE 2–2

Perform this refining process with the bubble diagrams developed in the previous exercise. It cannot be overstated that the successful development of each phase of professional quality space planning skills is directly related to the amount of time and effort put into it. Save these bubble diagram exercises to use in the development of rough floor plans recommended in Chapters Six and Seven.

BLOCK PLANNING

Another well established technique for this initial step into physical planning is conventionally referred to as Block Planning. Its use is particularly widespread in large scale retail and store planning. The process of development and the results are similar to bubble diagramming. Its primary advantage over bubble diagramming is that the result is more "floor-plan-like," and some planners feel more comfortable working with its more geometric quality. Its primary disadvantage in relation to bubble diagramming is that it lacks some of the free-flowing spontaneity and intuitiveness inherent in the bubble diagramming process, as well as a tendency to ignore curvelinear and other non-rectangular solutions. It is likely that most designers have made their choice of technique unwittingly, following the direction that they were first shown or taught. Despite block planning's rectangular nature, the use of a parallel edge and triangle are not recommended here, because they will tend to make the process slow and rigid. To get a general idea of what block-planning diagrams might look like, Illustration 2–3 contains one designer's use of this approach in the solution of Design Program 2S in Building Shell 2S, including a "refined" block plan at the extreme right.

Using the block planning approach, solve one or more of the 1500 square foot and 2500 square foot program/shell combinations in the Appendix. As before, select two or three of the "best" diagrams and refine them in the same manner selected bubble diagrams were refined. Again, save these exercises for continued use in the exercises recommended in Chapters Six and Seven.

A variation on the block planning technique some designers find advantageous is the use of paper templates for rooms and spaces, because the templates can be moved quickly and changes in planning relationships are seen immediately. The process begins with cutting and labeling a square or rectangular piece of substantial paper (such as coverstock) for each room or space, making sure it contains approximately the correct square footage. The templates are then moved about over the floor plan, leaving appropriate circulation paths or spaces, until some sort of workable solution is achieved. Illustration 2–4 shows a designer at work using this technique. Each reasonably workable solution must be recorded by a "hard copy" of some kind (a quick sketch or a Polaroid photo). Since the particular proportions of the cut templates may be very limiting in terms of achieving workable solutions, it is advisable to make two or three templates of varying proportions for each room, being careful to use only one template for a given room in each of the overall solutions. As with *all* of these first phase planning techniques, the process must be concluded with the refinement of the few most workable solutions into rough or abstracted floor plans.

It should be obvious that no single or "best" method exists for this phase of the space planning process. Because it is at the heart of that process, it is inherently creative and without confining definitions. Because it is creative, most designers ultimately develop a highly personalized method, which is specifically tied to their thinking process. Until a planner's experience builds to this level, the approaches shown here, if given enough time and practice, should provide one with adequate tools to solve most space planning problems.

Critiquing one's own work in this first planning phase is difficult. Graphic qualities are not the issue here; although graphic articulateness is of value, it is the planning qualities which are critical to a good solution to the problem. In a classroom, with the direction of a teacher, and with the ability to see and discuss the work of other students, the evaluation of first phase planning solutions is easily available. It is outside of the class-

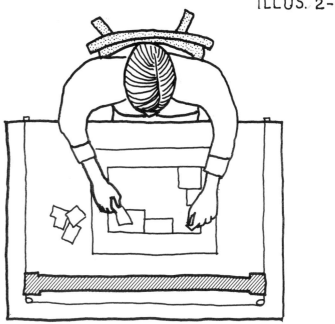

room where one must learn to evaluate the qualities of space planning solutions. Those evaluations must begin with the program material.

With the use of the project's Criteria Matrix, review the refined bubble diagrams or block plans for all the basic planning requirements. How well are adjacency requirements met? Will traffic flow easily? Are square footage requirements adhered to? Are windows well located in terms of daily functions? What about the needs for visual and acoustic privacy? Are basic esthetic/spatial desires attainable with the plan arrangement? Will basic equipment and furniture be easily accommodated? Etcetera. Use the results of the programming process as an objective evaluation tool in critiquing the first planning results. Has a basic function been forgotten? Are some inter-functional relationships not working well? Are code requirements a problem? Etcetera. Now is the time to make revisions, not later when plan changes become more difficult. In some aspects of the plan, it is possible that the physical planning process will create some new insights about the design program, and it may be the program, rather than the spatial layout, that demands revision. Make the revisions needed at this early stage, before other planning and design elements become incorporated and every small change has complex consequences.

BLOCK PLANS: DESIGN PROGRAM 2S

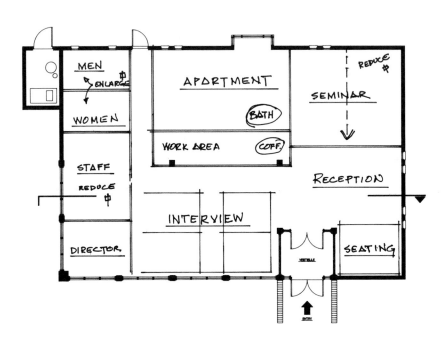

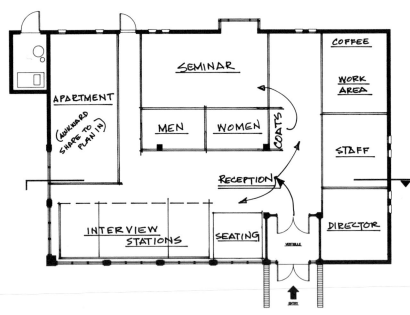

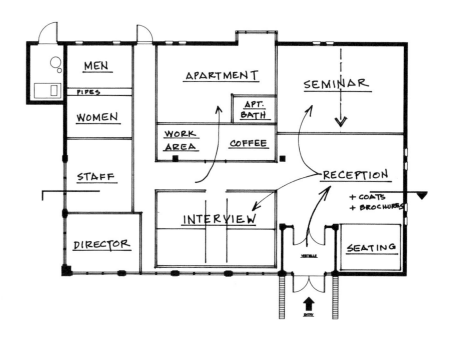

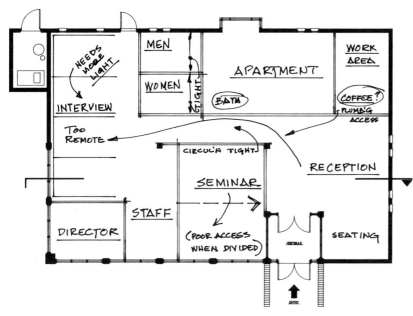

As the planning process progresses, the design program will again serve as an excellent evaluation tool. Throughout the space planning process, the planner/designer must learn the techniques of self-criticism in order to work well independently. Do not be too self-critical; remember that in space planning, perfection is a rare commodity. Strive for the blend of compromises that produces workable results.

Recommended Reading

17*, 21*, 22*, 28*

Books noted with an asterisk are also included in the Recommended Reading of other chapters.

Chapter 3 SMALL AND DIMENSIONALLY DEMANDING SPACES

Before attempting to solve conventional space planning problems, it is important to have a mastery of planning typical, small and dimensionally demanding spaces. To be more specific, competence should be achieved in planning typical residential spaces—kitchens, bathrooms, powder rooms, and laundries, and typical non-residential spaces—public restrooms and small serving kitchens. To a lesser degree, consideration should be given to such non-typical spaces as computer equipment rooms, dark rooms, and scientific laboratories. The common denominator for all these spaces is that they are equipment intensive and expensive to construct; hence, they are usually planned with an eye to maximum economy in their consumption of space.

Although the planning of these small spaces is not unusually difficult, if one is inexperienced in planning them, they can become a serious stumbling block in efficiently and effectively solving general space planning problems. Miscalculations concerning square footage requirements, misunderstanding of the detailed aspects of placing points of access, and

lack of knowledge concerning codes and standards related to plumbing and piping requirements are typical issues related to these specialized small spaces that impede the inexperienced space planner. Depending on one's current knowledge and skill in these areas, this chapter can be used as a refresher or as a primer before taking on the more complex qualities of general space planning.

EXERCISE 3–1

There are a lot of good, easily accessible resource materials concerning typical residential spaces of this kind (see the Recommended Reading at the end of this chapter). One of the best methods to establish these planning skills is to trace (or better, hand copy) *many* examples of residential kitchens, powder rooms, and bathrooms. In this process, one will become familiar with a variety of fixture and cabinet sizes, fixture and appliance planning relationships, and necessary details such as points of access, use of accessories, avoiding door swing conflicts, etc. After tracing or copying many plan arrangements, draw more without the aid of this kind of replication. One-quarter inch scale ($^1/_4" = 1'-0"$) should be used, since that is a scale commonly used professionally in their documentation. Despite the lack of manufactured templates, there is special value in drawing these spaces at larger scales ($^3/_8"$, $^1/_2"$ and $^3/_4" = 1'-0"$) because it allows us to better visualize and understand their detailed nature. Once some basic familiarity with typical arrangements has been established, a great deal can be learned from going beyond these basics by planning some non-typical kitchens and bathrooms, incorporating less common functions and equipment, such as bidets, whirlpool tubs, linen storage, laundry rooms or alcoves, cooking islands, food-processing centers, dining counters, etc.

By way of example, Illustrations 3–1A and 3–1B show several examples of small residential spaces with both typical and non-typical plan arrangements, drawn free-hand at $^1/_4" = 1'-0"$. Issues of drawing quality, while always important, are not a central issue in this part of the learning process, and discussion related to drawing technique and presentation matters are deferred for consideration until Chapter Seven. Note should also be made regarding the lack of concern for three-dimensional issues. For now, it is best to keep the focus on space planning; at the end of this chapter (and at a few additional points beyond) discussion of the three-dimensional reality, and its relationship to the planning process, will be explored.

Most of the equipment-intensive spaces discussed in this chapter involve the use of plumbing fixtures. Whenever plumbing is involved in buildings, knowledgeable consideration must be given to prevailing plumbing codes, as well as to good standards of practice related to piping and economy of construction. These issues will be dealt with in some depth in Chapter Four. For the present, observe the grouping of fixtures and the use of pipe chases in Illustration 3–2 as a visual example of these factors put into practice.

When some basic skills in planning small residential spaces have been achieved, the same approach should be taken for non-residential uses. Although resource material is not as plentiful for non-residential uses, several adequate sources are available (see the Recommended Reading at the end of this chapter). Some of the small utility spaces in non-residential settings, such as powder rooms and serving kitchens are only subtly different from their residential counterparts. The major differences are in restroom facilities, which are significantly more difficult to plan than residential bathrooms and require concerted effort to acquire skill in planning them well. In addition to the usual concerns of functional planning,

comfortable clearances, and traffic flow, a few special considerations must be accounted for in public restroom facilities:

1. *Visual privacy.* Avoid direct vision into toilet or urinal facilities through the use of partitions or vestibule spaces.
2. *Special accessories.* In addition to the basic plumbing fixtures, toilet stall partitions and accessories, such as soap and towel dispensers and trash receptacles, must be planned for comfortable use.
3. *Barrier-free design.* Federal law and most building codes require that public restroom facilities be designed for comfortable use by disabled users, including those who are wheelchair-bound.

Because barrier-free design standards are critical in the planning of public restrooms, the suggested planning exercise for restroom facilities (Exercise 3–2) follows the discussion and illustrations of barrier-free standards (see page 50).

In addition to relatively standard restroom facilities, many specialized, dimensionally demanding spaces in non-residential settings range from the fairly common (mailrooms, darkrooms) to the highly unique (scientific laboratories, medical treatment rooms). Occasionally, space planners become expert in a particular type of specialized facility and do not require the guidance of an outside specialist or consultant. However, in most cases, it is customary to call upon a consultant, either formal (paid) or informal (a manufacturer's representative). Consultants will provide information and direction from the programming phase of a project (square footage requirements, natural lighting needs, etc.) through the detailed completion of the design and documentation phases (equipment size and placement, electric lighting specifications, etc.). Gaining expertise with the more typical small spaces will help to make the planning of specialized spaces easier; but the help of a consultant for facilities such as commercial kitchens, central computer equipment rooms, or commercial laundry facilities is customary. Without any attempt at completeness, a few examples of preliminary plan sketches of specialized, equipment intensive functions demonstrate the similarities in approach with the more standardized restroom facilities, as seen in Illustrations 3–3A and 3–3B.

HUMAN FACTORS

Human factors is a broad field of scientific research that has many applications in architectural and interiors planning and design. Many of those applications lie far outside the concerns of space planning, such as the comfort factor in specifying a lavatory faucet handle, or the productivity and comfort factors in the lighting design of a computer facility. Conversely, many human factors research applications are directly related to

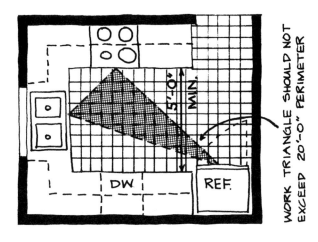

WORK TRIANGLE SHOULD NOT EXCEED 20'-0" PERIMETER

5'-0" MIN.

- U-SHAPED KITCHEN, 9'x 11'

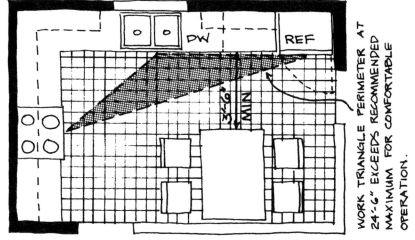

WORK TRIANGLE PERIMETER AT 24'-6" EXCEEDS RECOMMENDED MAXIMUM FOR COMFORTABLE OPERATION.

DW   REF

3'-6" MIN.

- L-SHAPED KITCHEN W/ DINING AREA, 10'x 15'

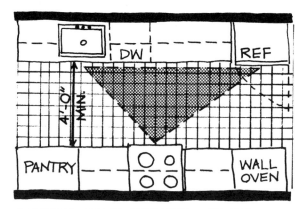

DW   REF.

4'-0" MIN.

PANTRY   WALL OVEN

- CENTER AISLE KITCHEN, 8'x13'

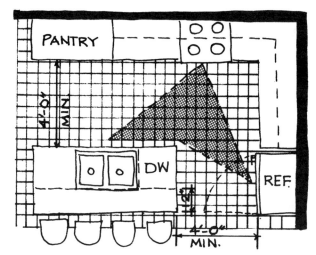

PANTRY

4'-0" MIN.

DW   REF.

4'-0" MIN.

- L-SHAPE KITCHEN W/CENTER ISLAND AND BREAKFAST BAR, 10'x 13'

RESIDENTIAL BATHROOM PLANS

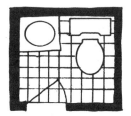

• POWDER ROOM
4'-6" x 4'-6" MIN.

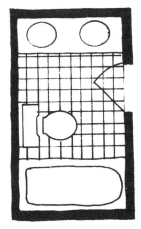

• FULL BATHROOM
5' x 9' MIN.

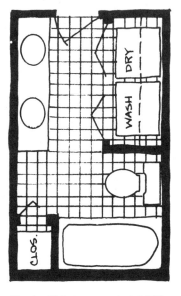

• FULL BATHROOM WITH
LINEN CLOSET AND
LAUNDRY 12' x 7' MIN.

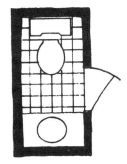

• POWDER ROOM
3' x 6'-6" MIN.

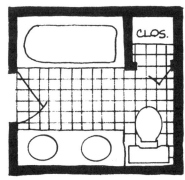

• FULL BATHROOM WITH
LINEN CLOSET, 7'-6" x 7' MIN.

PUBLIC RESTROOMS

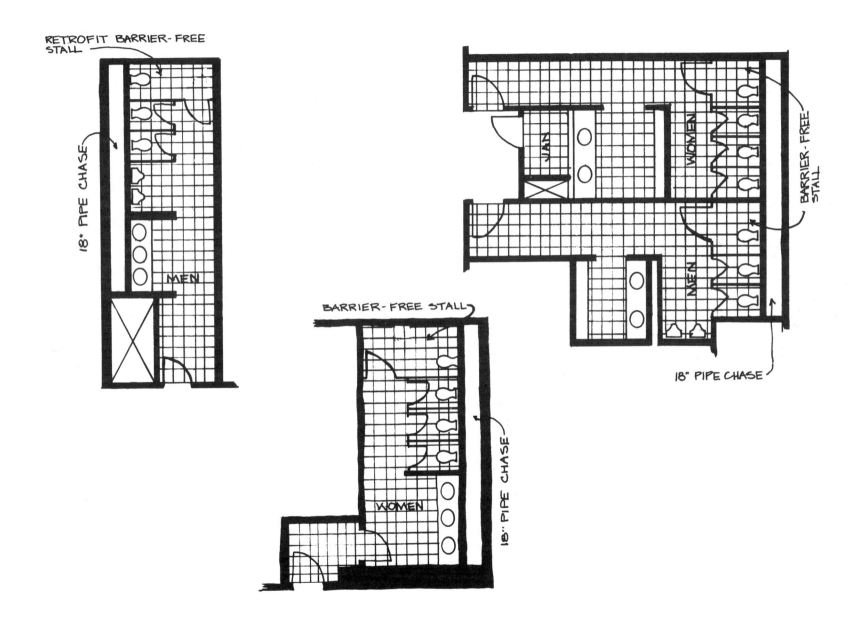

RETROFIT BARRIER-FREE STALL

18" PIPE CHASE

MEN

BARRIER-FREE STALL

18" PIPE CHASE

JAN.

WOMEN

MEN

BARRIER-FREE STALL

18" PIPE CHASE

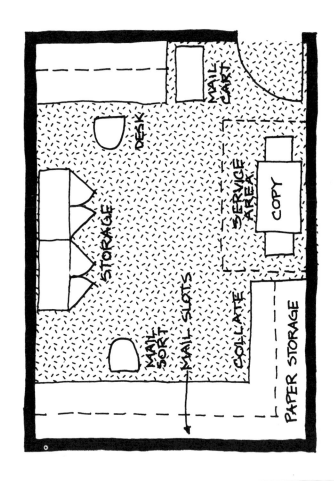

● MAIL / COPY

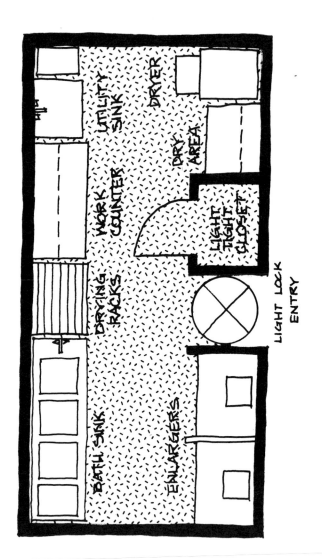

● DARK ROOM

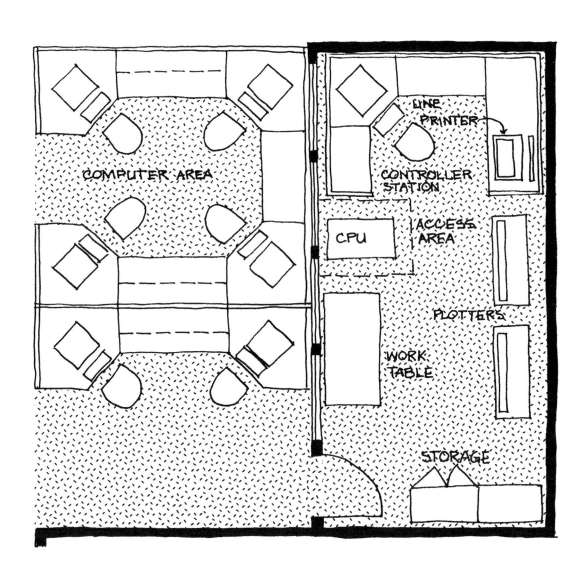

COMPUTER AREA

LINE PRINTER

CONTROLLER STATION

ACCESS AREA

CPU

PLOTTERS

WORK TABLE

STORAGE

• CONTROL ROOM WITH PLOTTERS AND COMPUTER STATIONS

space planning issues, within buildings in general, as well as in small and dimensionally demanding spaces. The most obviously applicable of these factors are those related to human dimensions, providing us with the necessary information about planning sizes and clearances. While most human factors research is related to the general adult population at large, some research has been related to "special populations," such as children and the elderly.

Space planners should be both sensitive to and knowledgeable about human factors, to know when such research data requires application and where to find the information. Because of the relative economy or tightness in their planning, these applications are used more frequently in small and dimensionally demanding spaces; but applications exist in most interior spaces, as in the placement of architectural element such as partitions and doors, as well as in the placement of conventional furniture and equipment.

Some of the issues involved in this area simply require common sense— avoiding the use of projecting sharp countertop corners in a tightly planned bathroom or restroom, or avoiding the placement of a toilet paper holder beyond comfortable reach. Other issues in this area will require some extensive human factors data gathering, such as the planning of a preschool day-care facility or a patient facility in a health-care setting. With an open-minded attitude towards human factors issues, sensitivity to the need for application of research will increase and knowledge of how to seek out data will broaden. The designer's need for human factors information goes far beyond space planning issues, and all professionals in the field should feel some responsibility to have a basic background in

this area. The Recommended Reading at the end of this chapter suggests books that provide an introduction to the field, as well as references for resource data.

BARRIER-FREE DESIGN STANDARDS

Accommodating people with physical disabilities, from minor (the early stages of aging) to major (wheelchair-bound) is often required of the space planner. This accommodation can be addressed from varying viewpoints: 1) philosophically, one could approach this issue in terms of satisfying a human and social need; 2) legally, code requirements must be fullfilled; and/or 3) pragmatically, barrier-free concepts could be seen as a means to plan more generous and comfortable interior spaces for all uses. The purpose here is not to address the conceptual or philosophical aspects of barrier-free design, but rather to present it as one necessary factor in the space planning process. A great deal of readily accessible resource material is available, as can be seen in the Recommended Reading list at the end of this chapter. For this reason, the related planning standards data illustrated in this text are extremely basic, assuming that appropriate references will be consulted as required. But designers should be made aware that code requirements and enforcement related to accommodations for disabled people are being regularly increased; the impact of the Americans with Disabilities Act will continue for many years to come. These code increases will relate to all categories of disabilities, including those related to sight, hearing, as well as physical movement and accessibility. Designers will be held accountable for this knowledge and its application.

Although all the aspects of planning for people with disabilities are important, in space planning terms, the controlling dimensional factor is wheelchair operation. The critical planning situations are:

ILLUS. 3-4A

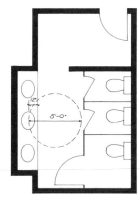

a. A 360° turn requires a 5'-0" diameter space (up to 12" of space under overhanging elements, such as a countertop, can be part of this 5'-0" diameter requirement, since very little height is needed for the wheelchair's footrest). See Illustration 3–4A.

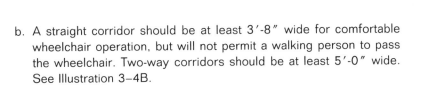

ILLUS. 3-4B

b. A straight corridor should be at least 3'-8" wide for comfortable wheelchair operation, but will not permit a walking person to pass the wheelchair. Two-way corridors should be at least 5'-0" wide. See Illustration 3–4B.

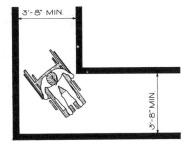

ILLUS. 3-4C

c. A right angle turn requires a 3'-8" radius for comfortable wheelchair operation. See Illustration 3–4C.

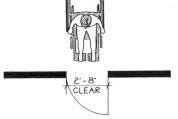

ILLUS. 3-4D

d. A minimum door opening should be at least 2'-8" wide, and 3'-0" is considered optimum. See Illustration 3–4D.

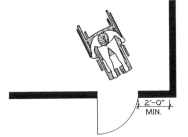

ILLUS. 3-4E

e. A minimum distance of 2'-0" should be maintained from the knob jamb of a door to an intersecting partition on the "pull side" of the door. See Illustration 3–4E.

Barrier-free requirements for public restrooms are important to account for in the early phases of planning, since they have a significant effect on square footage requirements. To demonstrate this point, the group of sketch plans shown in Illustration 3–5 provide some basic dimensional data needed for incorporating these accommodations. As mentioned earlier, several excellent resources provide complete data for these concerns. Residential considerations for the physically disabled deal with highly detailed issues and generally go beyond the concerns of space planning. Illustration 3–6 shows a typical residential kitchen accommodation for a wheelchair-bound person. So much non-space planning detail is involved in these residential facilities that further information for this specialized planning need is left to the reader's future research as those situations arise.

Planning for the physically disabled is complex and deals with a great deal more, both conceptually and in terms of nuance, than the simple dimensional issues presented here. While the design of all spaces is enhanced by a thorough integration of the floor plan with its vertical surfaces, the vertical element is absolutely crucial in planning for barrier-free concerns and should be made a part of initial planning studies. The Recommended Reading for this chapter includes several resources that will provide both conceptual thought and planning information in much greater detail.

EXERCISE 3-2

To become reasonably proficient in planning public restroom facilities, it is necessary to try one's hand at a broad variety of possibilities, starting with small and simple requirements and building to larger, more complex facilities for male and female users, imposing special criteria (use in office buildings, theatres, restaurants, etc.) as well. By incorporating specific planning requirements, such as a 160 seat restaurant or a 550 seat auditorium, this exercise can additionally provide some experience in using the prevailing building code to establish the number of plumbing fixtures required to serve the facility. Before starting this exercise, study the examples of such facilities shown in Illustration 3–2, as well as the examples found in the reference books suggested in this chapter's Recommended Reading. For each planning study, include an accompanying three-dimensional sketch which provides a graphic view of the plan's spatial qualities. From a learning viewpoint, this exercise is best done in $1/4'' = 1'-0''$ scale.

THE THREE-DIMENSIONAL REALITY

This text has focused and will continue to focus on the development of floor plan solutions. Do "good" floor plans always make for well designed interiors? Obviously not. Yet there is a strong inclination for the planner to get so involved in the space planning process and its two-dimensional, jig-saw-puzzle-like qualities, that the resulting three-dimensional qualities of the space become an afterthought.

Note was made in Chapter Two that it is entirely appropriate to include notations concerning three-dimensional or spatial ideas while developing bubble diagrams. But for most designers, the bubble diagram phase is too early in the process to attempt sketches—isometrics, perspectives, sections, or elevations—that develop three-dimensional ideas. But this chapter has dealt with specific floor plan arrangements, defining a proposed architectural reality, and whenever a floor plan arrangement emerges in any stage of the planning process, some form of three-dimensional sketch can be useful, no matter how rough or tentative.

It is not necessary to debate here whether a solidly functional floor plan is more important than visually satisfying spaces; both are crucial to create good building interiors. As the first rough floor plans emerge on your drawing board, they should be accompanied by first rough elevations, sections, perspectives, and/or isometric sketches, which might look like those in Illustration 3–7. No matter how well defined one's mental image of a space may be after drawing it in plan, more is seen and understood about that space after it has been sketched three-dimensionally. The meeting of planes and the visual inter-relationships that emerge on paper crystallize the mental image and permit the spatial concept to be more fully defined.

Recommended Reading

2*, 5*, 7*, 8*, 11, 14*, 15, 20*, 22*, 23*, 24*, 25*, 28*

Books noted with an asterisk are also included in the Recommended Reading of other chapters.

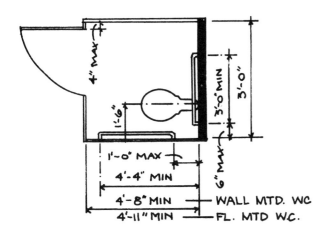

4" MAX

3'-0" MIN

3'-0"

1'-6"

6" MAX

1'-0" MAX

4'-4" MIN

4'-8" MIN —— WALL MTD. WC

4'-11" MIN —— FL. MTD WC.

● TYPICAL STALL
FOR HANDICAPPED

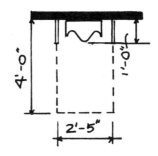

4'-0"

1'-0"

2'-5"

● URINAL FOR
CRUTCHES

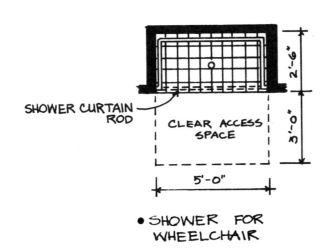

SHOWER CURTAIN
ROD

2'-6"

CLEAR ACCESS
SPACE

3'-0"

5'-0"

● SHOWER FOR
WHEELCHAIR

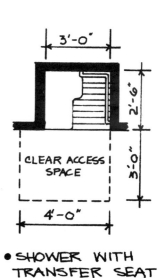

3'-0"

2'-6"

CLEAR ACCESS
SPACE

3'-0"

4'-0"

● SHOWER WITH
TRANSFER SEAT

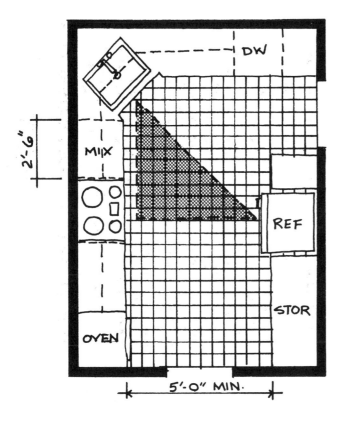

2'-6"

DW

MIX

REF

OVEN

STOR

5'-0" MIN.

• TYPICAL HANDICAPPED KITCHEN

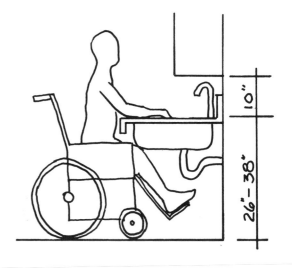

10"

26"-38"

• SECTION AT SINK

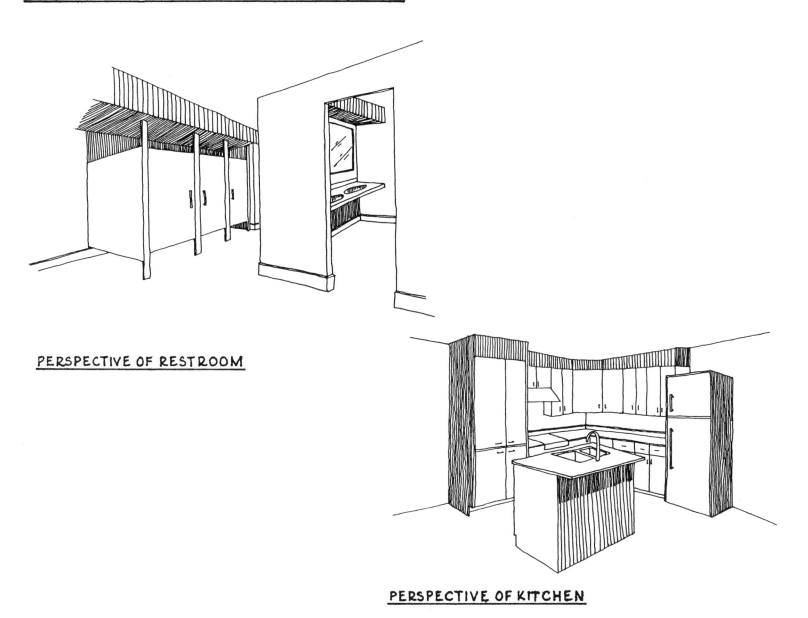

PERSPECTIVE OF RESTROOM

PERSPECTIVE OF KITCHEN

Chapter 4 THE BUILDING SHELL AND MAJOR SYSTEMS

The range and depth of knowledge an experienced space planner brings to a planning project is immense. It is the kind of knowledge rarely attained in the classroom, but rather through amassed experience in many and diverse projects over an extended period of time. Textbook or classroom processes cannot fully simulate the learning experience of repeated project research efforts related to the complexities and idiosyncracies of realistic situations. Throughout the course of any project, the space planner can call upon consultants and / or research information and application techniques related to building codes, acoustics, lighting, mechanical and electrical construction, historic preservation requirements, structural considerations, or interior construction techniques, as well as many others.

This chapter and Chapter Five are designed to provide an overview of each area of general planning and design background fundamentally important to the space planning process. As part of each overview, a general indication will be provided of the required level or depth of one's knowledge needed for that area. In addition, specific Recommended

Reading geared to develop that knowledge is identified at the end of the related chapter. Each of the areas discussed is complex and deserves separate coursework of its own. But a significant depth of knowledge in each area goes beyond the intent of this book; the focus here will remain on space planning.

General commentary must be made here on the use of consultants in most of the areas discussed in Chapters Four and Five. Customarily, professional planners make extensive use of engineers and other specialists throughout the planning and design process; the world of building design has become too complex for any professional to "know it all." Put simply, one of the most important facets of professional practice is to know when and how to use consultants. The issues discussed in Chapter Four would involve structural and mechanical engineers, in Chapter Five, lighting designers, code specialists, acoustic consultants, and furniture and equipment manufacturers representatives. The important message here is not to feel intimidated by the amount and depth of information required of the space planner; but rather, to know that no one is expected to have all the answers and that help is always available using specialized consultants. Once the consultant is at hand, the planner/designer must know enough to discuss intelligently the design issues and convey to the consultant what is expected of him/her. A great deal of the learning process will happen as one practices in the field during the first several years of professional experience.

THE BUILDING SHELL

Beyond the satisfying of user needs, no more basic influence exists on the planning and design process than the intrinsic qualities of the building shell containing those functions. It is extremely important that space planners and interior designers develop a thorough knowledge of and sensitivity to the basic qualities of buildings. Structural systems, construction materials, fenestration types, building shape and configuration, and architectural design and detail have a major effect on space planning decisions. Knowledge of and sensitivity to these aspects of buildings usually begin with school coursework. The Recommended Reading at the end of the chapter is geared to the further development of that knowledge. Further knowledge and sophistication can be gained through regular and keen observation of buildings. And over time, varied and repeated project experience in space planning and interior design will bring a full and authoritative knowledge in this area.

Planning within wood frame, masonry wall bearing, or columnar system buildings will determine the freedom with which one can manipulate interior space; interior bearing walls, masonry ones in particular, are often a serious impediment to creating floor plans that work and flow well. A building's basic structural materials, wood, masonry, steel, or concrete, will influence the ease with which wall and floor openings can be made, creating a major influence on the usefulness of a building for its intended new function. The length of a building's structural spans (bay size), often related to the building's age (generally, the more recent the building's structural technology, the longer the span) will determine the degree of flexibility and/or openness that can be created; obviously, small bays will restrict partition and furniture placement and limit traffic flow. A combination of structural system and materials factors will govern if, where, and how new door and window openings can be made in both interior and exterior walls. The relative simplicity or complexity of a building's shape or configuration will impact upon its usefulness for a given set of planning requirements; complex exterior wall configurations and peculiarly placed stairwells and elevator shafts can render a building unsuitable for a par-

ticular use. All of these issues may require consultation with architects and/or structural engineers, but basic background on the part of the space planner is necessary to intelligently discuss the issues with the consultants and ultimately make wise space planning decisions. Illustrations 4–1A and 4–1B demonstrate some of the basic aspects of the influence of the building shell on space planning.

Beyond these issues of structure and shell are the more subtle, but still important, ones of building history and design that have a bearing on space planning. Buildings of true historic significance are in a special category in which space planning decisions are dominated by architectural factors; this is true whether the historical significance is architectural, political, or social. But every building has its own connection with history—an expression of its time—that warrants sensitivity when replanning within it. The planner/designer needs to have knowledge of architectural and building-construction history to exercise appropriate design sensitivity; one should necessarily approach a traditionally based nineteenth-century building shell very differently from a 1930s Art Deco structure. These differences in historical context have relevance across the design spectrum, from major stylistic characteristics, to the details of trim and moulding. In most buildings of recent vintage, door and window trim have been kept to a minimum; consequently, new partitions can often be made perpendicularly flush with door and window jambs. But in many older buildings, where wide trim elements are carried around doors and windows, it is not only necessary to allow for the existing trim, but also to leave some wall surface adjacent to the trim before placing a perpendicular partition. Similar attention to detail must be given when planning in buildings with bay windows, when "crowding" a bay with a new partition can have a very unsatisfactory result. Both of these examples related to building design detail are demonstrated in Illustration 4–2. These are just two cases in which building design quality will have a significant influence on space planning decisions; almost endless examples can be cited, from incorporating monumental staircases and ornamental ceilings, to utilizing decorative floor patterns and traditional wall panelling. The importance of gaining a sophisticated background in architectural and interiors history, as well as in the art of building, cannot be overstated.

PLUMBING SYSTEMS

The placement of plumbing fixtures presents one of the most stringent constraints in the space planning process. A limited number of situations exists, such as one-story buildings with utility basements or crawl spaces below the floor, in which plumbing fixtures can be placed almost at will.

BUILDING CONFIGURATION INFLUENCES SPACE PLANNING

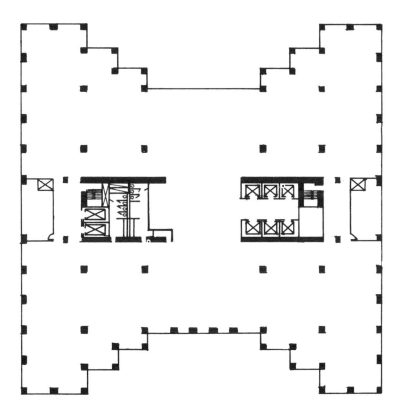

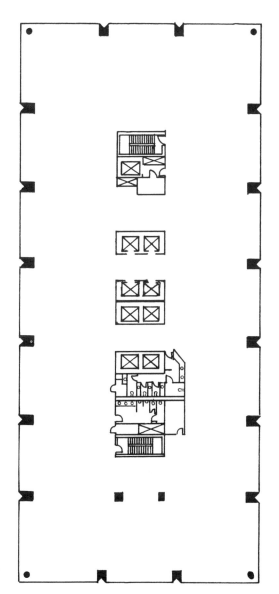

- MULTI-FACETED CONFIGURATION PROVIDES FOR MANY "CORNER" OFFICES, BUT CREATES SPACE PLANNING COMPLEXITIES.

- TYPICAL CENTER CORE BUILDING W/FEW INTERIOR COLUMNS PERMITS EASY SPACE PLANNING.

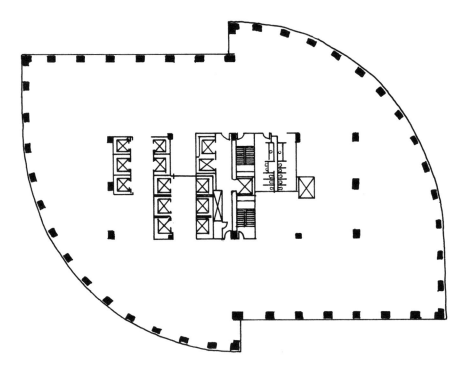

• MAJOR CURVED WALLS PRESENT
SPECIAL SPACE PLANNING PROBLEMS.

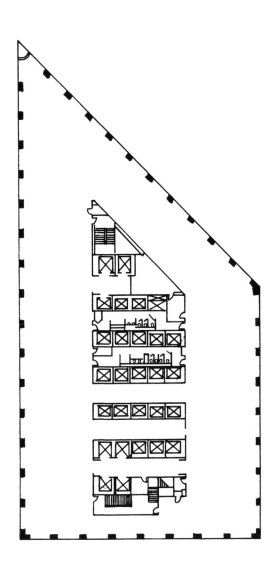

• ACUTE ANGLE IN BUILDING
SHAPE PRESENTS SPACE
PLANNING LIMITATIONS.

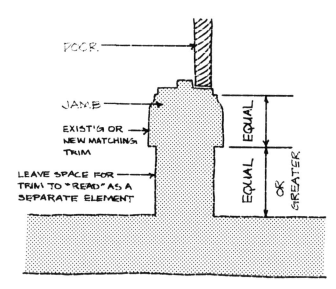

DOOR

JAMB

EXIST'G OR
NEW MATCHING
TRIM

LEAVE SPACE FOR
TRIM TO "READ" AS A
SEPARATE ELEMENT

EQUAL   EQUAL

EQUAL   OR GREATER

- POOR JAMB CONDITION

WHERE WIDE "TRADITIONAL" TRIM MUST
BE ACCOMMODATED OR MATCHED

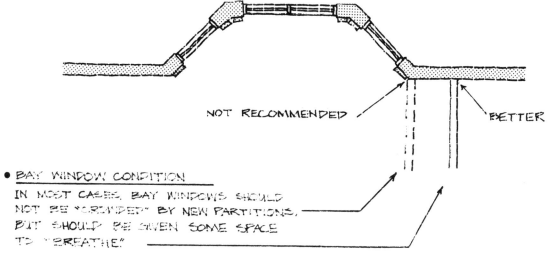

NOT RECOMMENDED   BETTER

- BAY WINDOW CONDITION

IN MOST CASES, BAY WINDOWS SHOULD
NOT BE "CROWDED" BY NEW PARTITIONS,
BUT SHOULD BE GIVEN SOME SPACE
TO "BREATHE"

In the great majority of situations, construction practicalities and cost factors require that fixtures be placed in close proximity to existing vented waste lines, limiting the location of typical rooms or functions requiring fixtures, such as restrooms, kitchens, and laboratories, as well as special situations as medical offices often requiring a dispersal of fixtures throughout the facility. The constraints on fixture placement are three-fold:

1. adherence to good plumbing construction practice;
2. compliance with the prevailing plumbing code;
3. grouping of fixtures for economical piping layouts.

Space planners do not have to know as much about plumbing as mechanical engineers or contractors; but a basic understanding of the three constraint issues cited is necessary. A great deal of the necessary knowledge is usually gained in the professional office and on the job site. Over time, the space planner should attempt to build that informational background in the following manner:

1. For good plumbing construction practice, become familiar with the terminology and principles of plumbing construction. Through reading, working with mechanical engineers and contractors, and observing piping layouts on the job site before they are covered up by finishing materials, the planner can gain an adequate understanding of the relationship between plumbing construction and the practicalities of space planning.
2. For plumbing code compliance, get to know the specific limitations on construction imposed by the plumbing code that has jurisdiction in specific project locations. This information should be sought from code enforcement officials and mechanical engineers and/or contractors before definitive space planning solutions are attempted.
3. For construction economy, become practiced and proficient with typical planning techniques for the grouping of fixtures. Typically, fixtures are placed along pipe chases to keep construction costs low and for ease of future building maintenance. See the left-hand sketch in Illustration 4–3 for a graphic example of this kind of fixture grouping.

EXERCISE 4–1

The recommended exercises in Chapter Three involving public restroom planning should be restudied from a plumbing systems viewpoint as well as a space planning perspective. Are the original exercise results practi-

cal and economical construction-wise? Rework the plans in terms of construction practicalities; ''real world'' projects will demand it.

In the very preliminary space planning phases of a project, before plumbing code information has been established, many space planners will use a rule-of-thumb for the preliminary placement of fixtures. For this early phase of planning, a reasonable rule-of-thumb approach would place flush fixtures (toilets, urinals, bidets) within 7'-0" of a vented waste line, and all other fixtures (sinks, bathtubs, clothes washers, etc.) within 10'-0" of a vented waste line, as graphically described in right-hand sketch of Illustration 4–3. If construction conditions permit the waste piping to run under the floor, these dimensions can be measured on a straight line from the center of the fixture to the vertical vent stack; otherwise, waste lines must be run in thickened plumbing walls or chases, with distances from fixtures to stacks measured along those lines. Like any other rule-of-thumb, this approach should not be used beyond a very preliminary planning stage.

HEATING, VENTILATING, AND AIR CONDITIONING (HVAC) SYSTEMS

Broad generalizations are difficult to draw concerning the relationship between the space planning process and HVAC systems, because the basic qualities of HVAC systems can vary greatly from building to building. The great majority of modern, nonresidential buildings have flexible HVAC systems exclusively contained in ceiling plenum spaces and/or exterior wall units. Because these systems are designed for maximum flexibility, they permit quick and easy changes and result in little impact on the space planning process. More specifically, new partitions can be located with almost complete freedom in terms of HVAC requirements. But this is not the case when working within older buildings or ones originally designed for specific or unique functions. Since the replacement of an entire HVAC system is usually very costly and time consuming, more often than not, existing systems are retained unless they are totally outdated or specialized beyond reuse. When older, inflexible systems are retained, HVAC requirements could place significant limitations on space allocation and partition placement. These older and/or unique buildings have many variables in configuration and HVAC system design, and no quick and easy rules-of-thumb or space planning techniques apply. In situations of this kind, it is important to consult with a mechanical engineer as soon as a survey of the existing conditions is available, and certainly before the bubble diagramming process has begun. Illustration 4–4 shows some of the typical and non-typical variables encountered in existing buildings.

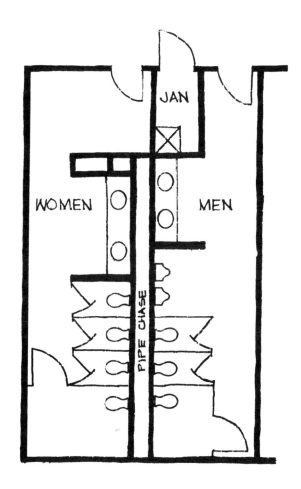

- PLUMBING FIXTURES GROUPED ALONG COMMON PIPE CHASE

CONSTRUCTION AND MAINTENANCE ECONOMIES DEMAND THIS TYPE OF ARRANGEMENT

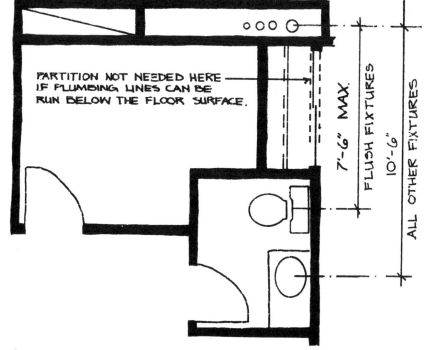

PARTITION NOT NEEDED HERE IF PLUMBING LINES CAN BE RUN BELOW THE FLOOR SURFACE.

7'-6" MAX.

FLUSH FIXTURES

10'-6"

ALL OTHER FIXTURES

- RULE-OF-THUMB FOR PLUMBING FIXTURE PLACEMENT

IN VERY PRELIMINARY PLANNING STAGE

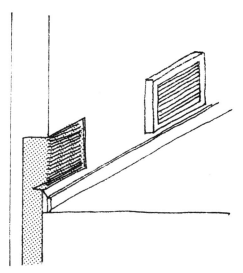

• HEAT BY RADIATION, FORCED AIR OR CONVECTION; SURFACED MOUNTED OR RECESSED.

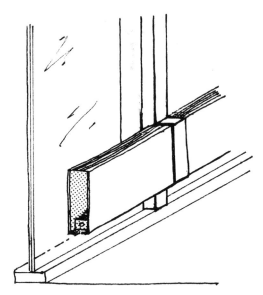

• MULLION OR WALL MOUNTED HEAT BY FORCED AIR OR CONVECTION.

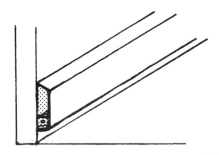

• BASEBOARD UNIT. HEAT BY CONVECTION.

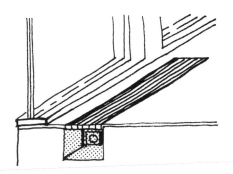

• UNDER FLOOR CONVECTOR UNIT.

- HUMAN COMFORT CONCERNS
  AVOID BAD DRAFT CONDITIONS

- PLACEMENT OF SUPPLY AIR
  REGISTERS AND
  RETURN AIR GRILLES

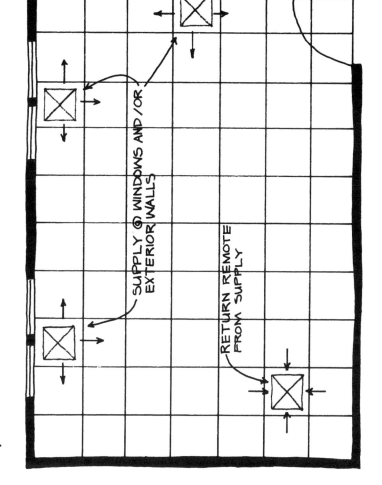

SUPPLY @ WINDOWS AND/OR EXTERIOR WALLS

RETURN REMOTE FROM SUPPLY

An understanding of the basic principles of HVAC systems, with particular emphasis on the air distribution elements of those systems, is the knowledge base for which the space planner should strive. More specifically, the planner should have knowledge of how supply diffusers and return grilles are placed in drywall and acoustic tile ceilings, plus an understanding of the principles that place supply air close to the offending exterior wall surface and return grills as remotely from them as possible to provide maximum supply air coverage and minimize short circuiting of the supply air. The top sketch in Illustration 4–5 demonstrates an appropriate application of these principles. In this one aspect of HVAC systems design, the interior designer is often the best or most appropriate member of the building design team, rather than the architect or mechanical engineer, to decide upon the final placement of such equipment. Detailed knowledge of specific or likely placement of furniture and related equipment permits the intelligent deployment of these HVAC devices, in terms of human comfort, within the space. Although much of this placement process occurs long after the space planning has been finalized, a general eye to ductwork and dropped soffit locations during the space planning phase will create better HVAC systems design in terms of human comfort. The bottom sketch in Illustration 4–5 shows one of the typical application problems encountered in this placement process. Note should also be made about the capacity of HVAC ductwork to carry sound and destroy otherwise well-planned acoustic environments. Wherever sensitive acoustic situations exist, HVAC systems must be designed to accommodate those needs.

Again, the interior planner/designer is not expected to be expert in the complexities of interior environmental control systems, but rather, to have enough understanding of basic principles and knowledge of basic terminology to be able to discuss intelligently project requirements with mechanical engineers and contractors. Initially, specific coursework and prescribed reading will build that knowledge base, and the Recommended Reading for this chapter should be helpful; beyond that, depth of knowledge is built through repeated project experience, both in the professional office and on the construction job site.

Recommended Reading

The Building Shell, 1*, 5*, 22*, 23*

Plumbing Systems, 1*, 5*, 19*, 22*, 23*

HVAC Systems, 1*, 5*, 19*, 22*, 23*

Books noted with an asterisk are also included in the Recommended Reading of other chapters.

Chapter 5   IMPORTANT INFLUENCING FACTORS

In addition to the building shell and major systems issues discussed in Chapter Four, several other factors have significant influence on the space planning process. The ideas raised in the three introductory paragraphs in Chapter Four, dealing with the planner's depth of knowledge and the complexity of factors bearing on space planning decisions, have equal application for the influencing factors discussed in this chapter. Each area discussed deserves a book or course of its own; but that kind of depth in each area goes far beyond the intent of this book. The focus here remains on space planning, and the reader will pursue additional knowledge in each area as his/her needs and circumstances require.

BUILDING CODES

Building codes deal with almost every area of building planning, design, and construction; consequently, they are very complex. To compound matters, their language is very technical, sometimes arcane, and generally difficult to penetrate for the uninitiated. Typically, interior designers'

primary code involvements are limited to the Articles on Use Group Classification, Types of Construction, Means of Egress, and Fire Resistive Construction, plus the issues of flammability and noxious fumes. During the space planning process, most building code involvement is limited to Means of Egress concerns, but that area will have major impact on most of the basic planning decisions that must be made.

Safe departure from a building during a fire or other panic situations is at the heart of means-of-egress standards. The basic principles and the details of these standards should be thoroughly understood by every interior planner/designer. That understanding begins with reading (and if necessary, re-reading . . . . and re-reading) the building code article. The following code concepts should not only be understood, but their typical forms of applications should also be known:

1. occupant load
2. exit capacity
3. door, corridor, stair width
4. two remote means of egress
5. length of exit travel
6. dead-end corridors

Despite many efforts to create one, a national building code does not exist. Which one should be read? Three major regional building codes exist, all of which are quite similar. Read and become familiar with the code used most prevalently in your region. Real depth of knowledge will come with applying the code concepts to specific space planning problems. With this end in mind, the following exercise is suggested as a first attempt at those applications. As one progresses through the space planning exercises provided in Chapters Six and Seven, the building code issues inherent in those design problems must be addressed and solved. As each of those future exercises is completed, they should be specifically reviewed and critiqued from a building code perspective.

EXERCISE 5-1

Using the Group #3 Building Shell plans (approximately 4,000 square feet in size) provided in the Appendix, sketch corridor pattern solutions for each that satisfy code requirements for egress (corridor widths, remote exits, length of travel, dead-end corridors), while maximizing usable (or rentable) square footage. This exercise can be extended by using shell plans of any multistory commercial or institutional building published in interior design and architectural publications.

Knowledge of prevailing codes related to the building process is critical to the space planner. Even aspects of zoning codes will have bearing on space planning problems. Despite this, no book is available that addresses these issues comprehensively. The Recommended Reading for this chapter provides some answers, but there is no substitute for digging into the codes themselves and learning how to use them. And, when necessary, learning whom to call upon for expert advice.

LIGHTING DESIGN

Both natural and electric lighting play a significant role in the space planning process. Although a sophisticated approach to lighting design would draw strong relationships between the planning of natural and electric lighting for a specific building and/or interior space, it is not necessary to integrate the two for preliminary space planning purposes, since that integration deals with subtleties of design that will not have bearing on the allocation of space. Consequently, they will be dealt with here as distinct and separate entities.

Natural Lighting

It is difficult and unnecessary to separate the issues of natural lighting, view to the exterior, solar orientation, and natural ventilation, as they relate to the preliminary space planning process. In some cases, only one of these issues will be a factor in providing a window, or windows, for a function or space; while in other cases, all four of these issues will be involved to determine the need for a window location. A well-articulated criteria matrix can and should be able to keep all of these issues clear during the planning process. Remember that building and/or housing codes generally require that all habitable rooms—code-defined as all residentially used spaces (except for mechanically ventilated bathrooms and kitchens)—must have natural light and air, typically requiring window area to be at least 8 to 10 percent of the floor area, and that one-half of that (4 to 5 percent) must be operable for ventilation, as shown in Illustration 5–1. Code issues aside, most rooms that people spend time in, residential or otherwise, psychologically need natural light and a view to the exterior, and these human factors should be the ultimate determinates in window placement decisions. One more factor to keep in mind is energy conservation, indicating that the use of natural lighting be maximized while maintaining an appropriate balance with heating and cooling needs.

The psychological and esthetic concerns of interior planning will have the strongest influence on the use of natural lighting. For both living and working spaces, the quality of natural light and a view to the exterior will, except for unique functions, be seen as highly desirable and often essential. Buildings with an abundance of windows and a minimum of deep interior regions far from exterior walls do not present problems in planning for natural light. But some buildings have limited windows and/or large interior regions far from windowed exterior walls. In these cases, planning for natural light can be a critical space planning element, in which difficult decisions must be made about which spaces get the windows and/or choice view and which go without. One graphically comparative example of this space planning "influencer" is demonstrated in Illustration 5–2.

Planning for natural lighting begins with the initial space planning analysis, as described in Chapter One. When organizing user and spatial needs, as in the development of a criteria matrix, priorities should be created for natural lighting needs, identifying those spaces for which natural lighting is: 1) essential ("habitable rooms, executive offices); 2) desirable (long-term work spaces, student lounges); 3) unnecessary (public restrooms, short-term conference rooms); and 4) undesirable (dark rooms, valuable

15' x 12' = 180 SQ. FT.
180 x 10% = 18 SQ. FT
2' x 4' = 8 SQ. FT x 3 = 24
     SQ. FT OF WINDOW

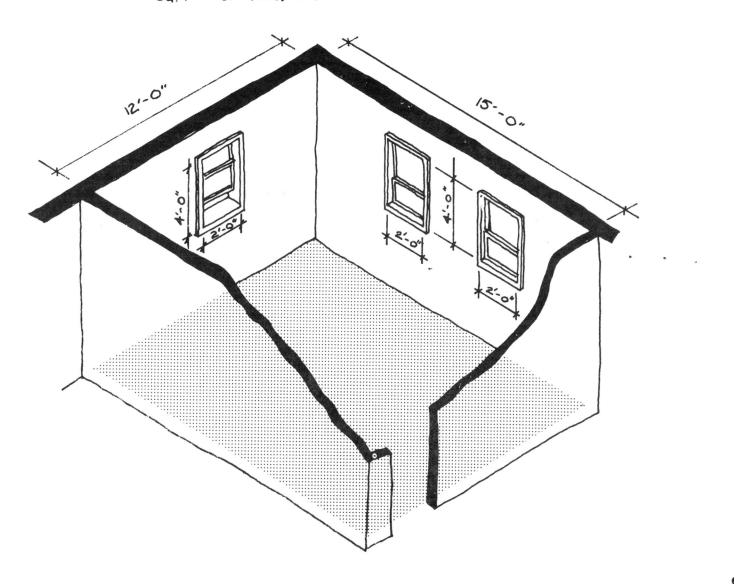

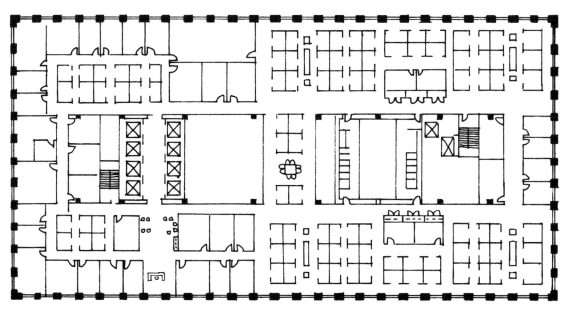

ILLUS. A

BUILDING WITH GENEROUS NATURAL
LIGHT/VIEW AVAILABILITY PROVIDES
DESIREABLE CONDITION FOR
MAJORITY OF EMPLOYEES.

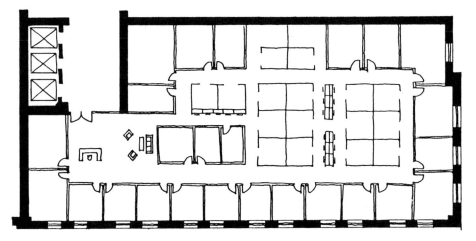

ILLUS. B

BUILDING WITH LIMITED NATURAL LIGHT/VIEW
AVAILABILITY CREATES DIFFICULT DECISIONS
CONCERNING PRIORITIES ON WINDOWED SPACES.

document storage). When windows are abundant, one may identify the desired direction of view and/or solar orientation for specific rooms or functions. In addition to the criteria matrix, relationship diagrams can easily reflect these needs and priorities. Decisions about natural light are made during the bubble diagramming or block planning phase. The final diagram or block plan must satisfy the natural lighting requirements, because it is usually impossible to reconfigure the building later to admit natural light when it is not available. Similarly, requirements for solar orientation and direction of view are determined at this very early planning phase, because it is impossible to rotate an existing building to satisfy these needs. Very often, the issues of solar orientation and selected views are not given high priority in the criteria matrix, particularly in non-residential buildings; but when they can be satisfied, a valuable esthetic element has been served.

Note should be made about the use of skylights. Their use is limited because they can only be used in one story buildings or in the top floor of multi-story buildings. When skylights can be used, they bring a unique and marvelous quality of daylight to a space that is quite different from the quality of light admitted by conventional windows. Unusually generous, flooding qualities of natural light can be admitted by relatively small skylights. Learning to use them effectively requires observation, informative reading, and project experience.

Planning for natural lighting is not technical or difficult, although as project size and scope increases, the sheer number of factors and priorities that must be kept in mind and satisfied can make natural lighting a problematic space planning task.

Electric Lighting
Unlike natural lighting, electric lighting is complex and highly technical—an area in which every interior designer should have significant background. As with natural lighting, electric lighting can have a significant effect on space planning decisions. From the outset, it should be remembered that most buildings must be planned for night-time as well as day-time use, therefore, natural lighting has only limited effect upon electric lighting planning and design.

For buildings without existing lighting systems (or when it makes economic sense to remove an existing system), the effects of lighting design on space planning solutions are usually not critical. In these situations, accommodation for lighting can wait until a rough, or first tentative floor plan, is established, indicating that lighting design need not have a significant effect on the early phases of space allocation or planning.

For non-residential buildings with existing lighting systems (most typically, part of an integrated suspended ceiling system), construction economy will usually dictate that the system be reused and conformed with. If that is the case, space planning cannot be accomplished without careful coordination with the existing system. More specifically, unless one is unconcerned with the coordination of partitions with the suspension system, or unconcerned with a fairly exacting location of lighting fixtures in relation to partitions, equipment, and furnishings, new partitions must be located with exacting relationship to the ceiling construction system. Once the bubble diagramming or block planning phase is complete, the building shell floor plan *and* the reflected ceiling plan must be worked with as an integral unit in the development of a rough floor plan. See Illustration 5–3 for reflected ceiling plans that demonstrate these issues of planning and design coordination.

Once a rough floor plan has been tentatively established, a first attempt at a reflected ceiling plan should be drawn. Basic ceiling configuration should be considered, including ceiling height(s), slopes, and soffits. The ceiling, despite its basic importance, is too often the "forgotten surface" in interior spaces. Now is the time to consciously address those design concerns, not after the floor plan has been so well established or refined that ceiling design considerations might be difficult to incorporate without making significant floor plan changes. In most buildings, particularly non-residential buildings, lighting is implemented through the ceiling construction, and lighting design decisions are integrally tied to the design of the ceiling. For that reason, a rough or first tentative reflected ceiling plan incorporating a first tentative lighting design solution should be prepared at this critical point in the space planning process. A method to incorporate this procedure in the space planning process is discussed and described in Chapter Six.

In professional settings, once the basic ceiling design issues have been considered and sketched, it is wise to consult with a lighting designer. Since lighting design has become very complex and technical, consultation with a specialist is desirable for all but the simplest of buildings. Under normal professional practice conditions, it is best to consult with the lighting designer at this very early phase in the planning process, and specifically before the final preliminary floor plan is started, to integrate the lighting design solution into the final design solution.

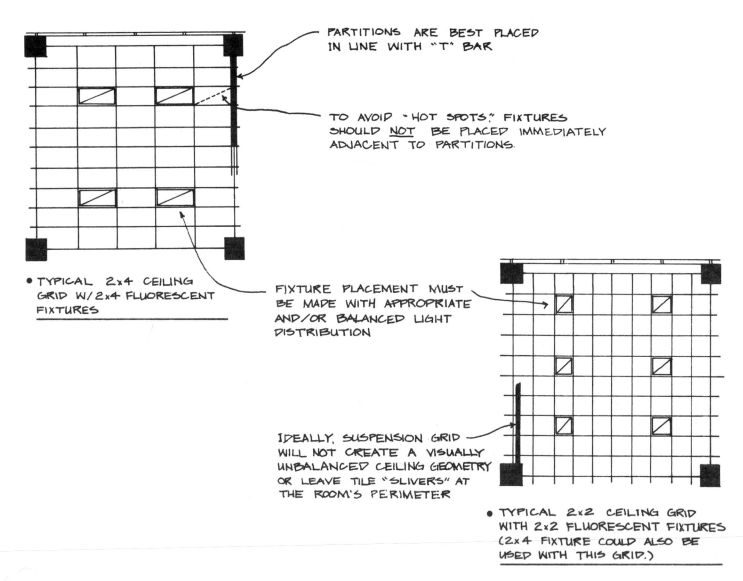

PARTITIONS ARE BEST PLACED
IN LINE WITH "T" BAR

TO AVOID "HOT SPOTS" FIXTURES
SHOULD <u>NOT</u> BE PLACED IMMEDIATELY
ADJACENT TO PARTITIONS.

FIXTURE PLACEMENT MUST
BE MADE WITH APPROPRIATE
AND/OR BALANCED LIGHT
DISTRIBUTION

• TYPICAL 2x4 CEILING
GRID W/ 2x4 FLUORESCENT
FIXTURES

IDEALLY, SUSPENSION GRID
WILL NOT CREATE A VISUALLY
UNBALANCED CEILING GEOMETRY
OR LEAVE TILE "SLIVERS" AT
THE ROOM'S PERIMETER

• TYPICAL 2x2 CEILING GRID
WITH 2x2 FLUORESCENT FIXTURES
(2x4 FIXTURE COULD ALSO BE
USED WITH THIS GRID.)

In a classroom, when the aid of a professional consultant is not available, it is excellent experience for design students to try their hand at a lighting design solution. Ideally, some background in lighting design coursework has already been accomplished; but even without that background, thinking through the lighting design issues is a valuable learning experience.

Lighting design is a field unto itself, requiring much knowledge and expertise. For space planning purposes, the interior designer's depth of knowledge need not be very detailed; only "broad brush" concepts and solutions are required. With all factors that require design integration with a consulting specialist, one must know enough to be able to work together intelligently with that consultant. If your knowledge and/or experience in this area need strengthening, some Recommended Reading is listed at the end of the chapter.

Note should be made that other aspects of electrical construction are not raised in this text. Although they represent major aspects of interior construction, they usually do not have critical impact on space planning because of the ease with which wiring is placed in chases, partitions and ceiling plenums.

ACOUSTICAL PLANNING

Although the field of architectural acoustics is complex and replete with a technology of its own, its application to basic space planning is relatively simple and essentially common-sense oriented. Except for relatively large performance spaces such as auditoriums, lecture halls, or cabarets, space planning for good or acceptable acoustics involves simple technical knowledge plus some basic interior construction information about what can be accomplished and its costs.

Good architectural acoustics begin with concepts of zoning and isolation, followed later by insulation and absorption. The planning process for acoustics begins with the initial space planning analysis, as described in Chapter One. When organizing user and spatial needs, as in the development of a criteria matrix, acoustic needs for privacy, isolation, and absorption should be identified. Creating quiet and noisy zones (often coinciding with private and public zones) can be accomplished during the bubble diagramming or block planning phase. Common sense tells one that it is inappropriate to put a school library adjacent to a band practice room or the company president next to a noisy mechanical equipment room. Wherever possible, acoustic conflicts or problems should first be addressed through appropriate and sensitive space allocation, as demonstrated in Illustration 5-4. Despite this, many acoustic conflicts cannot be easily resolved through space planning; working function and traffic flow adjacencies often require that acoustic conflicts be ignored, or even compounded, in terms of space planning, as is typically found in the necessary groupings of lawyers' offices, medical examining rooms, or meeting/conference rooms. In these cases, the acoustic interference must be dealt with through means other than zoning and isolation.

The transmission of sound through walls and partitions, except in the most extreme cases, can be limited to acceptable levels through established construction techniques. The greater the decibel level generated, the heavier, more complex, and costly are the construction solutions. For unusually noisy functions (banquet halls, music practice suites, etc.) when space planning cannot zone them away, buffer spaces (storage rooms, filing rooms, etc.) can be used if space planning adjacencies will permit, as demonstrated in Illustration 5-5. If it is difficult or inappropriate to use a buffer space for this purpose, the cost of a dense, isolating wall must be accepted.

Conventional groupings of rooms or spaces in which acoustic interference is common (offices, classrooms, conference/meeting rooms, etc.) require the space planner to have knowledge of the sound levels generated and the construction techniques needed to limit transmission to acceptable levels. This knowledge is not required because construction detailing will take place at this early phase of planning, but because the planner must know what degree of acoustic isolation can be practically accomplished through construction techniques. Basic information on these construction techniques is readily available in many reference sources (see the Recommended Reading at the end of the chapter). Illustration 5-6 indicates a sampling of information one needs to solve acoustic transmission problems through construction techniques. Detailed involvement in construction techniques to limit sound transmission or to absorb ambient sound within spaces, go far beyond the issues of space planning and are generally dealt with during the subsequent project phases of design and construction documentation. As mentioned in Chapter Four, HVAC construction can also play a critical role in achieving good acoustic results. An acoustic consultant's advice is often valuable in solving those HVAC construction detail issues.

When relatively large performance spaces are part of a planning project and affect the shape, height, and configuration of the performance space because of acoustic considerations, an acoustic consultant should be

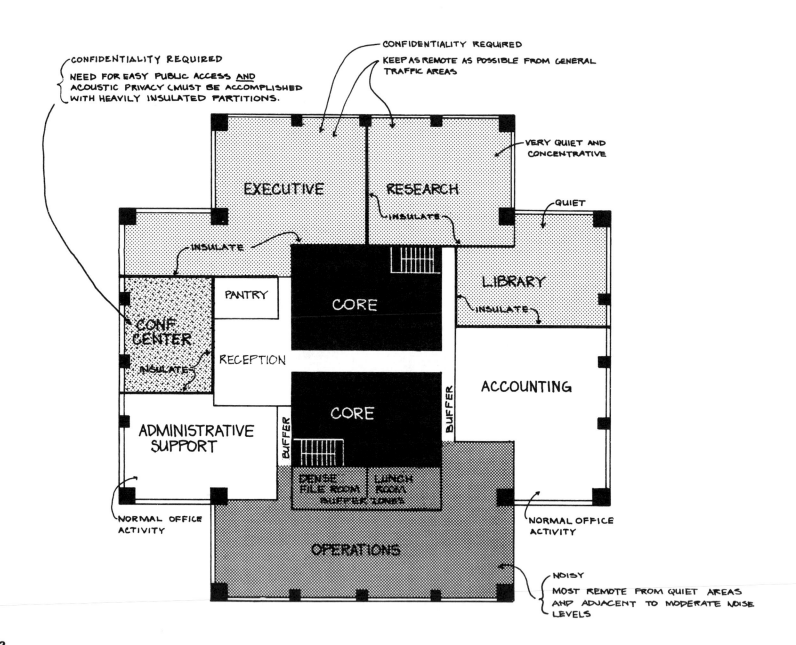

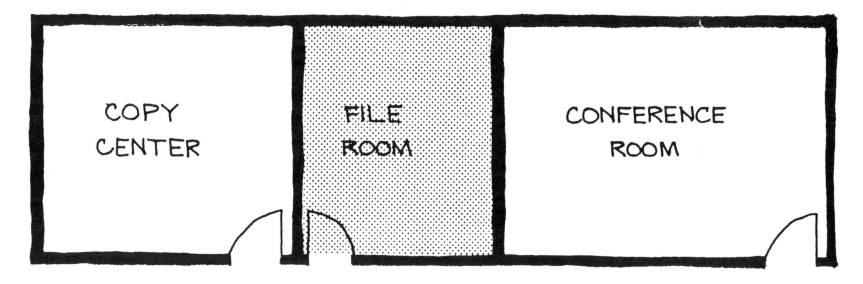

CORRIDOR = BUFFER ZONE

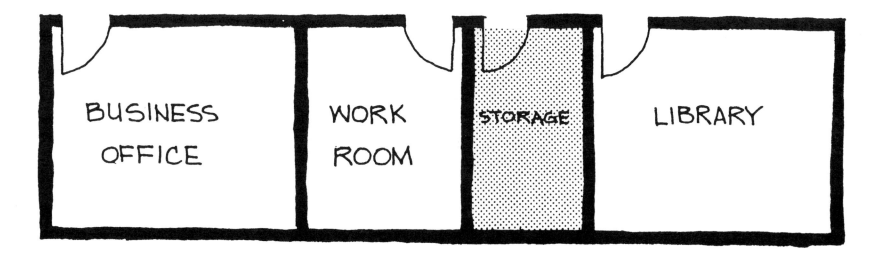

BASIC SOUND-RESISTIVE PARTITION CONSTRUCTION

ILLUS. 5-6

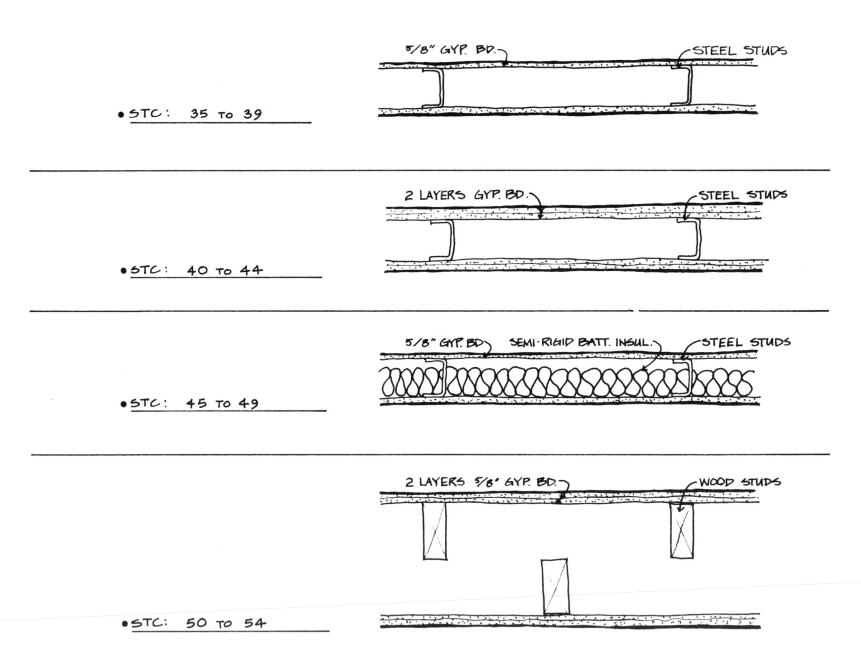

74

brought to the project at its earliest phases. Most designers and architects are not well enough versed in performance acoustics to design such spaces without the help of an experienced consultant who is able to provide design direction that will ensure acceptable acoustic results. In these cases, the unique shape of a performance space may have a profound effect on an entire spatial organization. The acoustic consultant's help is also invaluable in designing the details of those spaces and in the development of construction detailing when acoustic privacy and acoustic absorbancy are needed. These issues are usually addressed at later stages in most planning and design projects.

The need for multiple use of interior space occurs so frequently that space planners should also have general knowledge of the achievable sound transmission ratings of the several types of movable partitions available and the approximate costs involved in their installation. Multiple uses of space are most common in classroom, conference/meeting room, and banquet facilities but are not uncommon in many other types of interior uses. Surprisingly high acoustic ratings are achievable with these construction techniques but usually at very high cost. Illustration 5–7 diagrams the most commonly used types of movable partitions to separate spaces. Multiple space use is discussed again in this chapter, but from a perspective much broader than acoustic planning. (See section on Flexibility/Multi-Use, on this page.)

PLANNING RULES-OF-THUMB

Knowing the approximate size of typical rooms and spaces makes the preliminary space planning process easier and more efficient. It is impossible for the space planner to commit to memory square footage rules-of-thumb for every type of interior facility; but recurring spaces in most buildings have typical square footage requirements. It is for these spaces and functions that rules-of-thumb are worth developing and remembering.

Without any attempt at completeness, here is a beginning list of spaces and functions for which every space planner should attempt to remember an approximate space requirement:

Typical powder room (two piece)	20 to 30 square feet
Typical apartment bathroom (three piece)	35 to 45 square feet
Typical apartment kitchen (not studio or efficiency)	65 to 80 square feet
Lounge (hotel lobby, student center)	20 to 30 sq. ft./person

Waiting/Reception Room (doctor's office, school registration center)	15 to 20 sq. ft./person
Conference Room (business and professional offices, institutions)	20 to 30 sq. ft./person
Assembly Rooms (stack chairs for lectures—schools, hotels)	10 to 15 sq. ft./person
Auditorium (fixed seating)	8 to 14 sq. ft./person
Dining: high school cafeteria	10 to 15 sq. ft./person
a mid-priced restaurant	18 to 25 sq. ft./person
an elegant restaurant	30 to 40 sq. ft./person
Offices: minimal private work space	80 to 100 sq. ft.
standard work + consulting space	120 to 150 sq. ft.
executive office w/lounge seating	200 to 300 sq. ft.

Rule-of-thumb square footages are best thought of as approximations or a size range, rather than as specific numbers; perceptive judgment must be used to match the desired spatial quality with the appropriate part of the range. Keep in mind that rule-of-thumb figures can only apply to typical situations; if a conference room requires a significant guest or spectator area, the typical rule-of-thumb figure will not work. One should not try to store too much of this in his/her head; the prototypical plan sketch technique described in Chapter One, an integral step in preparing a criteria matrix, will always provide an adequate preliminary square footage figure if the specific requirements of a given space are known. When unique or special spaces require unconventional or specialty equipment, it is time to get out the appropriate reference sources and/or call in the specialist or consultant.

Reference sources are available (see the Recommended Reading at the end of this chapter) to help develop a store of useful square footage rules-of-thumb. Rote learning has severe limitations; rather than memorize numbers, work with the resource materials by sketching floor plans for a variety of situations and verifying the resource data; in this manner, the information will be more meaningful and long-lasting.

FLEXIBILITY/MULTIUSE

With the increasing cost of buildings, the demand increases for interior designers to provide functional facilities that maximize the use of interior space and permit it to serve more than one limited programmatic requirement. For example, in conference centers, classroom buildings, and ban-

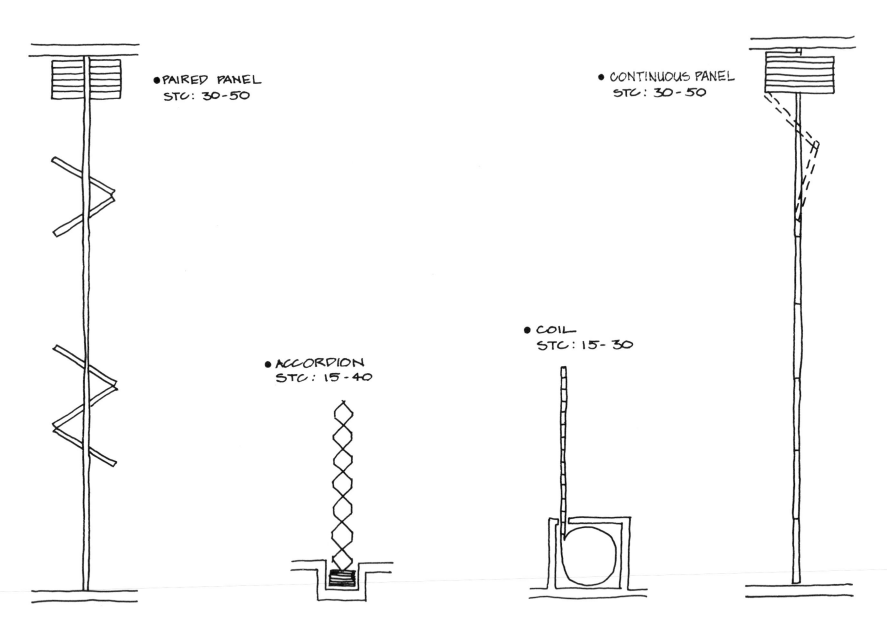

● PAIRED PANEL
STC: 30-50

● CONTINUOUS PANEL
STC: 30-50

● ACCORDION
STC: 15-40

● COIL
STC: 15-30

quet facilities the need for constantly changing room sizes is demanded. Similar kinds of flexible space are often required in less typical or less obvious situations. Through in-depth knowledge of programmatic needs, the space planner can often suggest space-saving planning techniques, such as combining two functions in one space when functional needs are not seriously compromised. For example, a combination of library/conference rooms for smaller law firms is common. When traffic and use is frequent, computerized time/use studies for specific planning situations will often reveal scheduling techniques that can eliminate unnecessary treatment, conference, or practice rooms, etc., when large numbers of spaces are planned within one facility.

The space planner should know the conventionally available building products and techniques to open and close spaces, including their approximate installed cost, approximate sound transmission qualities (discussed in the section on Acoustical Planning), and the relative ease with which they can be opened and closed (are maintenance personnel required and for how much time?). Sometimes, esthetic qualities are important in these product/technique decisions, since some products visually associated with institutional use are not acceptable in commercial or professional settings, or vice versa. As an example, the "nuts and bolts" appearance of a gymnasium's movable partition may be entirely appropriate for that use, but inappropriate for a high image law firm's conference room.

In addition to construction techniques, the planner should develop an awareness of programmatic situations that present possibilities for multiple use and space-saving scheduling of facilities. The professional planner/designer can more than earn his/her fee through just one space-saving "discovery" of this kind. Many valuable scheduling techniques are used by professional facilities managers, some of which are available in commercial computer software packages.

FURNITURE

Although the space planning specialist does not have to possess the same depth of knowledge about the furniture marketplace as the more typical specifying interior designer, basic knowledge about typical furniture and equipment sizes, and characteristics are essential. To some extent, this issue has already been discussed in Chapter One in relation to Prototypical Plan Sketches and will be raised again in Chapter Six that recommends exercises to strengthen furniture planning skills. The space planner

needs to know, or needs to know where and how to find, information on space requirements for specific furniture and furniture uses. It may be necessary to know how much space is required for a given number of seats in an airport lounge, or the size of the storage space required to stack chairs and folding tables in a banquet facility, or the size and capacity of filing cabinets for a law firm's central files, etc. Nothing is complex about this planning factor; a basic store of dimensional information and access to an adequate furniture and equipment catalog library is all that is needed. The development of that store of information usually comes quickly when one is space planning or furniture planning on a regular basis. The actual selection of furnishings is a complex and artful skill developed after much trial and error and is usually done after the space planning process has been completed.

SPATIAL QUALITY

Space planning has a natural consequence that is too often ignored or not given appropriate importance. As the space planner allocates and subdivides interior space, the basic spatial and esthetic qualities of that interior environment are determined, either consciously or unconsciously. There is a very strong tendency for the space planner to get so involved with the jig-saw-puzzle-like qualities of the planning task, that the three-dimensional experience of the people using the space is given little priority. Once the partition locations are established, the interior's basic three-dimensional design quality is essentially determined. Whether the space planner and the interior designer are the same person is of little importance.

The experienced space planner has an eye to spatial quality while the rough floor plan emerges on the drawing board and will often make decisions about the general plan organization based on the perceived three-dimensional qualities inherent in the plan. The experienced planner is regularly testing the concepts of entrance impact, room shape, spatial order, symbolic qualities, and the interior space-time experience of the users while making planning decisions. One of the best techniques to test spatial quality is the regular production of thumb-nail sketches (elevations, sections, isometrics, perspectives) while going through the planning process, shown in Illustration 3–7. If a planning solution looks promising, one should quickly sketch room shapes, travel or corridor vistas, view to the exterior, structural/internal detail coordination, etc. As the space planning solution develops, the basic spatial/esthetic qualities of the completed interior is in the planner's hands.

It is not uncommon for a rough study model to be built immediately following the establishment of a rough floor plan to better visualize the realities of the three-dimensional experience. This rough study model, usually constructed from illustration board and/or "foamcore," is much more time-consuming than drawing rough 3-D sketches; but the rewards are considerable, since so much more of the basic three-dimensional quality of the space can be visualized through this technique.

Regardless of the techniques employed, it is important to have a fairly accurate sense of the resulting spatial quality before final plan decisions are made. The most inventive decorative and detailed treatments cannot compensate for the opportunities lost in a basically unsatisfying spatial experience.

Recommended Reading

Building Codes, 2*, 5*, 23*, 24*, 25*, 32*

Lighting Design, 5*, 10, 13, 19*, 22*, 23*, 25*, 26

Acoustic Planning, 1*, 3, 5*, 9, 19*, 22*, 23*, 25*

Planning Rules-of-Thumb, 8*, 20*, 23*, 25*

Flexibility/Multi-Use, 23*, 25*

Furniture, 6*, 23*, 24*, 25*, 28*

Spatial Quality, 6*, 7*, 12*, 18*, 22*

Books noted with an asterisk are also included in the Recommended Reading of other chapters.

Chapter 6 DEVELOPING A ROUGH FLOOR PLAN

After the pre-design process has been completed, and bubble diagrams have produced a basic spatial organization, it is time to get to the heart of the matter and develop a floor plan that satisfies client/user needs. It should be restated at the outset that the planning process is a resolution of conflicting criteria resulting in a series of compromises. The process regularly involves the weighing of pros and cons of many varied configurations in which all user needs are rarely, if ever, satisfied. In simpler terms, the space planner would be unrealistic to expect a perfect solution satisfying all the program requirements in detail.

Even relatively small space planning problems are full of complex and often conflicting requirements, plus many demands for subtle and sensitive design judgments by the planner. Consequently, space planning skills are best developed in a progressive manner, starting with the relatively small and simple, slowly building to large, more complex problems. This chapter takes a step-by-step process in the development of a rough or first phase floor plan. The approach presented here makes a distinct sep-

aration between this first phase plan and the following development of a final preliminary floor plan, described in detail in Chapter Seven. The distinction between these two stages identifies the rough floor plan as an interim "design tool" phase, and the final preliminary plan as one that, after a refining process, develops into the presentation form, either for the classroom or client. At the end of this chapter, planning exercises using 1,500 square feet programs and shells in the Appendix are recommended. Planning exercises for the larger 2,500 square feet and 4,000 square feet sizes are reserved for Chapter Seven.

As stated at the outset, the progressive learning experience presented here assumes that the reader is reasonably proficient in furniture planning within single spaces—living rooms, bedrooms, private offices, conference rooms, etc. If those skills are lacking, or have not been used for some time, a methodical series of furniture-planning exercises in typical residential and non-residential spaces is essential before proceeding further. Experience with larger, more complex furniture arrangements, while not essential, is quite valuable while in the process of acquiring space planning skills. The larger arrangements include public lounges or waiting rooms, restaurant or club dining rooms, multiple desk or work station offices (both conventional and systems furniture), large-scale and / or multi-use conference and meeting rooms, etc. If one's competence in some or all of these areas is limited, a great deal can be gained by systematically going through a series of large-scale furniture arrangement studies before venturing into the development of a rough floor plan. The following exercise is recommended for that kind of practice experience.

EXERCISE 6–1

Draw at least one (and possibly more) plan sketch for each of the spaces listed below, including each of the size variations suggested. Although this may seem a laborious process, the plan sketches themselves may be quickly sketched (with reasonable accuracy), and the gain in skills can be considerable. Drawing quality is not of much importance in this learning experience, but this exercise can also be used to improve drawing skills, if desired. One can experiment with a variety of drawing techniques—hard line, free-hand, rendered, etc. Scale with the smaller size variations should be at $1/4'' = 1' = 0''$, while scale with the larger size variations should be at $1/8'' = 1' = 0''$; every planner / designer should feel comfortable working at both scales. Approach these exercises from a two-dimensional viewpoint; one may have an eye to three-dimensional implications, but the floor plan context should be the dominant focus.

- A corporate headquarters reception area to seat six people. Then try 10, 15, and 20 people spaces.
- A law firm's conference room to seat six people; followed by one to seat ten people, with modest accommodation for audio / visual facilities (front projection slides and film, large screen video); then try one for 20 people.
- An executive dining room (waiter service) to seat 16 people. Then try similar rooms for 24 and 40 people.
- A university meeting / conference suite for 40 people in a lecture setting, which can be divided by a movable partition to create two seminar rooms to accommodate 8 and 12 people, respectively. Then try a similar facility with lecture seating for 100, and seminar rooms for 12 and 24, respectively.
- A secretarial pool for six people at work stations, each equipped for word processing and containing 9 linear feet of letter files plus three box / storage drawers and 8 linear feet of book / catalog shelves. Then

try secretarial pools with 12 and 20 work stations with the same requirements.
- A public utility customer service facility with a central receptionist, waiting area for eight people, and six interview stations (each station to contain a CRT with keyboard, 4 linear feet of letter files, and two box drawers, plus two guest chairs). Try it again with waiting areas for 12 and 20 people and 8 and 15 interview stations, respectively.
- The situations described above are just a sampling of many furniture arrangement exercises. Try some others as well, using reasonably typical nonresidential settings; it shouldn't be too difficult to improve on many of the design results seen in existing facilities.

Useful rules-of-thumb are often developed from furniture arrangement studies. The rules-of-thumb extensions of the prototypical plan sketches described and recommended to establish square footage requirements in the development of a criteria matrix. Their value is not only numerical (how many square feet required for specific uses), but also visual and geometric (what room configurations are best for specific uses). The experienced space planner slowly compiles a mental list or vocabulary, sometimes recorded in notes and sketches, of space standards that help solve future planning problems more easily and efficiently. Although some standards of this kind are published (auditorium seating, cafeteria dining, etc.), a hands-on development of these rules-of-thumb provides the planner with a more flexible and useful working tool.

GETTING STARTED

When bubble diagrams have been completed and a "best" diagram has been selected with which to develop a rough floor plan, place the diagram over the building shell floor plan. (If a tracing paper or mylar film version of the shell plan is available, place the bubble diagram under the floor plan, so that the shell plan is more visually dominant than the diagram.) For continuity, the same design program (2S) and building shell (2S) used for descriptive illustration in Chapters One and Two will continue to be used for illustrative purposes here, with bubble diagram "D" in Illustration 2–2B (pages 32 and 33) used as the "best" diagram. Place a fresh sheet of paper over the shell plan, using a better quality paper than used for the bubble diagrams, because a lot of erasing is likely to occur in the development of a rough plan. (It is not necessary to use the best quality paper for this process because it is unlikely that this sheet will become the final or presentation preliminary floor plan.) As the rough plan emerges and divergences from the bubble diagram multiply, as they usually do, it may become desirable to remove the bubble diagram completely, since it is no longer relevant enough and it may be more of a distraction or nuisance than a help. Unlike the preceding bubble diagramming/block planning process, which is so strongly intuitive in nature, the development of a rough floor plan, while still requiring spontaneity and intuition, is decidedly more methodical and predictable. Although one can vary from the step-by-step process described below, the process through this phase of plan development should be highly organized. And just to stay on track, keep the criteria matrix within easy view throughout the process and make frequent reference to it. In other words, do not rely upon memory.

CONSTRUCTION REALITY

From the outset, the rough floor plan drawing should be realistic rather than diagrammatic. If it isn't, it is likely that dimensional inaccuracies will make the plan impractical or unworkable at a later stage. Partitions should be drawn with appropriate thickness; 4″ is a good nominal dimension for most preliminary floor plans, with 8″ thickness for partitions containing plumbing waste lines, and 1′-6″ to 2′-6″ for complex or multi-use pipe chases.

START WITH PLUMBING

The best approach is to start the planning process with the dimensionally demanding and plumbing-system-bound spaces, such as kitchens, bathrooms, restrooms, etc., since their sizes and possible locations within the shell are least flexible. Adhere to the increased square footage demands of barrier-free requirements. Illustration 6–1 demonstrates this first step.

MAJOR SPACES NEXT

In most cases, one or two unusually large or functionally dominant (heavily used) spaces exist. It's a good idea to work with these next, since they are of critical importance to the functioning of the whole and may only fit in limited number of locations within the shell, based on existing structural or building configuration conditions. A fairly accurate room size and shape, plus the location of access doors and other planning details, such as required equipment, built-ins or storage closets, are important to establish at this early stage. See Illustration 6–2.

CIRCULATION STUDIES

Look next to the circulation spaces—those defined by partitions (corridors and required exit stairs) and those that are traffic aisles within larger spaces. Circulation paths are often not well defined in bubble diagrams or block plans and can be deceptively space consuming. There are also very demanding building code requirements concerning paths of circulation and means of egress which are discussed in Chapter Four; these code requirements should be kept in mind throughout the rough plan development phase. See Illustration 6–3.

A common error made by inexperienced space planners is the unnecessary continuation of dead-end corridors, as shown in the "right" and "wrong" sketches of Illustration 6–4. In general, efficient use of circulation space should be a high priority planning criteria, so that valuable square footage is not wasted and to make traffic patterns within the space convenient for its users.

BASIC ROOM ALLOCATIONS

Proceed with the remainder of basic room allocations. Continue to keep program requirements in mind, including appropriate priority for spaces that demand light and air, privacy, and acoustic control (quiet zones). Don't lose sight of door swing conflicts in this early planning phase, because as the plan solidifies, it becomes more difficult to rectify those conflicts. The best way to guard against this is to draw door swings as the plan develops, rather than wait until later. See Illustration 6–5.

FURNITURE AND EQUIPMENT

As tentative decisions for partition locations are made to form rooms and spaces, the placement of basic furniture and equipment should follow shortly; if too much time goes by, it may be discovered that in one or more spaces, due to size and/or configuration (room shape, door and window locations, etc.), it is impossible to meet program requirements. It is not necessary or desirable to finalize furniture placement to the last detail at this stage; but it is very important to know that basic furniture arrangements will work well. The best approach is to try several furniture arrangements with sketch tracing paper overlays before committing an arrangement to the rough floor plan. See Illustration 6–6.

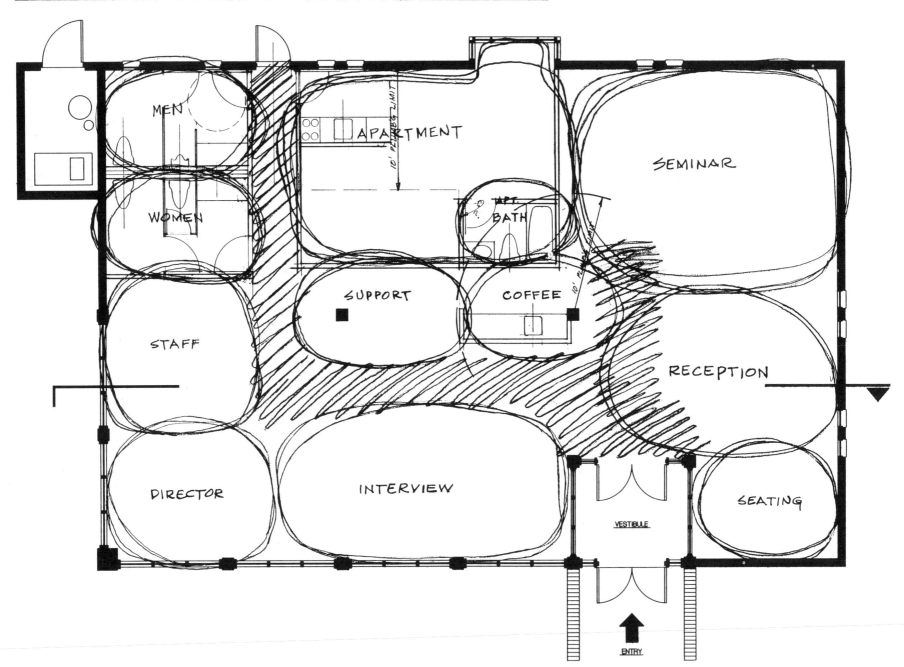

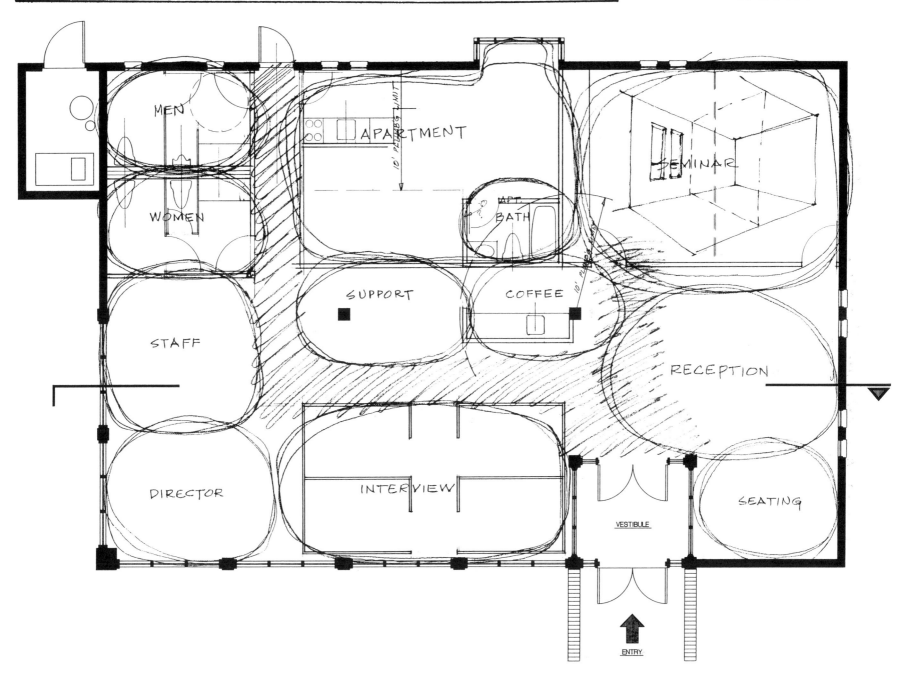

MEN

WOMEN

STAFF

DIRECTOR

APARTMENT

APT. BATH

SUPPORT

COFFEE

INTERVIEW

SEMINAR

RECEPTION

SEATING

VESTIBULE

ENTRY

10' PLBG. LIMIT

10' PLBG.

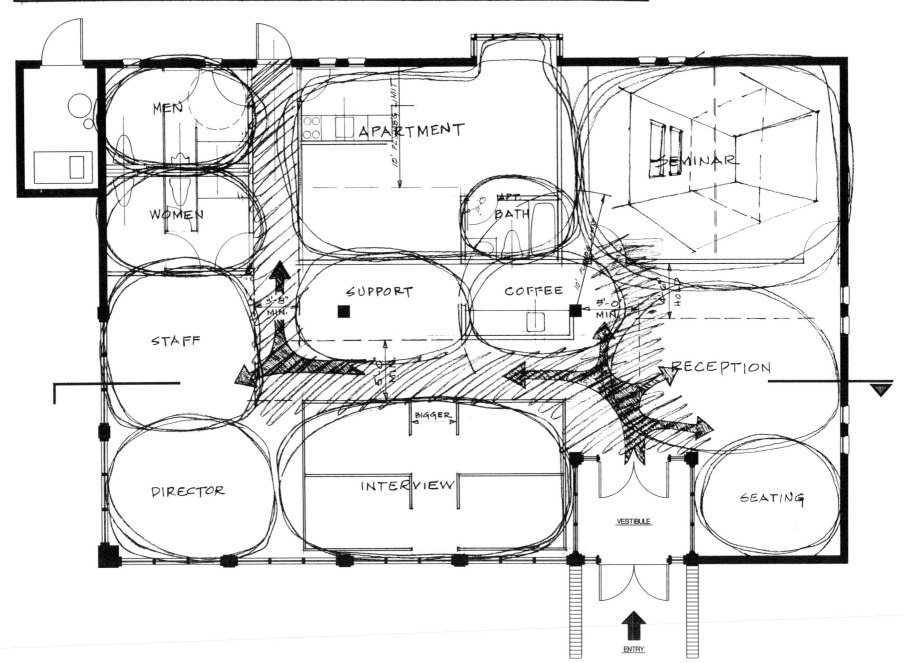

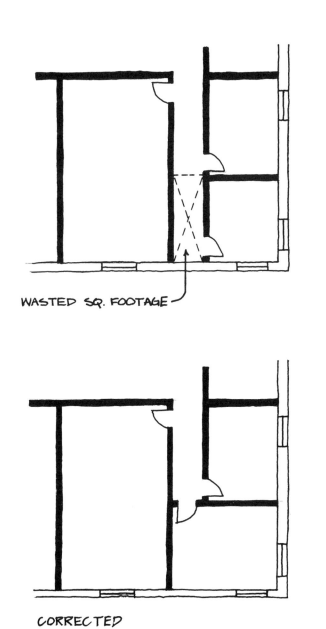

WASTED SQ. FOOTAGE

CORRECTED

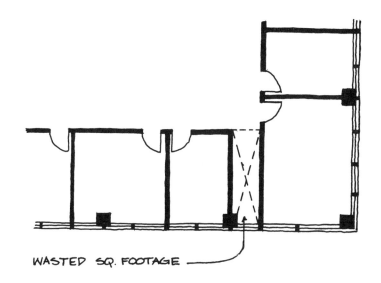

WASTED SQ. FOOTAGE

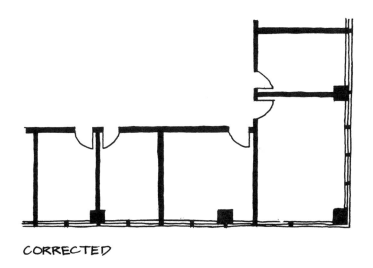

CORRECTED

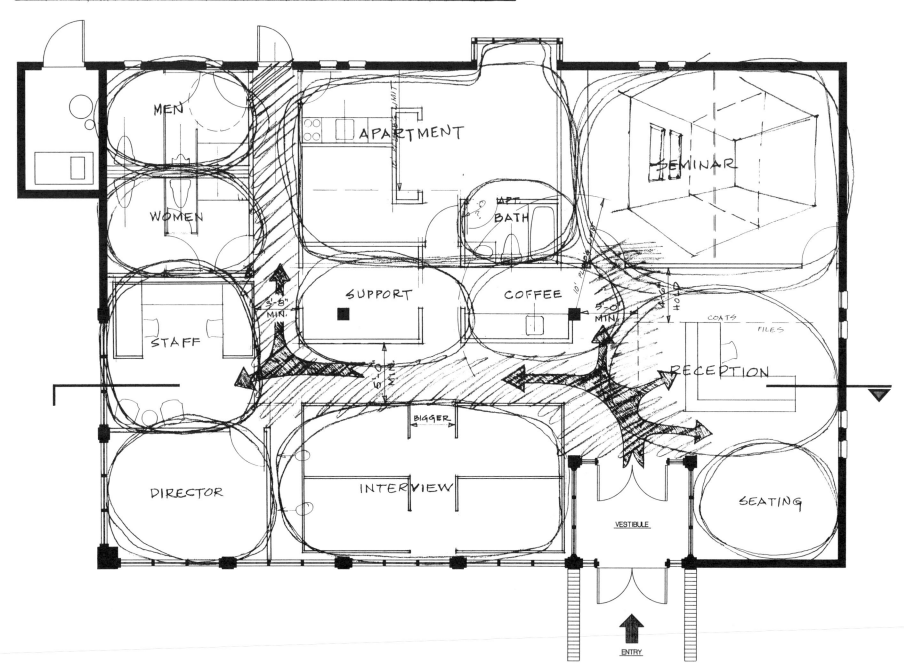

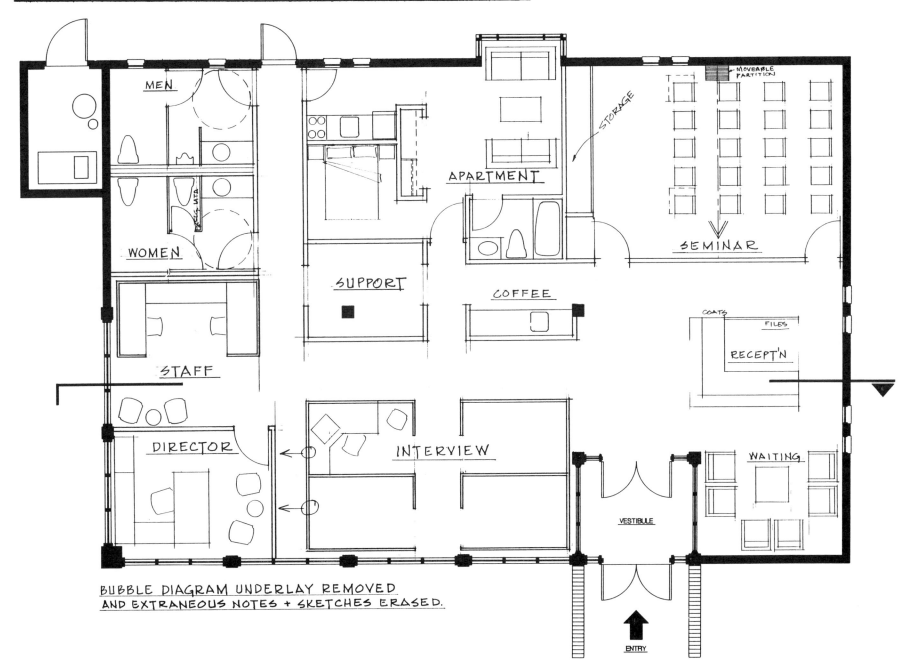

MEN

WOMEN

STAFF

DIRECTOR

SUPPORT

INTERVIEW

APARTMENT

COFFEE

STORAGE

MOVEABLE PARTITION

SEMINAR

COATS

FILES

RECEPT'N

WAITING

VESTIBULE

ENTRY

BUBBLE DIAGRAM UNDERLAY REMOVED
AND EXTRANEOUS NOTES + SKETCHES ERASED.

Remember that most furniture and equipment require adjacent space for appropriate use; too often these basic dimensional issues are forgotten—as examples, a conference table too close to an adjacent wall to permit comfortable seating, or sofas too close to coffee tables for comfortable access, or a bed placed so that it is almost impossible to be made easily. Some furniture and equipment have moving parts (such as drawers) or required servicing space (such as copying machines) that demand spatial accommodation. To forget these factors could result in poorly functioning rooms. A common example is not to provide proper allowance for the opening of file drawers, described in the "right" and "wrong" sketches in Illustration 6–7.

STORAGE AND FILING

Storage and filing requirements are often deceptive; make sure that program requirements for filing cabinets, storage closets, coat hanging space, stacking chair, folding table storage, etc., have been met. See Illustration 6–8.

SPATIAL QUALITY

The issues related to the importance of deliberately testing the three-dimensional consequences of the evolving floor plan early in its development have already been raised in Chapters Three and Five. How do the spaces feel to people moving through them? Is the size, scale, and proportion of a space appropriate to the number of people who will pass through it? Spatial use runs the gamut from intimate (a bedroom) to public (a theatre lobby). Does the scale of each space appropriately reflect its use in this sense? Have spaces with high ceiling height potential been taken advantage of? Have spaces been made visually varied and interesting using changing ceiling heights and soffit areas? When appropriate, are rhythmic or sequential spatial experiences provided? Are the proportions of walls and spaces pleasing? With the rough floor plan nearing completion, now is the critical moment to test and evaluate its three-dimensional potential. Realistically, look at the main entrance area, travel paths, major spaces, special spaces, etc. There is still plenty of time to adjust the plan to better satisfy spatial quality. See Illustration 6–9 for some reduced rough sketches of this type of preliminary spatial testing.

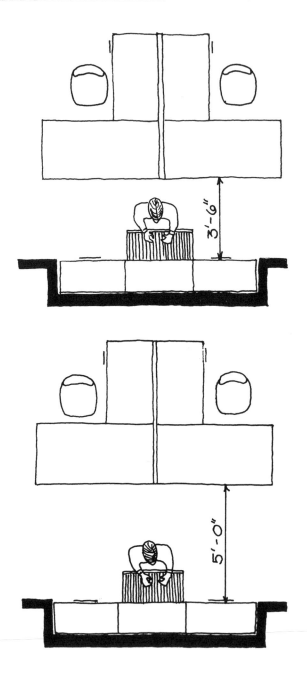

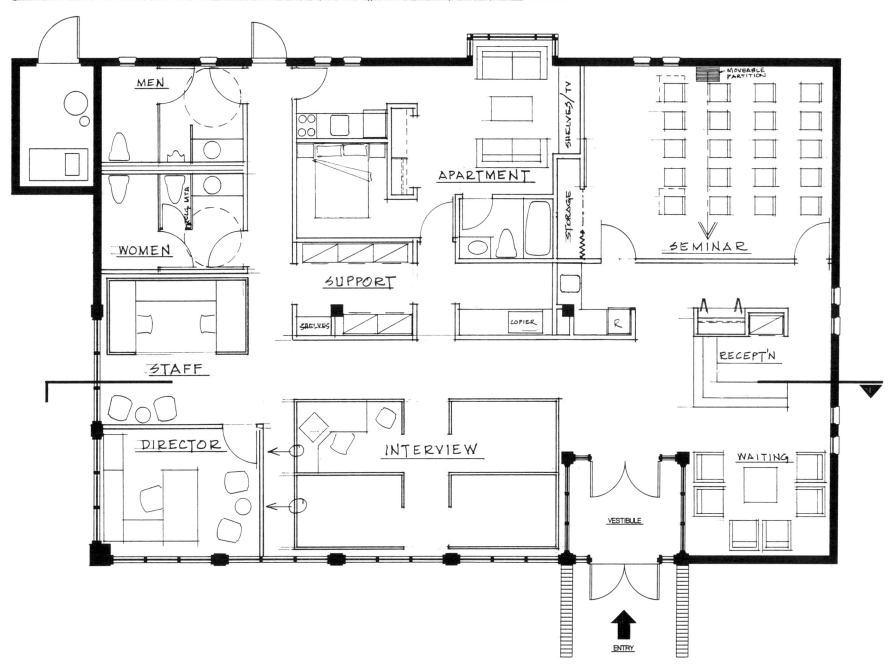

MEN

WOMEN

STAFF

DIRECTOR

INTERVIEW

APARTMENT

SHELVES/TV

STORAGE

SUPPORT

SHELVES

COPIER

R

SEMINAR

MOVEABLE PARTITION

RECEPT'N

WAITING

VESTIBULE

ENTRY

• VIEW FROM VESTIBULE
TO RECEPTION DESK

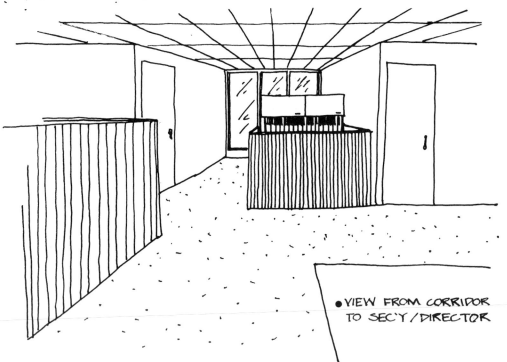

• VIEW FROM CORRIDOR
TO SEC'Y / DIRECTOR

REVIEW

A basic review is extremely valuable at the point when an entire floor plan can first be seen, no matter how sketchy it may be. This is a self-review in which one's skills in objective criticism should be called on and exercised. Get out a bold and/or colored pencil or marker and a role of sketch tracing paper for an overlay, or a print or photocopy of the plan, and make note of all the plan's qualities that are lacking or fail to meet the requirements established in the criteria matrix. Check the plan for the following:

Program Requirements

Does the plan satisfy the program requirements? Now is the time to catch a forgotten space, function, or a miscount in the numbers of people or operations to be served, rather than after a great deal more time has been spent in the further development and refinement of the plan. The criteria matrix technique for problem analysis, recommended in Chapter One, is an excellent tool at this point to see if the program requirements have been fulfilled, not just in numbers, but in basic issues of function and aesthetics as well, such as space adjacencies, acoustic isolation, or spatial quality.

Code Requirements

Are building code requirements complied with for safe egress from the building? Although code issues should be kept in mind throughout the rough plan development process, as the plan comes together as an entity for the first time, a basic overview for code compliance should be made. Now is the time to catch unacceptable lengths of travel or too long, dead-end corridors, not after significant plan refinement has been accomplished.

Barrier-Free Requirements

Is there compliance with barrier-free design standards required by law and/or client/user needs? To try to adjust a refined floor plan that has not accommodated barrier-free needs to one that meets those needs well, ranges from difficult to impossible. Now is the time to make the plan conform with these requirements.

Detailed Requirements

Do conflicts exist in the detailed aspects of planning—door swings, tight clearances between pieces of furniture, inclusion of required equipment (appliances, fixtures, communication devices), windows for habitable

rooms, corridor and stair widths, dimensions between plumbing fixtures and waste lines, etc? Although one has time to catch these details at a later point in the process, the more that can be accomplished now will save time and effort later.

As this review process comes to an end, the tracing paper overlay or marked-up copy of the rough floor plan probably looks something like the marked-up plan in Illustration 6–10. Revise the rough floor plan now, to correct as many of the planning flaws or inconsistencies as possible which are found in the review process. Keep in mind that not all the program requirements can be met; if all the major issues and most of the other basic requirements are resolved, the plan may come as close to problem resolution as possible. Illustration 6–11 shows the rough floor plan revised in accordance with most of the flaws noted in the previous illustration.

REVISIONS

After going through a long and often difficult process to arrive at this point with a revised rough floor plan, the planner may look at the result and believe that the recorded solution is too far removed from the best possible solution to consider it acceptable. The only recourse is to begin again with another of the refined bubble diagrams or block plans developed earlier. Despite this difficult decision, the second development of a rough floor plan will take much less time than the first. At the outset of a second start, the original plan development will provide insights to what will and won't work, and the second selection of a refined bubble diagram or block plan will be done with much more knowledge than the first. More importantly the time-consuming thought and data search efforts that went into the first try will not have to be repeated. These comments about a second attempt at a rough floor plan are not meant to be discouraging; the basic process recommended here is usually successful, but one should not fear making the tough judgment to repeat the process. The fundamental success of an interior planning solution lies in the workability and aesthetic qualities of the spatial arrangements contained in the rough floor plan; your design solutions deserve your best efforts in this critical phase of the design process.

It is early in the planning process to consider non-space planning issues, but once a workable rough plan has been developed, it is extremely valuable to develop a rough reflected ceiling and lighting plan. The ceiling

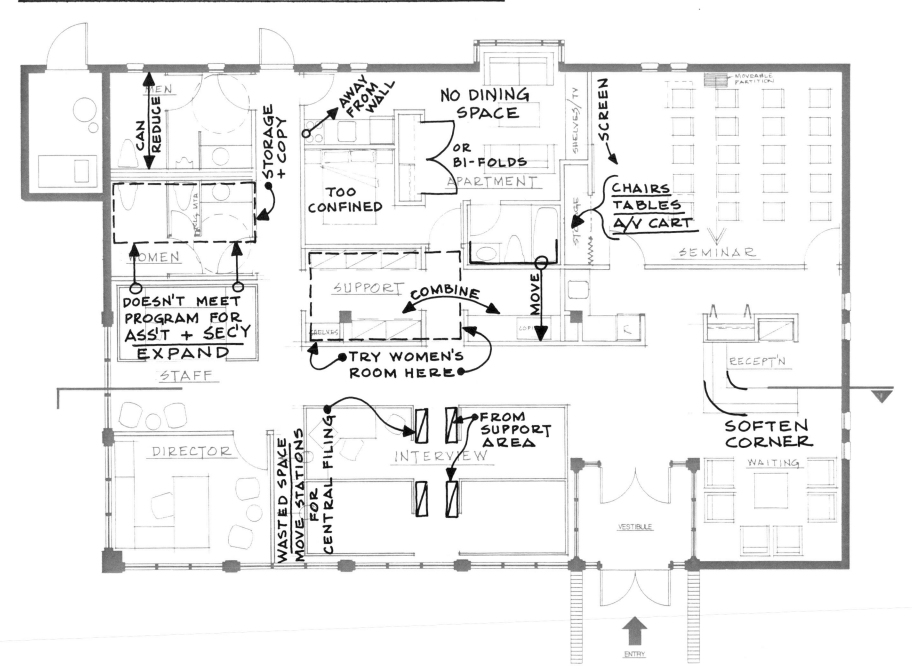

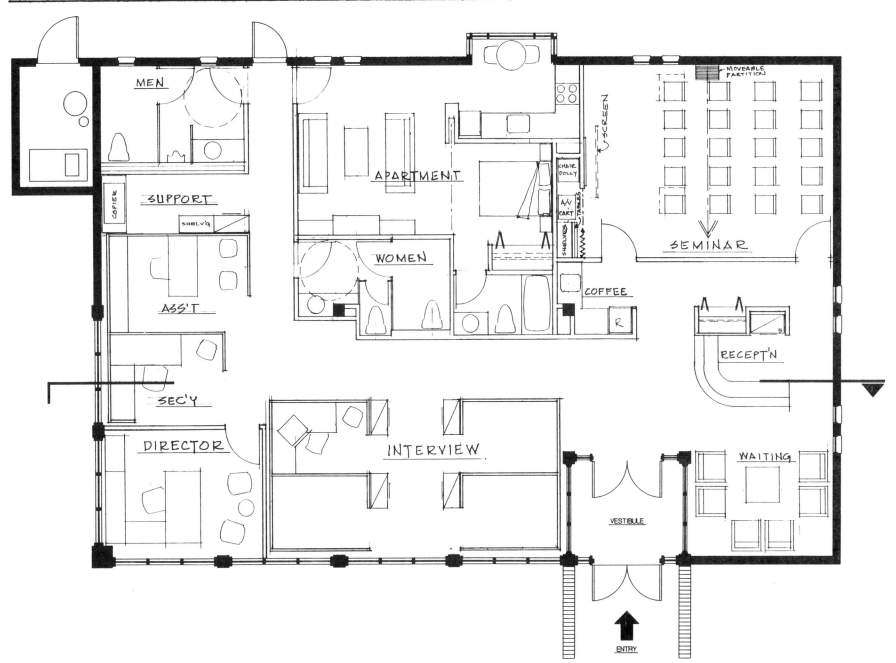

MEN

SUPPORT

COPIER

SHELV'G

ASS'T

SEC'Y

DIRECTOR

APARTMENT

WOMEN

INTERVIEW

CHAIR DOLLY

A/V CART

TABLES

SHELVES

COFFEE

R

SCREEN

MOVEABLE PARTITION

SEMINAR

RECEPT'N

WAITING

VESTIBULE

ENTRY

configuration has such great potential to create sculptural quality, that this aspect of the reflected ceiling plan should be given major priority while the three-dimensional characteristics of the space are still malleable. From a lighting design perspective the simple and/or standard rooms or functions can be given rudimentary attention at this point, but more complex spaces or functions requiring multiple lighting systems or multi-level ceilings can and should receive design attention. All aspects of the ceiling configuration (soffits, sloping surfaces, skylights, acoustic tile grids, etc.) and the use of luminaries (recessed, surface, pendant, wall mounted, etc.) may clearly suggest revisions in the rough floor plan which are best made now, before the plan becomes solidified and difficult to change. Illustration 6–12 shows the kind of rough reflected ceiling plan which is appropriate at this stage of planning development.

In a typical professional setting, this is the ideal time to have the first discussions with appropriate consultants, such as engineers, contractors, and specialists (acoustic, food service, etc.), to get their first input concerning spatial needs, adjacencies, accommodation of equipment, and any other issues bearing on space allocations, while it is still easy to make changes to the rough floor plan. The details of these issues can wait until after the final preliminary floor plans and other design development drawings have been approved by the client. Beyond that point, the next round of meetings with consultants is usually scheduled, but a first meeting with consultants during the rough floor plan phase can be invaluable in saving a great deal of time and energy in revising plans after the design development documents have been completed.

The suggestion that one should develop a rough reflected ceiling plan and consider specialized space and equipment needs (with or without consultants) at this early point in the space planning process may seem divergent in nature, tending to pull one away from the primary task of developing a preliminary floor plan. However, despite the step-by-step space planning process suggested here, do not forget that the entire design problem solving process is highly creative and cannot appropriately be confined to a simple deductive reasoning process. As discussed in Chapter One, designers must learn to think in a "lateral" (rather than "vertical" or "hierarchical") manner, permitting complex, divergent, and sometimes conflicting factors to bear appropriately on the solution. Although the complexities presented by the consideration of these non-space planning issues may be difficult to deal with because they introduce new sets of factors to an already formidable tangle of factors, it is best to raise them now, rather than permit them to come as a surprise later.

The classroom presents a unique opportunity for evaluation and critique rarely experienced again in professional practice. Just the fact that there are peers working on the same or a similar design problem at the same time is not likely to be repeated again. In addition to the valued insights and critique that the studio instructor has to offer on a one-to-one basis, many other forms of beneficial feedback, both formal and informal, are offered in the classroom. Particularly at this rough floor plan stage in the development of a space planning problem, major insights are to be gained from discussion and comparison of both the planning process and the interim results of this first tentative plan. Such an exchange of ideas can be as informal as one-to-one conversation with another student, or small group discussions and comparisons, or classwide critiques or "pin-ups" of work-in-progress. Learning opportunities of this kind will be hard to find in the professional setting; make maximum use of them now. Chapter Seven will include follow-up discussion of critiquing the final preliminary plan and critiques in the "real world" beyond.

The rough floor plan process described in this chapter must be put to work and experienced before it can have real meaning or value. The exercises following are geared exactly to that purpose. Before reading Chapter Seven in which the next, and final, step in the space planning process is described, it is important to try at least two or three rough floor plans without attempting to refine or finalize them beyond a rough sketch drawing stage. If put to proper use, these exercises are the most valuable aspects of the entire process presented here.

To this point, no mention of time has been made—how long should it take to develop a rough floor plan, or how long should it take to acquire professional quality space planning skills? Ultimately, the time it takes to complete a task is of importance to all professionals because of the economic factors inherent in professional practice; but during the learning process, the development of speedy techniques can be counterproductive. Speed will come with experience; for now, without wasting time, be more concerned with solving these problems well, not fast. Take the same attitude in the overall development of space planning skills. In general, if the exercises provided within the text are performed thoroughly over several weeks to a few months, a reasonable level of professional skill will be attained. Professional project experience is necessary for the full development of space planning skills. For those still in the student/learning process, growth and sophistication will happen in the not-too-distant future. Diligent application of energy to the solution of these exercises is critical to gain professional competence.

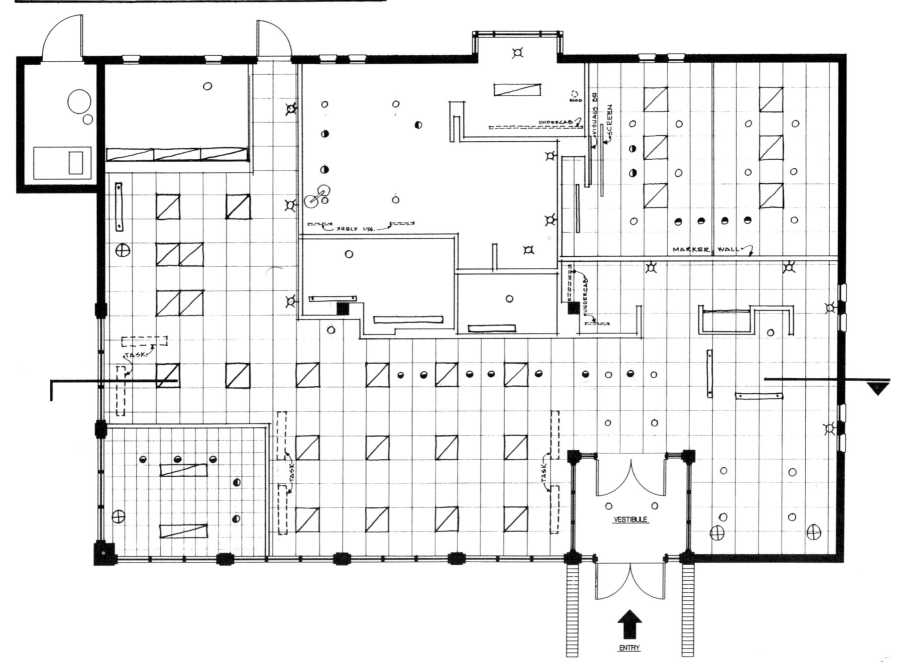

The criteria matrixes and bubble diagrams or block plans developed for the exercises in Chapter One and Two may be used now for the rough floor plan exercises recommended here; or new matrixes and diagrams can be developed. With this material in hand, develop and draw a rough floor plan for at least two or three of the 1500 square feet program / shell combinations provided in the Appendix. Most importantly, work with the process at this small scale, until it feels known and comfortable. Ideally, informal and / or formal critiques should be part of the process, to put one's best efforts to work in the final preliminary plan development described in Chapter Seven.

One could immediately move on to develop rough floor plans for the 2,500 square feet and 4,000 square feet program / shell combinations; but it is recommended here that the development of final preliminary floor plans at the 1,500 square feet size be accomplished first. Exercises for rough and final preliminary floor plans at the larger sizes will be recommended in Chapter Seven.

It should be noted that the aggregate of program and building shell exercises provided in the Appendix are planned to give you experience with as broad a variety of interior uses and spaces as is practical. The programs run the gamut from intimate residential through typical office and working uses, to public settings used by large numbers of people. The building shells range from residential wood-frame construction through typical low-rise, steel-frame commercial / institutional structures to high-rise office building shells. In addition to solving the mechanics of the problems presented, be aware of and sensitive to the issues of usage, scale, and architectural context when working with the exercises of this chapter and Chapter Seven. As a professional, you will be called on to appropriately respond to these issues and, to a lesser degree, the NCIDQ examination will also test your competence in these areas of customary professional concerns.

Recommended Reading

6*, 8*, 22*, 28*

Books noted with an asterisk are also included in the Recommended Reading of other chapters.

Chapter 7 REFINING THE SOLUTION

Chapter Six left the rough floor plan in an almost complete but unpresentable form. In terms of presentability, even the most informal preliminary plan expectations, such as a first phase critique in the classroom, or an in-house staff review in the professional office, would anticipate something more finished. (The rough floor plan ''pin-up'' suggested in Chapter Six would rarely happen outside of a learning oriented classroom; sketchy plans of this nature would seldom, if ever, be shown at a staff review session or to a client in a professional office.) Preliminary floor plans can be completed in a simple, unpretentious manner or in a complex, flamboyant style, with possibilities ranging from one extreme to the other, depending on the requirements of the setting or situation.

The manner of completion is usually determined by the nature of the project. In the classroom, project assignments are usually given in a variety of manners, from the quick sketch problem to the full-blown design project requiring a range of presentation techniques from basic black and white drawings to a large set of fully rendered and colored, exhibit-quality display boards. The professional setting also demands the same broad range of techniques, from the simply drawn preliminary plan presented informally to the client across a desk or drawing board, to the large, formal, and complex presentation of a major project in a formal conference room with many client representatives evaluating the design solution.

The primary concern of this text is space planning, not design presentation. Despite this, the language of space planning is the floor plan, and its graphic qualities cannot be entirely ignored. One of the premises of the planning methodology presented here is that the transition from the rough floor plan to the preliminary or presentation floor plan is part of the planning process, not just a graphic refinement. The transition phase of the process will be described first, and in full detail, and some comments on drawing quality and presentation technique will be added and interjected as a natural supplement to the planning process.

REFINING THE ROUGH PLAN

The development of the rough floor plan, as described in Chapter Six, suggests significant review and evaluation within the plan development process. Assuming that has been done, the concluding phase of the space planning process, the development of a "final" preliminary plan, should begin now.

First, tape down the rough floor plan, and then tape down a high-quality tracing paper over it. In a professional office, the high-quality paper may be a high-rag content tracing paper with a lot of "tooth" to grab the pencil, or a tracing vellum with little or no "tooth," ideal for ink, but still often used with pencil, or less frequently, a plastic film, such as Mylar, designed for use with plastic leads, but often used with conventional pencil leads or ink. (These plastic films are most often used for contract documents because of their durability.)

The drawing medium may be conventional pencil leads of varying hardness; or plastic leads, again of varying hardness; or drafting pens, such as Rapidograph, or one of several varieties of sealed-cartridge plastic-tipped pens. The basic drawing technique can range from a meticulous hard-line drafted style to a loose free-hand drawn style. The selection of paper, drawing media, and basic drawing style should be based on the desired style and quality of the preliminary drawing being presented. Ideally, experienced designers have several media/style techniques in their repertoire and call on the appropriate combination to suit the specific situation. In the learning process, a variety of media and style combinations can be experimented with to develop a personal repertoire. In the beginning, it makes sense to use basic tracing paper and pencil with a simple drafted or free-hand style and to move on to other techniques as one's experience grows. Note that the pencil, in addition to its potential for subtleties of shading, has the forgiving quality of being easily erase-able, a characteristic not found in wet media. Drawing reproduction techniques will often play a role in the selection of style and materials, discussed later in the chapter. The illustrations presented on the following pages have been drawn to demonstrate a variety of those basic approaches and techniques.

Placing a fresh sheet of paper over the rough plan presents an opportunity to see it from a fresh vantage point, almost demanding a closer look at the plan details for the first time in the space planning process. This opportunity should not be wasted. Although major plan changes at this point would be counterproductive, minor changes, refinements rather than revisions, are both possible and productive. Use this fresh vantage point to discover plan refinements that enhance the solution without having to re-think the basic plan arrangement. This process is not unlike the final editing technique one uses with written material, when moving from first to final draft. The kinds of plan refinements appropriate at this point are:

- the addition of incidental furnishings, such as an end table or floor lamp;
- the change of a closet door from sliding to bifold;
- the minor relocation of a partition by a few or several inches to better accommodate furniture, people access, or several other possible reasons;
- the relocation of a door to provide better access to a room or appropriate wall space for an anticipated signage system;
- the creation of a niche to accommodate a built-in unit or a decorative element;
- the expanding of a pipe chase to better accommodate the plumbing system.

If time pressures do not exist, this refining process can be done in a slow, methodical manner; but even if time is short, one can make several small but significant changes at this time. As suggested before, it is best, while in the learning process, to avoid the highly pressured time frame to get the most out of each planning step. It is recommended here that you incorporate this refinement phase into your basic approach to space planning and assume that it will become an integral part of your personal space planning process.

THE PRELIMINARY FLOOR PLAN

As one begins to draw the final version of a floor plan, starting at the top of the drawing and working down is best, keeping a critical eye out for possible plan refinements as one proceeds. Working down in this manner will minimize working over completed portions of the drawing, making it easier to maintain sharp and clean pencil lines or avoid going over wet ink or marker lines. Some designers have a difficult time keeping a pencil drawing sharp and clean; if this is the case, try using pounce or a crumbled eraser compound, and/or keep finished portions of the drawing covered with an inexpensive tracing paper while completing the balance of the sheet, to avoid rubbing over lines with hands or drafting tools. The dual process of refining the graphic language of the plan and the design quality of the planning solution results in a presentation or final preliminary plan drawing that is usually the fundamental or central element of a typical interior design project presentation.

DRAWING QUALITY AND TECHNIQUES

The subject of drawing quality warrants some basic comment here. The original end product of space planning is a floor plan, which can only be expressed in graphic form, making the connection between planning and graphic quality inescapable. The quality of one's planning efforts cannot be expressed in words but is expressed in a unique drawing language universally understood by designers, architects, engineers, contractors, and others who work in the world of building environments. It follows that the planner/designer should know that language well, and that working on the exercises presented here should be seen as an opportunity to concurrently develop drawing skills and a repertoire of techniques.

Good drawing quality will provide a readable floor plan and create a positive impression upon critics/jurors in a classroom or clients in a professional practice setting. Remember that a floor plan is really a horizontal section taken through a building (normally assumed at 4'–0" above the floor) and should present a good pictorial view of the building from above, after the portion of the building above the section line has (in theory) been removed. Good and consistent line quality should be maintained, and line weights should appropriately express the degree of importance of the building or furnishing element being drawn. More specifically, the architectural elements being cut through by the drawing plane section line (walls and partitions) should be drawn with the darkest and boldest line; major items of furniture and equipment (such as plumbing fixtures) should be drawn with a strong medium-weight line; and minor elements of the plan such as door swings, area rugs, floor tile patterns, or wood grains should be drawn with the lightest lines. The experienced designer, over time, develops drawing techniques with a broad range of graphic subtleties that represent a complex and articulate language rivaling all of the intricacies and shadings of one's verbal language.

When drawing with pencil, varying line weights can be accomplished primarily by using a relatively soft lead for the darkest lines, a medium weight for the middle value lines, and a relatively hard lead for the lightest lines, although the degree of pressure exerted by one's hand is also a factor in controlling line weight. It's impossible to recommend specific lead weights, because the type of paper being used and the personal tendency to apply hand pressure when drawing present unknown variables. Generally, when using conventional pencil leads on good quality tracing paper, an F or HB lead should work well for the darkest lines, a 2H or 3H is appropriate for the middle-weight lines, and a 4H or 5H usually works well for the light lines.

The greatest value in using ink is its boldness and clarity; the negative factor is the lack of varying tones of gray. Line weight must be controlled by line thickness only. Although conventional wisdom often advises against mixing pencil and ink techniques, no absolute rule exists against it. That combination can be very effective, particularly if, rather than use the original drawing the final product is to be reproduced. Similarly, despite conventions to the contrary, a combination of drafted or hard-line and free-hand techniques is often quite effective, particularly when the hard-line is used for the architectural elements and the free-hand line is used for furnishings, equipment, and other graphic notations, such as material indications. Clearly, the development of drawing skills requires repeated experimentation over considerable time.

A note about drawing templates. On floor plans, they are normally used for door swings, plumbing fixtures, and furniture. They are invaluable, in terms of time expended, for uniquely shaped furniture (a specific chair), equipment (a toilet or bathtub), or repetitive items (auditorium seating). Despite this, one should be selective in their use and generally opt to draw the item rather than use a template. In addition to providing visual consistency in the drawn quality of the plan, drawing these items by hand will avoid the amateurish or unsophisticated "look" too often lent by oversimplified or inappropriately shaped template forms, such as a rectangle for a sofa or an obviously traditional furniture shape in a nontraditional setting. Remember that beds and most upholstered furniture have soft or round corners.

The first two Illustrations, 7–1 and 7–2, of a refined and completed preliminary floor plan (developed from the rough floor plan shown in Illustration 6–11) represents a very simplified and "bare-bones" approach to the final step in the initial planning process. Note that the first example (7–1) uses a conventional drafted technique, and the second (7–2) is drawn free-hand. Although you should ultimately strive for a more developed drawing product, these drawing techniques are reasonably communicative and should be adequate for many informal purposes, from classroom presentations to professional setting uses. Many occasions call for this kind of simple plan drawing, and where something more descriptive or complex would be inappropriate.

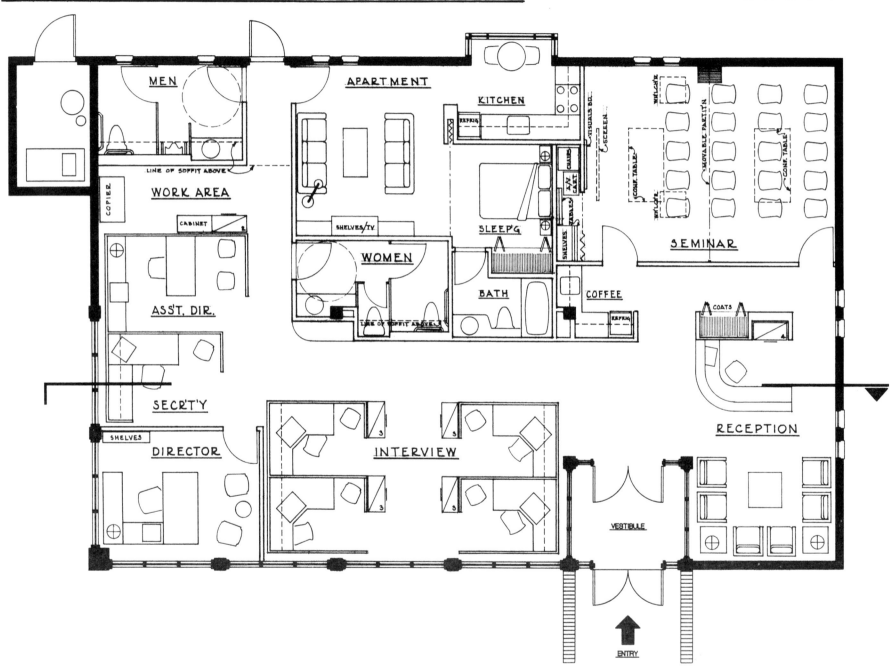

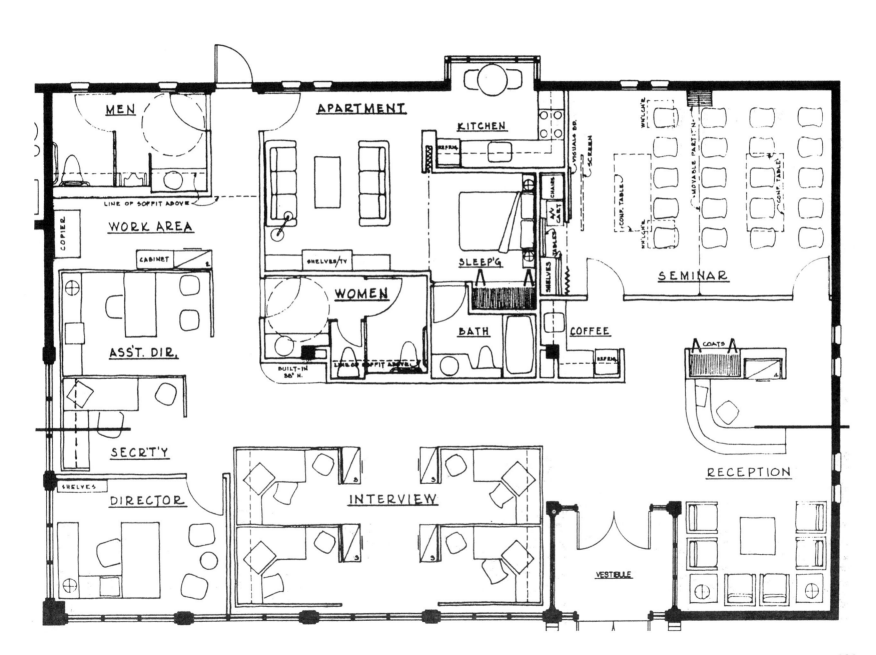

Make note of several detailed aspects of these two drawings:

- Each drawing is consistent in using one technique exclusively. Another quite successful approach is to use the hard-line of Illustration 7–1 for the architectural elements and the free-hand of Illustration 7–2 for furnishings and other nonarchitectural elements.
- Line weights vary in relation to their building and furnishings use and importance.
- A few plan refinements have been made. The Men's Room is a little smaller and the Guest Apartment Living Room is a little larger; the door to the Guest Apartment Bathroom has been relocated to create a more comfortable use of the bathroom space; and a few table and floor lamps have been added.
- The south wall of the Women's Room has been thickened from 4″ to 9″ to accommodate plumbing lines.
- Except for a few standard items, furniture and equipment have been drawn without the use of a template.
- The low partition behind the receptionist's filing cabinet has been furred out to accommodate the actual depth of the cabinet.
- The position of the conference tables in the Seminar Room are shown with a dotted line to indicate that the varying program requirements have been met.
- Storage space for Seminar Room tables and chairs has been refined.
- Room names are boldly lettered and underlined in each room to clearly identify each space.
- Several small lettered notations have been added to clarify the use of the space and its furnishings. Some designers may argue that these notes are not necessary on a preliminary drawing, tending to ruin the visual simplicity of the presentation. Strong arguments to the contrary state that the visual language of the floor plan is not complete without them and requires augmentation with verbal notes. This issue can be decided by the designer, either as a general rule or case by case. The approach presented here favors a judicious use of verbal notations.

The bare-bones approach of Illustrations 7–1 and 7–2, while adequate and appropriate for many classroom and professional purposes, is far from the most articulate graphic language available. It is quite reasonable to strive for a descriptive and readable drawing quality that will create a more positive impression of one's professional skills to critics, jurors, clients, or anyone making evaluations or judgments. A presentation enhanced beyond this bare-bones level will have many appropriate class-room and professional applications. It takes little time to add the elements shown in Illustrations 7–3 and 7–4, and the added degree of readability and professionalism is quite significant. Make note of the added elements:

- The *full-height* partitions have been filled in with a tone; this technique is usually referred to as "poché" (pronounced "po-SHAY"). The pochéing technique is applied with a lead pencil, or better, a hard wax colored pencil, using a black, gray, or essentially neutral tone. (Occasionally, a situation may call for a distinct, or even bold color poché, but in most cases, the bold color is too distracting in terms of drawing content.) The poché can be done on the front or back of the tracing paper; if the tracing paper is the final presentation medium, apply the poché to the back of the paper for a more even appearance of the tone. If the tracing paper drawing is to be printed for presentation purposes, such as a black line Ozalid print, neither the color nor side of application is of any consequence. The darkness of the tone can vary from very light to black, depending on the pressure with which the poché is applied; a middle-depth tone is recommended for most purposes. Broad or chisel tipped markers are often used for presentation poché, but they (and other wet media) are again recommended with the warning that they are not erasable.
- Floor tile patterns are shown in the kitchen, bathroom, and restroom spaces to better identify them in a graphic manner. In most cases, an 8″ to 12″ grid is appropriate for kitchens, and a 3″ to 6″ grid is appropriate for bathrooms and restrooms. Use a very light line for this purpose.
- Wood grain patterns are shown on items of built-in and conventional furniture to separate the plane of the item from the plane of the floor below. Make these the lightest lines of the drawing.
- Area rugs, shown in the Reception Area and in the Guest Apartment Living Room, provide a greater sense of scale and detail. Again, these should be drawn very lightly.
- Dotted lines are drawn *and noted* to indicate dropped ceiling soffits in the otherwise uniform ceiling height, as seen in the Men's and Women's Rooms and the corridor between the Men's Room and the Guest Apartment. A light-to medium-weight line should be used for this purpose.
- Additional lettered notations describe and/or clarify detailed elements of the plan. As noted earlier, it is possible to overdo such notations. Allow the circumstance to dictate this decision. Keep in mind that in many classroom and professional office related

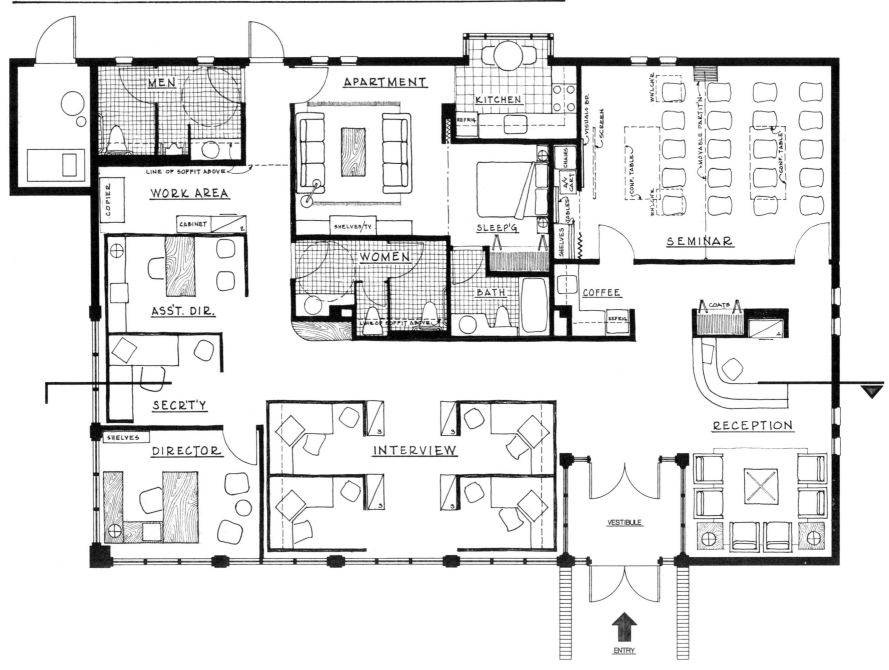

instances, the drawing will be left behind, and no verbal explanation of the drawing or its details will be available for an instructor or client.

While all the subtleties of an original drawing cannot be fully captured in reproduction processes, reproduction techniques are used commonly as an integral part of the graphic presentation approach to planning and design projects. Several reasons for this are:

- If a need or desire is to use color on the plan (beyond a poché tone or color within the thickness of the walls) for either representational or diagrammatic purposes, the color applied to a tracing paper drawing would make simple, inexpensive black line or copier prints difficult to read.
- Since most color media are difficult to erase, if a mistake is made in the color application to an original drawing, one must start over again.
- Sometimes floor plans are purposely left unfinished, and then prints are made on either opaque or translucent/printable paper. Different categories of information are added to each print, resulting in a series of floor plans in which each drawing describes a different aspect of the plan.
- Sometimes one wants to experiment with presentation techniques and/or color schemes before committing to a final choice.

For these reasons, reproduction techniques of many kinds, on several kinds of paper or film, from inexpensive Ozalid techniques to costly photographic processes, have become a part of the designer's presentation repertoire. Within the limits of affordability, students should be encouraged to learn about and experiment with these additional and valuable presentation tools.

How long should it take to accomplish this combined plan-refining and presentation-drawing process? Many factors are involved in this time frame question, such as size of project, complexity of presentation technique, imposed deadline requirements, and the varying ways in which individuals work and produce. As suggested in Chapter Six, it is counterproductive to rush while learning. If possible, one should leave enough time to accomplish this last phase in the space planning process in an unhurried and deliberate manner. The fact that both student and professional designers often procrastinate by putting off design decisions and

project completion until the last hour is a reality that cannot be dealt with here. But "real world" pressures are often as stringent as these self-imposed pressures; it is not uncommon for the essential work of a consultant to arrive days to weeks late and force a hurried completion of a project, or for a client to plead for an unreasonably tight completion date because of an external business pressure. Every designer must learn to work quickly and efficiently and sometimes at break-neck speed. For now, in the process of learning how to refine a floor plan and how to present it well, take enough time to learn these tasks thoroughly.

Some practice for those hurried professional situations can be valuable; one-day sketch problems based in space planning are an excellent learning experience. The NCIDQ exam, for either professional society entrance or professional licensing, has become a reality for interior designers; the time pressures of the space planning portion of that exam are quite stringent and should be known and practiced several times before it is taken.

The issues of plan evaluation must be dealt with again. This is true for both classroom and professional settings, although their modes are vastly different. Is the plan a good one? Does it work well? Although one may feel far removed from the original problem analysis by the time the final presentation plan is completed, value exists in going back to the criteria matrix for one last self-critical look at the space planning results. The designer should know a plan's shortcomings before someone else points them out. Beyond this self-critical look, the classroom and professional processes vary greatly. Criticism can be difficult to accept, but students should benefit from the learning opportunities presented by individual and classroom critiques, remembering that one often learns as much, or more, from the critique of other students' work. In most cases, student projects are terminated after the presentation of final preliminary drawings. The professional process is basically different because the "real world" projects are carried beyond this drawing phase to include construction and furnishings installation, so that the consequences of presenting final preliminary drawings to a client are very different. Whether presented to an individual or a group; or to non-professionals, an in-house designer or facilities manager; the results of the presentation must be acted upon. It is unusual in "real" situations to come away from a first presentation without some direction for revisions; and on some occasions, for many revisions. Learning to work with clients is an artful skill normally learned after one's formal education; but students should have some awareness of what the professional designer faces in client relationships and its relevance in the assessment and revision of space planning solutions.

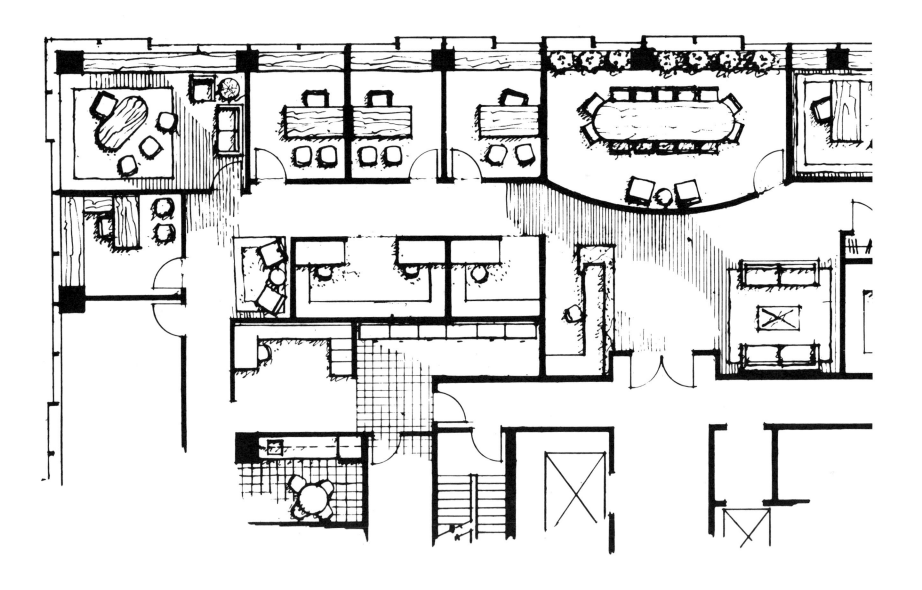

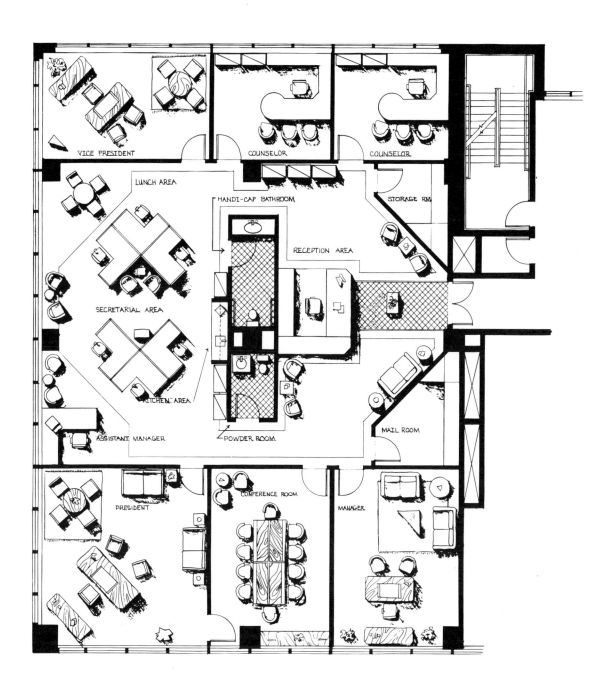

EXERCISE 7-1

To get started with this final phase of the space planning process, take two or three of the rough floor plans of the Group #1 planning exercises recommended in Chapter Six and go through the specified refinement and presentation steps with each of them. If necessary, complete more of these Group #1 exercises, to the point when the full execution of planning problems of this scale feels familiar and comfortable. With each project, some form of individual and/or classroom critique should be incorporated, so that constructive criticism can be used to improve skills in each step along the way.

EXERCISE 7-2

Now move on to the Group #2 planning exercises, using the criteria matrix and bubble diagram material from the exercises developed in Chapters One and Two. First go through the development of a rough floor plan with each program/shell combination, and then move directly into the refinement and presentation phase, allowing this last step in space planning to become routine. During this exercise, experimentation with drawing/presentation may be attempted to begin the development of a personal style. The number of exercises performed before moving on to the final group (Group #3) is a matter of individual judgment—feeling familiar and comfortable with problems of this scale should be the primary measure. Critiques are invaluable to the learning process and should be made an integral part of each exercise at the critical predesign, diagramming, and rough plan turning points, as well as at the completion of the exercise.

EXERCISE 7-3

Finally, starting from scratch, work on the Group #3 exercises, which present the greatest planning challenge of this text. It would be misleading to imply that mastering these 4,000 square foot planning exercises will prepare one for any other space planning challenges that may be encountered. A 20,000 square foot space will probably bring complexities requiring additional growth of one's skills. Specialized interiors with unique equipment or operational procedures will require research and special know-how not covered by these exercises. And the idiosyncracies of "real" spaces and client problems will bring new challenges. These new challenges will not require a basically new methodology or planning process different from what was learned in these exercises.

A few final comments on drawing and presentation skills are appropriate at this point. The learning process described in this text demands many hours at the drawing board. If one's drawing skills are not at a level that is personally satisfying, it would be a shame to pass up this opportunity to sharpen those skills. Relatively few people have strong natural drawing skills, yet many designers have developed them to a high level in their professional training and development. Though not a difficult task, it takes considerable time to repeatedly practice each of the detailed aspects of a design presentation.

The drawing skill development process is primarily one of emulation. Whenever an admired plan drawing is encountered, its techniques should be experimented with—not once, but a few times. The result will probably not be identical to the admired original, but rather a combination of the original and one's previously gained techniques. Each time this imitating process takes place, drawing quality and range of skills will expand. Sources of good quality floor plan drawings include the monthly interior design magazines, books related to interior design and architecture, and the work of colleagues, other designers, and architects. Purely by way of showing some additional preliminary floor plan drawing techniques, Illustrations 7-5A and 7-5B demonstrate a few high-quality drawings by the hands of other designers.

The use of three-dimensional simulation presentation techniques, (perspectives, isometrics, etc.), have not been discussed in this chapter, not that they are unimportant, but, when applied to the final presentation phase of a project, they serve as a "selling tool," not a "design tool." The development of presentation quality perspective drawing skills is a complex and time-consuming process to which many texts have already been devoted. These skills should be encouraged in all design students, but are essentially unrelated to acquiring space planning skills.

Recommended Reading

4, 18*, 22*

Books noted with an asterisk are also included in the Recommended Reading of other chapters.

Chapter 8 DEVELOPING SKILLS BEYOND THE BASIC LEVEL

From a learning viewpoint, the 4,000 square feet space planning exercises are a practical point of achievement. Although space planning problems of larger size may be more complex and take more time to solve, the methods and techniques for their solution presented here are fundamental and will serve one well as project demands become larger in scale and programmatically more complex. Once a basic approach to this kind of problem solving has been mastered, hands-on experience will be the best learning mode to expand one's skills to comfortably deal with larger, more complex spaces. This final chapter is presented with the intent to provide basic ideas and directions to develop skills beyond the basic level of achievement called for in the program / shell exercises presented here.

BASIC IMPLICATIONS

To understand the scale of the 4,000 square feet space in appropriate perspective, a typical floor in most new mid-and high-rise speculative office buildings ranges from 15,000 to 25,000 square feet of rentable floor space. The typical business or professional firm usually requires from 125 to 250 square feet per person to accommodate its personnel; the variables that create that range of square footage are the programmatic needs of the personnel employed, the number of outside visitors, and the amount of equipment space needed. To understand the programmatic quality of the program / shell exercises presented here in appropriate perspective, they have intentionally dealt with functions that are essentially typical or common and without the need of specialized equipment or building systems.

It is not uncommon to find a relatively large facility, accommodating many people, that performs only a few simple functions. The space planning for that kind of user/client may be no more difficult or time consuming than it is for a much smaller but relatively complex user/client. Typically, space planning for the larger user is more complex and difficult, but it should be understood that programmatic complexity or uniqueness can have as much or more bearing on the degree of problem solving difficulty as size does.

Generally, larger spaces serve a greater number of functions, and the complexities of inter-functional relationships multiply. These complexities become compounded when large numbers of both employees and outside visitors are involved, particularly when outside visitors must be isolated to specific areas. Often, specific work-flow processes must be accommodated, requiring exacting spatial adjacencies between functions and departments. It is interesting to note that with the increased use of computer data storage and retrieval, that "paper flow" has become decreasingly important. Particularly with high-tech users, the accommodation of equipment has become as important as the accommodation of people, not only in occupied space, but also in adjacency to mechanical and electrical services.

Special planning challenges are presented by unique facility functions, such as in television production, specialized medical treatment, or scientific laboratories. In addition to the fact that their detailed functions are beyond most people's experience, they often require the use of specialized equipment; these issues of function and equipment normally require a significant amount of research prior to and during the space planning process. Probably the most difficult and complex building type to plan is the large hospital. It incorporates all the elements that contribute to complex and potentially problematic space planning: large numbers of staff and visitors, separation of staff and visitors, many diverse functions, specific functional processes demanding specific adjacencies, and a great deal of large equipment that must be exactingly placed in specific proximity to mechanical and electrical services. For these reasons, hospitals are always planned with the assistance of specialized consultants. Most specialized facilities require the involvement of at least one, and often several, consultants. The comments related to the use of consultants, expressed in the introductory paragraphs to Chapter Four, have equal application to the planning of specialized buildings and facilities. Getting out of mainstream design practice and into specialized facilities provides the potential for an interesting and challenging professional career.

Learning to plan larger, more complex spaces can only be accomplished through real project experience. As pointed out earlier, the uniquenesses and eccentricities of "real" projects cannot be simulated by planned exercises. It would take many long, detailed case study documents to begin to explain the variables that the planner/designer must deal with in planning projects of even moderate size. Existing building conditions may present an unusual floor/ceiling construction assembly, or a peculiar door detail, or an HVAC system that is particularly inflexible. Local building and zoning code requirements will often place limitations on space planning options. Even without considering the problems of personal communication with clients or those created by the typical client's lack of understanding of the design process, the variables and uniquenesses of each client's operating procedures will often be difficult to uncover, understand, and analyze. Ideally, each planner/designer will have the opportunity to learn progressively, to plan facilities of gradually increasing size and complexity. In that manner, one is able to adapt and modify the basic planning methods and techniques presented here, until a personal repertoire of methodologies is developed that can meet the variety of challenges and opportunities available to interior designers.

PROGRAMS WITHIN PROGRAMS

When faced with the problems of planning a facility to accommodate many people who perform a large variety of functions, it is impractical to account for every person and task when you start the planning process. The well-worn analogy of not being able to see the forest for the trees is quite applicable to that situation. With any large, complex problem solving task, it is important to first break down the problem to a manageable number of parts.

If a particular problem calls for accommodating 156 people in 14 departments on a 23,500 square feet high-rise office building floor, start with planning the departments, not the offices and work stations for 156 people. The 14 department elements can and should be manipulated in relationship diagrams and bubble diagrams in the same manner that rooms are manipulated when planning smaller facilities. Even a criteria matrix for departmental needs and inter-relationships should be made as a separate and distinct analytical tool; the issues of adjacency, square footage requirements, traffic/circulation flow, work process, privacy, acoustics, etc., apply to departments in a manner very similar to individual rooms and spaces. Illustrations 8–1A and 8–1B show a relationship diagram and a bubble diagram for a departmental arrangement of spaces. Diagrams of this kind are very much like zoning diagrams, in which a spatial zone is set aside for each departmental function. An intentional "zoning concept" is a valuable first step process with large scale facilities.

Accommodating one organization on a number of floors within the same building is a common occurrence. In that situation, a vertical bubble diagram is best used that graphically identifies the functions and/or departments to be located on each floor, as shown in Illustration 8–2. Multi-floor

DEPARTMENTAL RELATIONSHIP DIAGRAM

ILLUS. 8-1A

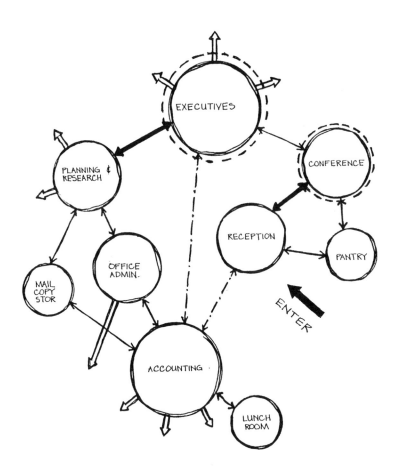

LEGEND

- INTERCONNECTED
- INTERACTIVE
- INTERMITTENT
- ACOUSTICAL ZONING
- WINDOWS / VIEW

facilities are not related to the size of the organization involved; many relatively small organizations are housed in traditional urban town houses or older, small commercial buildings. Determining the functions to go on each floor must be accomplished before the space planning on individual floors is begun. It should be pointed out that the vertical bubble diagram can be graphically misleading, because the bubbles are not a proportional indication of the size of each function; correct proportions cannot be seen without the use of a conventional bubble diagram. To compensate for this shortcoming, vertical bubble diagrams should include square footage figures, as shown in the illustrated example.

Generally, large space planning problems are fairly unique; despite some similarities, it is difficult to find two which are the same. As problems become larger and more complex, it is often necessary to devise or invent new problem solving techniques to cope with new problems. In most cases, remember that the basic technique of breaking down a large problem into smaller, manageable parts is of great value. This process can also be seen as developing *"programs within programs."* Although it is necessary to eventually analyze and accommodate each person and task, it can be helpful to separately analyze the department-to-department or zone-to-zone relationships.

OPEN PLAN/SYSTEMS FURNITURE

It is unusual to find a large business or institutional office facility that does not use systems furniture. By way of definition, systems furniture can be described as an integrated combination of partition panels, work surfaces, storage elements, and wire management raceways that can be combined in a variety of configurations to accommodate most functional office-use requirements. Because the space planning problems presented in this text are of relatively small size, they do not touch significantly on major uses of systems furniture.

Although systems furniture is often used in small office situations for as few as two or three workstations, its essential purpose is to spatially articulate office areas accommodating several to many workstations. In addition to their spatial organization qualities, these systems are well geared to solve the complex problems of wire management for today's electronic office *and* offer to its users a high degree of flexibility. Such flexibility can quickly and easily permit reconfiguration of workstations to change functional needs at relatively low cost compared with the demolition and rebuilding of new conventional partitions. In addition to these

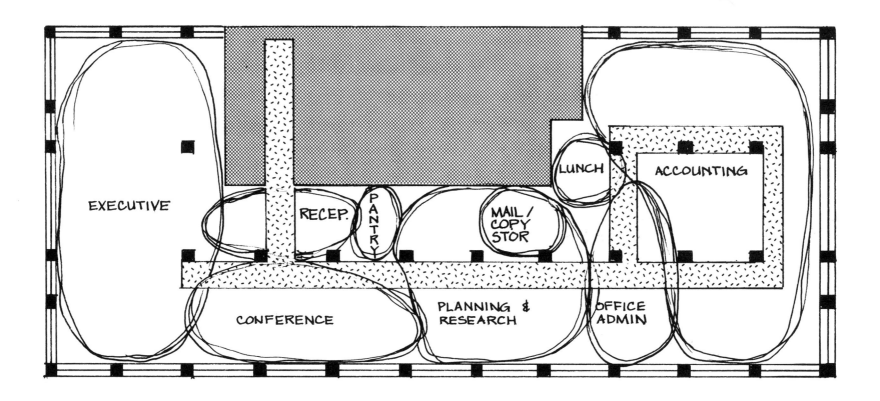

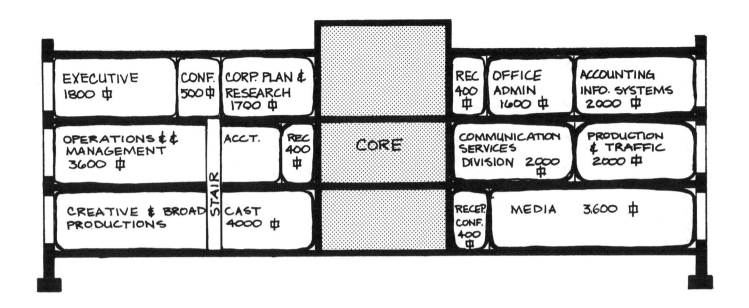

practical advantages, the proponents of systems furniture also claim that significant benefits exist in the human and personal aspects of open planning by encouraging interaction among people who work together.

Three major office-planning problems not solved with systems furniture are:

1. a high degree of acoustic control and privacy;
2. security / confidentiality of documents;
3. the conventional image of prestige or status offered by the private office.

Clearly, it is difficult to imagine the acoustic privacy needs of a lawyer's office, medical examining room, or executive conference room being met by systems furniture. Payroll offices, personnel records management, research and development staffs, to cite just a few, require confidentiality and security not offered by systems furniture. Regardless of the amount of space allocated, few executives are satisfied with the privacy, image,

or status provided by systems furniture. For these reasons, most office facilities use a combination of systems furniture and conventionally constructed partitions to solve their space planning needs.

Many interior designers' professional involvements are normally related to non-office facilities, such as the hospitality industry or small scale healthcare facilities. In these situations, the need to learn to plan with systems furniture may not be necessary. But most designers who work in other-than-residential settings need to know how to plan and design with systems furniture. Planning and designing with systems furniture is a process more akin to space planning than to furniture placement or planning, and to learn it is much like learning space planning.

Ideally, one should start with relatively small spaces and numbers of stations and gradually increase in size and numbers to large office facilities, including several non-workstation functions such as informal conference areas or filing / storage areas. The fact that so many systems are being manufactured can make learning to plan with them both trying and diffi-

113

cult. Although most tend to be very similar to one another, each system has its own unique module, panel connections, or configuration potential, making planning generalizations elusive for the uninitiated.

It is not possible to bring a systems-planning solution to completion without detailed knowledge of the dimensions, details and configurations of the particular system being specified. After one has worked in detail with several systems over time, it is possible to do some general space planning without having selected a specific manufacturer's system; even then however, the final space planning must wait until the specific system has been chosen. The implication here is clear; it will take several projects and detailed investigation and planning with several systems before one can easily and confidently manipulate systems elements within a space, with reasonable assurance that the scheme will work as well in the final detailed plan.

The manufacturers of systems furniture are interested in having designers become fully familiar with their products. Many of them offer planning manuals and/or seminars on the use of their systems to encourage designers to learn to use them. Particularly for the uninitiated, these learning tools can be very helpful. Contacting the manufacturer or manufacturer's representative of the systems of interest can bring a great deal of valuable planning information.

THE SPECULATIVE OFFICE BUILDING

Large volumes of office planning and design work are the "bread and butter" projects for a major segment of interior design professionals. A great deal, if not most, of that work is performed in multi-tenant, developer-built buildings in settings from suburban office parks to urban high-rises. Despite the major professional involvement within such buildings, this text and its planning exercises have dealt very little with those kinds of interiors, for the same reasons of scale that systems furniture has not been fully addressed. Every designer who expects to work with office interiors should become thoroughly familiar with the speculative office building, from its general plan configurations to its details of construction, including their mechanical systems for HVAC and plumbing.

Some buildings are designed and constructed with little accommodation for future change. Hotels, hospitals, and most institutional buildings are in this category of relatively fixed interiors, as are some buildings intended for specific business uses. Planning new interior uses within these buildings usually presents many limitations on the planning process because many elements are relatively fixed and expensive to adjust or relocate.

Speculative buildings are the antithesis of fixed-use buildings. Within the limitations of economical construction techniques, they are designed for maximum flexibility and adaptability, to accommodate as broad a variety of functions and users as possible over many years and tenants.

For these reasons, standardized and modular component systems are used for ceilings, exterior wall/window construction, lighting, electrical distribution, and HVAC control. (The one exception is the major use of steel stud and gypsum drywall partitions because of their low cost and ease with which they are demolished.) Learning to work with this unique building type is essential to significant involvement in office planning and design. This learning should include the unique building code requirements for egress and compartmentalization, as well as the economics and practicalities of leasing policies devised by the buildings' developers and their rental agents.

Space planning within the speculative office building is quite often done in two stages. The first establishes a general space plan or feasibility plan to confirm the appropriateness of the space for the tenant and to bring the tenant to the point of lease signing; this phase is sometimes referred to as tenant planning. The second stage refines the general space plan and completes the design process down to its final details. Some design firms and some in-house design departments specialize in the first stage general space planning; these firms or departments are often excellent training grounds to develop professional space planning skills.

FUTURE EXPANSION

Planning for the future is usually a significant factor of most space planning problems, regardless of their size. It has not been dealt with to this point, because it is a factor containing many conditional or indeterminate elements and is difficult to specify in the kind of pre-planned programmatic exercises presented here. Ideally, it should be a basic planning factor from the first phases of problem data gathering and analysis and should be included as an element in a criteria matrix (see Illustration 1–2a) and/or other pre-design programming documents, such as relationship diagrams.

Despite its importance, many clients have great difficulty in dealing with future planning, to the point where they resist discussing it in concrete terms. This is understandable, because no one really knows what the future will bring; and equally important, planning for the future usually contains major elements of financial commitment.

If the client will identify, quantify, and place a time frame on future growth or change, and commit to the place it will happen (leasing additional floor space, setting aside land for a future addition, etc.), the space planning problem is usually not too difficult. Too often however, clients are absorbed in current problems and are not interested in or sensitive to the need for addressing future space planning requirements.

Despite the discomforts of specifying needs for an unknown future, most clients are better served if the designer will be assertive and press for an articulated future direction of the organization. Even if the programmatic information for the future is rather vague, a general sense of the functions likely to change or grow will permit the current placement of functional units in a manner that could make future re-planning immeasurably easier. In addition to these space planning issues, many designers believe that an involvement in programming for the future will help to cement a long-standing client/designer relationship.

It should be pointed out that planning for future needs is as important to and difficult for the small client organization as it is for the large client organization and probably most difficult for the relatively new organization, regardless of size. Generally, no easy answers exist to resolve these issues, since the difficulty lies in making economic, not space planning, decisions. Again, real project experience is the best learning mode; after one has grappled with these future planning issues with a few clients, the designer can be a valuable consultant to their clients in this unique area of decision making.

COMPUTER-AIDED DESIGN AND DRAFTING (CADD)

From a practical point of view, CADD has been in use since the early 1970s. At first, it was used primarily for the nongraphic aspects of pre-design programming, such as adjacency and traffic flow studies and some first generation studies in three-dimensional modeling and layering of production drawings. With each succeeding year, both refinements of existing techniques and whole new processes have been added to the repertoire of CADD applications to interior design and architectural practice. While most design professionals agree that CADD is still in a development mode, at this point many interior design firms with a significant volume of work have some CADD capability, and for many, CADD is a primary factor in almost all its design related functions, particularly in the production of contract documents.

Despite the tremendous growth in CADD techniques and their acceptance in professional practice, most aspects of the space planning process continue to be performed in the traditional pencil-on-paper manner. In large projects with large numbers of people and functions, adjacency and traffic flow studies are often (and best) tabulated and analyzed by computerized methods, using programs specifically geared to analyze the complexities of inter-relationships in large organizations. Once basic space allocation figures have been established, computer graphics are sometimes used to present the results of the bubble diagramming or block planning process. After a basic floor plan has been established, it is often ''drawn'' on the CRT screen for the purposes of plan manipulation and refinement, permitting the final details of floor plan development, such as the exact placement of partitions and doors, to be performed by the exacting capabilities of the computer.

As the technology continues to develop, the entire space planning process may conventionally be performed with CADD programs. For now, the pencil-on-paper tradition is the best technique to learn how to manipulate space for the development of successful floor plans.

PLANNING NEW BUILDINGS

The process of designing a new building is quite similar to designing a new interior in an existing building. Despite the similarities in process, the design of a new building involves several major and complex considerations not part of the interior space planning process. Without attempting to enumerate the myriad of details related to each of those considerations, the elements of site, exterior form and image, building structure, and the placement of basic environmental control systems, demand knowledge and expertise not involved in the typical interior space planning project.

The reasons for the separation in both training and practice of architects and interior designers are many, including the magnitude and complexity of the architect's task in designing new buildings. It is relatively unusual to find a fundamental integration of the building design and interior design processes. With architectural firms usually in control of the building design process, the interior designer is too often brought into the process at such a late point in the planning phase that their expertise in interior space and detail is relegated to secondary importance, rather than being integrated into the whole of the building design, as would be more functionally useful.

Skillful interior space planning is accomplished only with great attention to detail, both in program development and the physical planning process itself. The task of designing buildings has become more complex, and it is unlikely that most architects will be able to devote the time to develop well-honed interior space planning skills. Likewise, the design of building interiors has become extremely complex, and it is equally unlikely that most interior designers will acquire architectural expertise or credentials. Ideally, a more productive coming together will happen, both in thought and practice, of these two inter-dependent specializations in the field of creating the built environment. This coming together requires greater knowledge and understanding of interior programming and systems, as well as furniture and interior materials, on the part of architects and an equal growth of knowledge and understanding of site, structures, and environmental control systems on the part of interior designers. Clearly, the result will be better buildings.

An interdisciplinary approach should go far beyond the interaction of architects and interior designers. Most design professionals have broad concerns for environmental issues, from intelligent use of our planet's natural resources, to the detailed components that determine the day-to-day quality of contemporary life. Making a meaningful effort to implement these concerns will require a knowledgeable global view and a willingness of all design disciplines to work together.

A FINAL NOTE

Becoming professionally proficient in interior space planning is a challenging enterprise. Although a major time investment is required, the rewards are commensurate. Not only is one prepared then to take on the full range of interior design projects, but the basic problem solving skills in organization, analysis, and synthesis are adaptable and useful lifelong tools for a profession and a world that will surely change.

Recommended Reading

8*, 16, 28*

Books noted with an asterisk are also included in the Recommended Reading of other chapters.

Appendix

DESIGN PROGRAMS
AND BUILDING SHELLS

DESIGN PROGRAM I-A:
Suite for Dual Pediatric Practice

A partnership of two pediatricians requires a new office facility. Their practice is neighborhood-oriented, dealing with a complete range of pediatric care. Although the atmosphere should be professional and businesslike, the primary concern in terms of ambience is to create a relaxed atmosphere throughout to minimize the typical anxiety that most people, parents and children, feel when entering a doctor's office. The practice employs a receptionist/secretary, a medical technician, and a part-time bookkeeper for billing and other business functions. A medical equipment manufacturer has been selected; their representative has prescribed the size and shape of the typical exam room and the nurse's station.

SPECIAL REQUIREMENTS

1. The receptionist controls the movement of patients; consequently, that station must be centrally and uniquely situated to perform that function.
2. The exam rooms and the consulting offices must have acoustic privacy.
3. The business office and work room functions may be combined into one space, assuming that all the detailed requirements are met; if not combined, they should be adjacent to one another.
4. Where the building configuration permits, the partners would like an "escape hatch" exit, where they can leave without walking through the reception/waiting area.
5. Exterior view and natural light are desirable, but not at a premium—first priority is for the waiting/reception area, and second priority is for the consulting offices.
6. All patient areas shall be barrier-free in concept and dimension.

PROGRAM REQUIREMENTS

A. Reception/Business Office
1. The reception station is the hub of most patient activity, checking-in there upon arrival and making or arranging for payment before leaving.
2. Primary work surface of at least 12 s.f., secondary surface of at least 8 s.f., transaction counter for patients 4' to 6' long, two box/file drawer pedestals, personal computer (22"w × 19"d × 21"h).
3. 60 l.f. of lateral files in easy reach of receptionist.
4. Part-time bookkeeper's station with 10 to 12 s.f. desk surface, plus a return for a computer identical to the receptionist's, two box/file drawer pedestals.
5. Two secretarial task chairs.
6. Easy eye contact between the two work stations is desirable.

B. Work Room
1. Desk top copier (26"w × 20"d × 14"h) on base 30"w × 24"d.
2. Storage closet or cabinet, min. 18 l.f. of 12" deep shelves and min. 18 l.f. of 18" deep shelves.
3. Coat closet, 3 l.f. hanging rod.
4. Work Table, 10 to 12 s.f.
5. Computer printer stand (24" sq. × 32" high).

C. Waiting Area
1. Seating for five adults and three children.
2. Magazine rack or display.
3. Set aside approx. 60 s.f. for a children's play area.
4. This area presents the greatest challenge in creating psychological comfort for patients, particularly considering the children's age range from infancy through puberty.

D. Nurse's Station
1. Regularly shaped space of 70 to 80 s.f., with a min. dimension of 7'-0".
2. Station shall present a transaction counter to entering patients that shall be directly in the line of vision when entering from the Waiting Area, and the station must also conveniently serve the three exam rooms.
3. Station shall contain a laboratory sink on one of its long walls.

E. Exam Rooms (three)
1. Regularly shaped spaces of 85 to 95 s.f. with a min. dimension of 8'-0".
2. A regular or irregular placement of rooms is acceptable; comfortable access for patients and staff is the first priority.
3. Plumbing tie-in requirements are not restricted by conventional distance requirements to the plumbing waste lines, despite the installation of a lavatory in each room.

F. Consulting Offices (two)
1. Comfortable spaces for talking to patients and parents, as well

as private desk work; atmosphere should be informal, even residential in ambience.

2. Desk with 12 to 15 s.f. surface, plus credenza or return with 5 to 8 s.f. secondary surface; and two box/file drawer pedestals. Allow for future placement of a personal computer.

3. Swivel-tilt desk chair and three guest chairs.

4. 36 l.f. of book/artifact shelves, 12" deep.

G. Powder Rooms (two)

1. Lavatory and toilet (only one room shall be barrier-free).

H. Storage Closet

1. Approx. 50 s.f., placed for easy access to both Work Room and Nurse's Station.

DESIGN PROGRAM I-B:
Township Youth Organization

A suburban township has decided to establish and support a youth organization for its sizable and growing population. To a great degree, the organization's purpose will be to provide a meeting place for several established small organizations and programs. In addition, it will coordinate programs with the township's schools and fill gaps where programmatic voids exist. The organization will generally serve an age range of 8 to 16, with primary hours of activity during the afternoon and evening during the week and daylight hours during the weekend; a complete seven-day-a-week schedule will be maintained during the summer vacation period. The range of activities is immense, including a chess club, a hiking/camping club, an intramural-level sports competition, a debating club, dance competitions, a community newsletter, theatrical productions, martial arts instruction, and even some supervised overnight activities. Flexibility of space and equipment is essential, informality of atmosphere is a given, and a critical eye to easy maintenance will make the day-to-day operations run more smoothly.

SPECIAL REQUIREMENTS

1. The director's office must be strategically placed so that it is near the entrance door and that a glass vision panel will permit supervision of the multipurpose room. When the door is closed, acoustic privacy must be accomplished.
2. Except for the kitchen, the entire facility shall be barrier-free in concept and dimension.
3. Storage of tables, chairs, and equipment is an important aspect of planning the center. Access to and the removal and replacement of stored items must be accomplished with ease and efficiency; the storage location(s) may not be remote, and the maneuvering of stored items must be kept to a minimum.

PROGRAM REQUIREMENTS

A. Multipurpose Room

1. A room of maximum flexibility and diversity of use, capable of seating at least 30 in a classroom arrangement or at least 24 at a few or several modular tables (for games, dining, or small group use), or at least 20 at a central table in a conference arrangement.
2. A pull-out or fold-down reception desk (24" × 48") near the entrance door for those occasions when entrance must be monitored.
3. Two locker alcoves (boys and girls), each with 30 half lockers, 12"w × 12"d × 36"h.

B. Toilet Rooms

1. Boys: two lavatories, one urinal, and one toilet stall.
2. Girls: two lavatories and two toilet stalls.

C. Kitchen

1. Essentially residential in design, to serve a broad range of functions, from afternoon snack service to prepared dinners.
2. Min. 14 s.f. countertop with full complement of base and wall cabinets.
3. 30" wide double bowl sink, 30" wide range/oven, 32" wide refrigerator, 24" wide undercounter dish washer.

D. Director's Office

1. 12 to 15 s.f. desk surface, 5 to 8 s.f. return or credenza surface, two box/file drawer pedestals.
2. Personal computer (20"w × 17"d × 18"h).
3. Swivel-tilt desk chair and two guest chairs.
4. 30 l.f. of book/artifact shelves, 12" deep.
5. Closet, 5'w × 2'd; half for hanging rod and half for shelves.
6. Private barrier-free bathroom, compact but comfortable, with lavatory, toilet, and stall shower.

E. Storage

In closets or cabinets, store the following items out of sight, but easily accessible for use.
1. 24" sq. dolly capable of holding 30 stack chairs.
2. Folding leg tables to accommodate 20 people (table size based on multipurpose room plan).
3. 12 sleeping bags in bins 18"w × 18"h × 24"d.
4. A/V equipment on 12 l.f. of 18" deep shelves (one shelf 18" high and the other two shelves 12" high).
5. Games and equipment on 12 l.f. of 12" deep shelves, 12" high, and 8 l.f. of 18" deep shelves, 15" high.
6. Supplies on 8 l.f. of 12" deep shelves, 12" high, and 12 l.f. of 18" deep shelves, 15" high.

DESIGN PROGRAM I-C:
A Small Accounting Firm Suite

A small, well-established accounting firm must relocate its offices. Their practice is fairly conventional, with most of their client involvement in the business and small corporate areas. The two partners operate with a two-person staff: a secretary/receptionist and a per diem accountant. Their desired ambience is one of comfortable formality, reflecting their success, but without a hint of pretentiousness. Although visitors are frequent, it is unusual for more than two or three to be there at one time, except for occasional conferences or meetings of five or six people.

SPECIAL REQUIREMENTS

1. The issues of privacy and confidentiality are of major concern. The partners' offices and the conference room must have visual and acoustic privacy.
2. The four permanent work spaces should ideally have exterior view and natural light.
3. The per diem accountant's work area should have some degree of privacy, not only for confidentiality, but also because the work function often demands long uninterrupted hours of concentrated work.
4. One of the partners is wheelchair-bound. The entire suite must be barrier-free in both concept and dimensional reality.
5. If possible, the partners would like to have a secondary "escape hatch" exit, where they can leave without passing through the reception area.

PROGRAM REQUIREMENTS

A. Receptionist/Secretary
1. Minimum 15 s.f. primary work surface, with minimum 10 s.f. return, two box/file drawer pedestals, telephone, personal computer (23"w × 20"d × 21"h). A transaction surface is needed to provide privacy of paper work and to screen desk clutter.
2. Secretarial task chair.
3. Minimum 24 l.f. of lateral files.

B. Waiting Area
1. Seating for four visitors.
2. Coat storage for six, in closet or cabinet.

3. Convenience surface(s), i.e., an end table for magazines and visitors' articles.

C. Partners Offices (two)
1. Minimum 18 s.f. working surface, plus "kneehole" credenza or return surface for personal computer (20"w × 17"d × 17"h), minimum two box/file drawer pedestals.
2. Executive swivel-tilt chair and two guest pull-up chairs.
3. Minimum 12 l.f. of lateral files.
4. Minimum of 40 l.f. of book/artifact shelving, 12" deep.
5. Partner A prefers an informal, conversational conference area, with lounge seating for four.
6. Partner B prefers small conference table or round conference extension of main desk work surface, capable of seating four people.
7. Each office requires a small personal clothes closet.

D. Per Diem Accountant
1. Work area or station with minimum 15 s.f. of primary work surface, plus a secondary work surface of at least 10 s.f., a personal computer (23"w × 20"d × 21"h), at least two box/file drawer pedestals, and a minimum of 12 l.f. of wall-hung shelves above the work surfaces.
2. Operational task chair and one guest chair.
3. Minimum of 12 l.f. of lateral files.

E. Conference/Library
1. Conference table and chairs to comfortably accommodate six people.
2. Credenza for beverage service and paper/pencil storage.
3. Legal book shelves lining most wall surfaces; minimum 90 l.f. of shelving, 12" deep, 12" high.

F. Copy/Storage/Work Room
1. Free-standing copier (42"w × 25"d × 38"h) that requires a 55" wide space.
2. Collating work surfaces (min. 10 s.f.) with storage below.
3. Minimum of 30 l.f. of lateral filing.
4. Lockable storage (cabinets and/or closet) with min. of 18 l.f. of 12" deep shelving and a minimum of 18 l.f. of 18" deep shelving.
5. Prefab "executive kitchen" unit for beverage service and refrigeration (42"w × 25"d × 36"h). Sink must be tied into plumbing lines as a conventional plumbing fixture.

G. Restroom
1. Lavatory.
2. Toilet.

DESIGN PROGRAM 2-A:
Regional Management Office

A national financial services firm must relocate a regional management office. This regional facility serves three functions: 1) the management of executive activities for the region, 2) marketing center for potential clients, and 3) a home base for account executives who spend most of their time on the road. Because of the executive and marketing activities, a reasonably impressive atmosphere is desired, so that the success of the firm is clearly conveyed and visiting clients are made to feel comfortable.

Visitor traffic is normally limited to the reception area, the three private offices, and the conference room, with the remainder of the facility being primarily for in-house use. The office manager, in addition to being responsible for the day-to-day in-house functions, is also the interface between the public/executive functions and in-house functions. Ideally, all personnel areas should have easy access to exterior view and natural light, except for the account executives' area, where those people will typically spend only a few hours a week in their shared work stations. The accounting staff requires a degree of separateness from other functions, while the support staff are the most accessible personnel and are directly supervised by the office manager. Restroom facilities must be strategically located to serve employees and visitors. The beverage center must serve the daily needs of employees as well as guests in the conference room.

SPECIAL REQUIREMENTS

1. Acoustic privacy is required for the three private offices, the conference room, and the office manager.
2. All facilities shall be barrier-free in concept and dimension.

PROGRAM REQUIREMENTS

A. Reception/Waiting Area
1. Receptionist shall greet visitors, control visitor traffic, and handle a part-time secretarial work load.
2. Desk shall have a primary work surface of 12 to 18 s.f. and a return of 7 to 10 s.f., plus two box/file drawer pedestals.
3. Personal computer (22"w × 18"d × 20"h).
4. 12 l.f. of lateral files within easy reach.
5. Secretarial task chair.
6. Visitor seating for five, plus convenience surfaces.
7. Coat closet or cabinet for visitors.
8. At least one major, unbroken exhibit wall for display of the company's services, 5 l.f. min.

B. Regional Manager's Office
1. Desk with 18 to 20 s.f. surface and two drawer pedestals.
2. Credenza with kneehole, 10 to 12 s.f. surface and maximum filing and storage capacity above and below the work surface.
3. Personal computer (19"w × 17"d × 16"h).
4. Executive task chair and two pull-up guest chairs.
5. Lounge seating for four and convenience surfaces to create an informal conference area.
6. Personal clothes closet, with at least 3 l.f. of hanging rod.

C. Private Offices (two)
The office needs of the Marketing Manager and the Accounts Administrator are the same:
1. Desk with primary work surface of 20 to 24 s.f., containing a round conference extension to accommodate three visitors, plus a return or credenza with 8 to 12 s.f., and one box/file drawer pedestal.
2. Open or closed book/manual shelving of at least 8 l.f., placed above and/or adjacent to the credenza/return surface.
3. Personal computer (19"w × 17"d × 16"h).
4. Management task chair and three pull-up guest chairs.
5. 12 l.f. of lateral files.

D. Conference Room
1. Central table to seat ten people.
2. Credenza for beverage service, pencil/paper storage, and the control panel for the video A/V system. (A ceiling-mounted video projector, directed toward the projection screen, is the only A/V system to be considered.)
3. A motorized, ceiling-recessed, projection screen, 4'-6" wide.
4. A marker-board wall, at least 8' long, placed to not conflict with the projection screen.

E. Office Manager
1. Desk with 12 to 15 s.f. work surface, return with 7 to 10 s.f. surface, two box/file drawer pedestals, 8 l.f. of book/manual shelving, 12 l.f. of lateral filing, and a personal computer (22"w × 21"d × 20"h).
2. Management task chair and two pull-up guest chairs.
3. Glass vision panel for supervision of support staff.

F. Support Staff (four)

These four people work together as a team; their work stations should be arranged to facilitate that relationship. It is assumed that systems furniture will be employed, with partition panels not exceeding 60″ in height.

1. Typical work stations: 45 to 60 s.f., containing at least 16 s.f. of work surface, a box/file drawer pedestal, 6 l.f. of lateral filing, 4 l.f. of overhead binder bin, and a personal computer (20″w × 20″d × 20″h).
2. Operational task chair.

G. Accounting Staff (two)

1. Two identical stations arranged as a working group with a common bank of files consisting of 36 l.f. of lateral files.
2. Typical station: 65 to 80 s.f. containing at least 18 s.f. of work surface, a box/file drawer pedestal, 6 l.f. of lateral files, 8 l.f. of overhead binder bin, and a personal computer (20″w × 20″d × 20″h). Management task chair and a guest chair.

H. Account Executives (three)

1. Three stations for part-time use by six on-the-road account execs; their periods of time in the office will not often coincide.
2. Typical station: 40 to 50 s.f. containing at least 14 s.f. of work surface, two box/file drawer pedestals, 4 l.f. of binder bin, and a personal computer (20″w × 20″d × 20″h). Operational task chair.

3. This area shall also contain a "huddle" space: a small, open conference space to seat four at a table, for informal and/or impromptu conferences. The huddle space is available to all personnel.

I. Work Room

Centrally located for easy access by all personnel.

1. Free-standing copier (46″w × 26″d × 35″h); requires a 54″ wide space for maintenance purposes.
2. Central computer printer (20″w × 21″d × 12″h), on stand.
3. Closed shelving for supplies, at least 18 l.f., 12″ deep and at least 18 l.f., 18″ deep.
4. Work table (60″w × 24″d × 36″h), for collating, sorting, etc.
5. Employee coat closet with 5′ long hanging rod.
6. 45 l.f. of lateral filing capacity.

J. Beverage Center

1. Min. of 8 s.f. of clear work counter, with full complement of base and wall cabinets.
2. Single bowl sink, 17″ wide, small range/oven, 20″ wide, stand-up refrigerator, 24″ wide, cabinet-hung coffee maker.

K. Restrooms

1. Men: one lavatory, one toilet stall.
2. Women: one lavatory, one toilet stall.

DESIGN PROGRAM 2-B:
Popular Culture Institute

A large urban university in a suburban-like setting at the edge of the city limits plans to house a new Popular Culture Institute. With an established reputation in the social sciences and several esteemed faculty involved in popular culture and futurism, the university expects to become part of an international network of similar institutions participating in the exchange of traveling exhibits and programs. In addition to regularly changing exhibits, the institute will initiate many conference and seminar programs. Because the nature of the exhibits will take on many formats and media, it is necessary for the exhibit space to provide maximum flexibility.

The general atmosphere generated by the interior planning and design should be one of energy and currency, avoiding any suggestion of institutional quality or museum stodginess. Most traffic will flow from the entry/reception space to the main exhibit area and the meeting room, with secondary traffic to the curator's and assistant's offices. Exhibit deliveries are infrequent enough so as to not require a separate service entrance; but if the potential for a separate service entry exists, direct access from that point to the work room is desirable.

SPECIAL REQUIREMENTS

1. The meeting room and the curator's office require acoustic privacy.
2. The curator and the administrative assistant work closely together, and their offices should be arranged to accommodate that relationship.
3. The administrative assistant will supervise shipping and receiving, as well as the part-time employees involved in exhibit construction/installation in the work room.
4. Natural light and view are desirable for all of the spaces/functions, but window placement in the main exhibit space must be carefully planned to not limit exhibit design and planning potential.
5. The building code requires that rooms or spaces seating more than 30 people shall have two remote means of egress.
6. The entire facility shall be barrier-free in concept and dimension.

PROGRAM REQUIREMENTS

A. Entry/Reception
1. A reception desk, at least 4'-6" wide, serviced by work/study student help, as an entry point information desk; desk shall contain pedestal drawers for the storage of hand-out literature.
2. A bench(es) to seat three to four people should not encourage lengthy occupancy.
3. Literature rack with face size of about 15 to 20 s.f. (4" deep).
4. Bulletin board for coming events and announcements, about 20 to 24 s.f.

B. Meeting Room
1. Flexible lecture/seminar room to seat 24, auditorium style, or 14 at a centrally placed conference table.
2. The room should be divisible by a folding partition of high acoustic value to accommodate small conferences of six people in each part.
3. Credenza for beverage service and storage of pencils and paper; the credenza should be available when the room is used as one large space or as two smaller spaces.
4. Ceiling-recessed projection screen, 6' wide, placed for classroom viewing when the room is set up to seat 24 people.
5. A marker-board wall, at least 32 s.f. in size, shall be placed for classroom viewing.

C. Main Exhibit Area—650 s.f.
1. An open, flexible space for a variety of exhibit formats. The ceiling grid shall be designed to accept the verticals of a modular exhibit system. Track lighting is the primary illumination system.
2. In special circumstances, the space will be used for lectures or presentations, seating up to 45 people.
3. Ceiling-recessed projection screen, 8' wide, located for lecture/presentation viewing.

D. Curator's Office
1. Primary desk surface of at least 18 s.f. with secondary surface of at least 10 s.f, personal computer (19"w × 18"d × 19"h), at least one box/file drawer pedestal.
2. Lateral files, 18 l.f.
3. Book shelves, 30 l.f., 12" deep.
4. Managerial task chair and three guest chairs.

5. A casual seating/conference arrangement is preferred (the curator does *not* have to sit *behind* a desk).

E. Administrative Assistant

1. A functional work station with 20 to 25 s.f. of work surface, a personal computer (19″w; × 18″d × 19″h), and two box/file drawer pedestals.

2. Lateral files, 24 l.f.

3. Book/manual shelves, 12 l.f., 12″ deep.

4. Operational task chair and one guest chair.

F. Work Room

1. Work bench (72″w × 36″d × 36″h) with 12 l.f. of 8″ deep shelves above.

2. Modular steel shelving, two units @ 36″w × 12″d × 78″h and two units @ 36″w × 18″d × 78″h.

3. Storage area for modular exhibit system parts (56″w × 28″d × full height); this area shall be separated from other work room areas by a partition or permanent panel.

4. Storage area for two-stack chair dollies 24″ sq. and six folding tables with 72″ × 36″ top surface.

5. Central work table (78″w × 42″d × 36″h).

6. Four work bench/table stools.

7. Lumber/crate storage, two divided spaces, each 48″w × 30″d × full height; areas to be separated from other areas by a partition or permanent panel.

8. Two portable coat racks (60″w × 18″d × 58″h).

G. Serving Kitchen

1. Min. of 12 s.f. counter, with full complement of base and wall cabinets.

2. Single bowl sink, 25″ wide; two burner commercial coffee urn; cabinet hung microwave, under-counter warming oven, 30″ wide; stand-up refrigerator, 32″ wide.

H. Restrooms

1. Men: two lavatories, one urinal, one toilet stall.

2. Women: two lavatories, two toilet stalls.

DESIGN PROGRAM 2-C: Meeting/Marketing Facility

A successful publishing firm wishes to create its own small meeting and marketing facility. The new facility is expected to serve a variety of functions from in-house training sessions to sales and marketing presentations to potential buyers. While maintaining a strongly professional image, this facility is expected to reflect the firm's success and impress visitors through its design quality.

From a functional viewpoint, the most important planning and design issue is the creation of optimal presentation/classroom/conference spaces. The only regular staff housed at the center are the reception personnel, both of whom are trained to operate the A/V equipment. Presenters, workshop leaders, conveners, etc., will come from their own offices to use the conference center. Special attention should be given to corridor and aisle spaces, since relatively large numbers of people will be entering or leaving a space at one time, as well as moving from one space to another as a group.

SPECIAL REQUIREMENTS

1. Acoustic control is of primary importance; each meeting/conference space must provide acoustic privacy.
2. The entire center shall be barrier-free in concept and dimension.
3. All A/V equipment is video-based. Each presentation/classroom conference space shall have a ceiling-mounted projection unit directed toward a projection screen.
4. Although not required, preference has been expressed for the large and small conference rooms to be placed adjacent to one another, with their common wall being a folding partition of high acoustic performance, making it possible to have a combined conference area capable of seating 18 at a central table.

PROGRAM REQUIREMENTS

A. Reception Station

1. Critically located for maximum control of visitor traffic; ideally, the station should be visible upon entry to the center. Reception personnel should always be easily available for information purposes.
2. A two-person reception desk, with 10 to 12 s.f. of clear work surface and a box/file drawer pedestal for each person and a shared personal computer (20"w × 19"d × 17"h).
3. Transaction surface for visitors in front of each desk area.
4. Immediately adjacent storage wall, 8' to 10' long by 6'-6" to 7'-0" high by 1'-8" deep, containing 12 l.f. of lateral files, an enclosed computer printer, and closed cabinets for the storage of supplies and hand-out literature.

B. Waiting Area

1. A comfortable lounge atmosphere in visual contact with the Reception Station.
2. Seating for seven (min.) to eight visitors.
3. Coat storage for 70 winter coats.
4. Table(s)/convenience surface(s) for magazines, mugs, etc.
5. Display rack for company literature, 3'w × 4'h × 4"d.

C. Equipment Room

1. Central control and equipment storage for all of the presentation/classroom/conference spaces located immediately adjacent to (or at least very nearby) the Reception Station.
2. Provide a 90 to 100 s.f. room with lockable door (and desirably without windows), minimum dimensions of 7'-6", for a permanent control panel, equipment shelving, tape storage, and space for four 22" by 34" equipment carts that will be used in the presentation/classroom/conference areas.

D. Presentation Room

1. A conventional lecture/presentation space with comfortable fixed seating for 24 people.
2. A speaker's lectern or a panelists' table and chairs (for four at the front of the room.
3. A motorized, ceiling-recessed projection screen, 6' wide, at the front of the room.
4. A marker-board surface across the entire front of the room.
5. A closet for four stack chairs and the panelists' table.

E. Training Room

1. Seating for 16 people at eight training tables, 72"w × 24'd.
2. Each table shall contain a personal computer (20"w × 20"d × 18"h).
3. A speaker's lectern at the front of the room.
4. A motorized, ceiling-recessed projection screen, 5' wide, at the front of the room.
5. A marker-board surface across the entire front of the room.

F. Large Conference Room

1. A central, modular conference table for 12 people. (The modular table design will accommodate the adding of the small conference table, if space planning permits.)
2. A credenza, at least 8' long, for beverage service and pencil/paper storage.
3. A motorized, ceiling-recessed projection screen, 5' wide, at the front of the room.
4. A marker board, at least 10' long, for one side of the room.

G. Small Conference Room

1. A central, modular conference table for six people.
2. A credenza, at least 5' long, for beverage service and pencil/paper storage.
3. A motorized, ceiling-recessed projection screen, 4' wide, placed for easy viewing.
4. A marker board, at least 8' wide, for a side of the room other than the projection screen side.

H. Coffee/Break Area

1. A centrally located break space for intermission periods of presentation, class, or conference programs.
2. A primarily open space for standing or seating, with stool, bench, or leaning surfaces for 12 to 18 people; comfortable seating is specifically not desired.
3. Buffet or counter surface(s) (one or two totaling 8 to 10 l.f.) for beverage and snack/hors d'oeuvres service.
4. Adequate wall surface for diverting graphics or other visual material. A view to the exterior is also important for this space.
5. Ideally, this space should be adjacent to (and flow into) the Waiting Area, so that the combined spaces can serve for larger social/reception functions.

I. Kitchen

1. A serving kitchen only (no food preparation), centrally located to serve the Presentation Room and conference rooms, as well as the Coffee/Break Area.
2. At least 12 s.f. of counter space, with a complete complement of base and wall cabinets.
3. Single bowl sink (25" wide), two burner commercial coffee urn, small four burner range/oven (20" to 24" wide), and a 28" wide stand-up refrigerator.
4. Enclose space to contain noise and odors.

J. Restrooms

1. Men: two lavatories, one urinal, one toilet stall.
2. Women: two lavatories, two toilet stalls, make-up bar.

DESIGN PROGRAM 2-S:
University Career Counseling Center

The University Career Counseling Center will become an integral part of this medium sized, state supported university and will provide curriculum and career counseling for all levels of students. Seminar type instruction will be provided for college and high school level educators, who are themselves counselors. In addition, the director and the director's staff are considered the university's primary resource for career information and employment opportunities for graduates and have a major role to play with each of the institution's departments of professional education. The center not only serves the adjacent campus but three other branch campuses located in other parts of the state. This statewide activity often brings overnight guests to the center, creating a need for a guest apartment, which would generally be used for one or two night stays.

The bulk of the center's traffic is generated by a fairly constant flow of students and recent graduates, most of whom come with a specific appointment time. Several times each week, groups ranging in size from six to thirty come for conferences, seminars, lectures, and group counseling. The Director and Assistant Director will each see several visitors on a typical day, usually coming alone or in pairs.

SPECIAL REQUIREMENTS

1. The general atmosphere of the center should essentially reflect its connections to the business and corporate worlds, rather than its institutional/educational connections. Each visitor's experience, from reception through interview or program, should emulate a "real-world" or professional experience. Jeans and T-shirts are discouraged attire for visitors.
2. Wherever possible, full advantage should be taken of exterior view and natural light in areas where staff or visitors spend a considerable amount of time.
3. Except for the kitchen and bathroom in the Guest Apartment, all spaces and functions shall be accessible to wheelchair-bound users.

4. The Director's office, the Seminar Room, and the Guest Apartment require acoustic privacy.
5. The Guest Apartment is expected to have an appropriate residential environment, avoiding the typical "hotel plastic" character. The entrance to the apartment should avoid a public or prominent location.
6. The Director, Assistant Director, and Secretary tend to work as an administrative team and should have their work spaces clustered together. The receptionist is the "greeter" and "traffic cop" for the center. The interviewer's locations need only be convenient for visitors; their other internal working relationships are not frequent or critical.

PROGRAM REQUIREMENTS

A. Reception Area
1. The reception station shall include an uninterrupted work surface of at least 12 s.f.; a transaction surface for visitors, 40″ AFF; a standard office typewriter; a personal computer (20″w × 19″d × 21″h); a return surface for the typewriter and the computer; two box/file drawer pedestals; a small console telephone; and a secretarial task chair.
2. Immediately adjacent to the station, 12 l.f. of lateral files; a computer printer (19″w × 19″d × 10″h); and a fax machine (18″w × 16″d × 9″h) must be accommodated.
3. Guest seating for five to six visitors.
4. Coat storage for 30 people.
5. Wall hung literature rack (40″w × 60″h × 5″d), easily accessible by visitors.

B. Interview Stations (four)
1. Stations shall be created through the use of systems furniture work surfaces, acoustic partition panels, and storage elements; panel height shall not exceed 65″.
2. Primary work surface and return shall provide a combined surface of 18 to 20 s.f. per station.
3. Provide two box/file drawer pedestals; a minimum of 4 l.f. of overhead storage bin; and a personal computer (20″w × 19″d × 18″h) per station.
4. One operational task chair and one guest chair per station.
5. A minimum of 48 l.f. of lateral files shall be accessible to all four stations.
6. Without creating "offices," each station should, through the use of acoustic partition panels, create a sense of separateness from the other stations.

C. Director

1. A comfortable, no-frills, executive office consistent with institutional standards.
2. An executive, double pedestal, recessed front desk with matching "kneehole" credenza for placement of a personal computer (20"w × 19"d × 18"h).
3. An executive swivel-tilt desk chair and two guest pull-up chairs.
4. Minimum of 20 l.f. of book/artifact shelving, 12" deep.

D. Assistant Director

1. A management work station created through the use of systems furniture; acoustic panels shall not exceed 65" in height.
2. 12 to 15 s.f. primary work surface, plus credenza or desk return (at least 8 s.f.) and two or three box/file drawer pedestals.
3. Overhead bin storage, at least 4 l.f.
4. Personal computer (20"w × 19"d × 18"h).
5. A management task chair and two guest pull-up chairs.

E. Secretary

1. Primary work relationships are with the Director and Assistant Director. This station monitors access to the Director's office.
2. An operational work station created through the use of systems furniture; this station should have a high level of visual accessibility.
3. Minimum 12 s.f. primary work surface, min. 6 s.f. return, two box/file drawer pedestals, min. 4 l.f. overhead shelf or bin; personal computer (20"w × 19"d × 21"h).
4. Operational task chair and one guest chair.
5. Min. 6 l.f. of lateral filing.

F. Work Area

1. Free-standing copier (44"w × 27"d × 38"h) requiring 54"w space.
2. Storage cabinet, 36"w × 18"d × 78"h.
3. Min. 6 l.f. of lateral files.
4. Remote computer printer (19" × 19"d × 10"h) that can be placed on top of lateral file.

G. Seminar Room

1. Multipurpose presentation, conference, and encounter activities, with flexible arrangement potential. Provide classroom seating for 20, conference/seminar for 12 at one central table, or (through the use of a folding partition) two small conference rooms, each to seat at least six at a central table.
2. Beverage serving surface, plus paper/pencil storage below it; this should be available when room is set up as one large space or as two small spaces.
3. Storage for tables and/or chairs that are not in use, plus storage for roll-away A/V equipment cart.
4. 6'-0" wide ceiling-mounted projection screen (elec. operation).
5. 48"w × 48"h × 5"d visuals board (96"w when open) placed for use when room is set up as one large space.
6. Tackable wall surface, min. 8 l.f. placed for use when room is set up as one large space.

H. Public Restrooms

1. Men: two lavatories, one urinal, one toilet stall.
2. Women: two lavatories, two toilet stalls.

I. Coffee Station

1. For daily staff use and for support of Seminar Room activities.
2. Minimum of 8 s.f. of work counter (not including sink) plus base and overhead cabinets.
3. Double burner commercial coffee urn, sink, undercabinet microwave, 24"w stand-up refrigerator.

J. Guest Apartment

1. Living area: comfortable lounge seating for four or five, coffee table for informal serving, and entertainment center (TV, VCR, music) with books/artifacts shelving.
2. Dining area: minimal in size; can be part of living area or kitchen; table surface to double as desk/work surface.
3. Kitchen: small but serviceable for occasional food preparation, with sink, small four burner range/oven (20" to 24" wide), and adequate countertop and cabinets.
4. Sleeping area: can be an alcove rather than a separate room; double bed, night table and lamp; 3 to 4 l.f. of closet space, drawer storage, and space for a luggage rack.
5. Bathroom: basic, but comfortable, apartment bathroom, with lavatory, toilet, and tub or stall shower, plus small linen closet or cabinet.

DESIGN PROGRAM 3-A: Market Research Group

A small and prosperous market research group is planning to relocate its offices to larger quarters because they have outgrown their current facilities. Their new design program, which was researched and written by a space planning consultant, incorporates an estimated growth factor for the next five years. Because the firm represents a broad spectrum of services, their facility must accommodate a large number of varied tasks for a relatively small business concern. Telephone survey is the only company function not handled from this office.

Comfort and productivity for employees and visitors are the dominating planning factors here; image for its own sake is not desired. Visitors are generally limited to the reception area, group survey rooms, conference room, and the three private offices. The Vice President for Operations is the supervisor of day-to-day functions and must be located appropriately. The work room should be reasonably convenient to all working functions, while the reference library gets limited use and may be placed in a relatively remote location. The beverage center must be strategically located to serve the needs of employees and visitors in the survey and conference rooms; the beverage center and the lunch/break room could be combined in one space.

SPECIAL REQUIREMENTS

1. The conference room, group survey rooms, three private offices, and the lunch/break room require acoustic privacy.
2. The group survey rooms require maximum acoustic absorption.
3. The three private offices should be arranged to permit easy interaction between those three people.
4. Access to natural light and exterior view is very desirable for all offices and workstations.
5. All facilities shall be barrier-free in concept and dimension.

PROGRAM REQUIREMENTS

A. Reception/Waiting
1. This working reception station greets visitors and controls visitors' traffic, and provides some limited secretarial services.
2. Total work surface must be at least 20 s.f., accommodate a personal computer (21″w × 21″d × 17″h), and provide at least one box/file drawer pedestal.
3. A transaction counter is required for arriving visitors.
4. Lateral files, 18 l.f., must be within easy reach.
5. Waiting area shall include seating for 12, plus coat closet or cabinet (5 l.f.), and a magazine rack or display surface. Waiting periods can occasionally be lengthy; so therefore, comfortable upholstered seating is desired.

B. Group Survey Rooms (two)
1. Survey Room A shall be set up as a conventional conference for 12 people. Seating should be appropriate for survey sessions of up to three hours in length.
2. Survey Room B shall be set up in a comfortable conversational circle for ten people, with one part of the "circle" open for reference to the marker wall or video screen.
3. Each room shall contain a marker wall (at least 8 l.f.), a ceiling-recessed (and motorized) screen (6′ wide) to drop in front of the marker wall, and a credenza (at least 6′ long) for beverage service, video controls, and supply storage. A video projector will be ceiling mounted and directed toward the screen.

C. Conference Room
1. Central table to seat ten.
2. Credenza for beverage service and the storage of pencils/paper and A/V equipment and controls.
3. A clear wall surface or a ceiling-recessed projection screen for the viewing of slides.
4. Marker-board wall surface, 8 to 10 l.f.
5. Storage closet, at least 10 s.f., for a video monitor cart, newsprint pad easel, and other A/V paraphernalia.

D. President's Office
1. Executive desk, 18 to 22 s.f., credenza with kneehole space and able to accommodate personal computer (18″w × 17″d × 16″h), two box/file pedestals and book/artifacts shelves (above), 16 to 20 l.f.
2. Executive task chair and 2 pull-up guest chairs.
3. Conversational conference area with lounge seating for four, plus appropriate space for the two pull-up chairs to become part of the conversational grouping, when needed.
4. Shelving for books and artifacts, with at least 50 l.f.

E. Private Offices (two)

Except for the shelving requirements, the office needs of the Executive Vice President and the Vice President of Operations are the same and are as follows:

1. Desk surface of 20 to 26 s.f. containing a rounded conference extension to accommodate three visitors, plus a return or credenza with 7 to 10 s.f., personal computer (18"w × 17"d × 16"h), and one box/file drawer pedestal.
2. Management task chair and three pull-up guest chairs.
3. Lateral files, 12 l.f.
4. Shelving:
   a. for Exec. V.P.—60 l.f. for books and artifacts.
   b. for V.P. for Operations—16 l.f. for books.

F. Account Executives (two)

1. Management workstation with at least 20 s.f. of desk surface, personal computer (15"w × 17"d × 16"h), and two box/file drawer pedestals.
2. Management task chair and two pull-up guest chairs.
3. 9 l.f. of lateral files.

G. Administrative Assistants (four)

1. Workstation with at least 16 s.f. of desk surface, a personal computer (18"w × 17"d × 16"h), and two box/file drawer pedestals.
2. Operations task chair and a guest side chair.
3. 6 l.f. of lateral files.

H. Work Room

1. Free-standing copier (47"w × 27"d × 38"h), requires a 56" wide space for maintenance.
2. Mail sorting table, 60"w × 24"d × 36"h, with a wall hung mail sorter above the table 48"w × 26"h × 9"d.
3. Lockable supply shelving in cabinets or closet, containing 36 l.f. of 12" deep shelving and 36 l.f. of 18" deep shelving.
4. Two computer printers, 21"w × 22"d × 32"h.
5. Employee coat closet with 6 l.f. of hanging rod.
6. General storage closet, 30 s.f.

I. Beverage Center

1. At least 10 s.f. of open counter space, plus a full complement of base and wall cabinets.
2. Single bowl sink, 19" wide; small range/oven, 20" wide; stand-up refrigerator, 28" wide.
3. Undercounter dishwasher, two burner coffee maker, and a cabinet hung microwave.

J. Lunch/Break Room

1. Flexible table arrangement for eight to ten people, accommodating groups from two to six people.
2. Service station for supplies, condiments, etc., plus trash receptacles below.

K. Rest Rooms

1. Men: two lavatories, one urinal, one toilet stall.
2. Women: two lavatories, two toilet stalls.

DESIGN PROGRAM 3-B:
The Cosmopolitan Club

Following the lead of other metropolitan chapters, the local chapter of a national business and professional organization has decided to initiate its own private dining club. The club's purposes are to provide a meeting place for members, a place to entertain non-member friends and business associates, and a dining place of predictable fare and atmosphere where one is known. The design program was established after lengthy consultation with the managers of other dining clubs within the national organization and a local food service consultant.

The overall ambience should be friendly, businesslike, and more formal than informal. Lunch is the major meal of the day, although dinner will be served as well. Previous experience indicates that men and women diners will be equal in number. The bar and lounge activity is expected to be limited; again, previous experience indicates that members expect the lunch hour to be limited, without the luxury of an extended midday break. Because the membership is fairly diverse in nature, a strong theme in cuisine or decor is not desired. The general traffic patterns are obvious, but in circumstances where a separate service entrance is not possible (as in the case of a high-rise office building), service deliveries and garbage pick-up must be routed with minimal passage through public spaces and strictly scheduled for nondining hours. The manager's office should be located fairly close to the entry and, ideally, it should have access to food preparation areas without having to travel through the dining area.

SPECIAL REQUIREMENTS

1. The private dining rooms and the manager's office must provide acoustic isolation.
2. The bar is primarily a service bar, and a 5′ long portion of the bar length must be reserved for waiter pick-up.
3. Priority for natural light and view must be given to the dining areas; the same are desirable but not necessary in the bar/lounge and the manager's office.
4. All public areas shall be barrier-free.

PROGRAM REQUIREMENTS

A. Entry
1. Seating for four to five people; the comfort level need not be very great.
2. Maitre d' stand, about 3 s.f. in size, strategically placed to view both the bar/lounge and the main dining room.
3. Small decorative table, 6 to 10 s.f., for the display of club literature.
4. Self-service coat room or alcove with at least 20 l.f. of hanging rod, plus umbrella stand, hat rack, and boot rack.

B. Bar/Lounge
1. A traditional bar with at least 8 l.f. of undercounter work area and a back bar with storage and bottle display, space for six bar stools, and a waiter pick-up space of 5′-0″ in length.
2. Flexible table area for eight to ten people, to accommodate groups of two and four.

C. Main Dining Room
1. Seat 40 diners at tables for 2 and 4, with the flexibility for occasional arrangements for 6.
2. Service station, 6 l.f. of clear countertop, plus storage trays for flatware and shelves for china service, glasses, table linens, etc.; allow 50 s.f. for the station.

D. Private Dining Rooms (two)
1. One room to seat 6 and the other to seat 12 (at one table).
2. Each room shall have a service buffet of at least 5′ and 7′ long, respectively, with service storage below the buffet surface.

E. Manager's Office
1. Desk with 12 to 15 s.f. work surface, return with 7 to 10 s.f. surface, two box/file drawer pedestals, 8 l.f. of book/manual shelving, and a personal computer (22″w × 21″d × 20″h).
2. Lateral files, 30 l.f.
3. Management task chair and two pull-up guest chairs.

F. Restrooms
1. Men: two lavatories, one urinal, one toilet stall.
2. Women: two lavatories, two toilet stalls, 2 seat grooming.

G. Food Service Facilities
Allow 1,000 s.f. for total food service area, including receiving desk, employee lockers and toilet facilities, dry and cold storage (including waste refrigeration), food preparation kitchen, dishwashing area, and waiter service line. View of kitchen should be screened from diners and kitchen noises should be contained in the work areas. At least one major wall shall be adjacent to an existing plumbing stack.

DESIGN PROGRAM 3-C:
Community Counseling Consortium

The Community Counseling Consortium (CCC) has found a new space in which to house their offices and meeting facilities. The space must accommodate the administrative and counseling offices for CCC, a community seminar/conference room, and a Hot Line Center (HLC).

CCC is a non-profit, community-funded organization that counsels both families and individuals "in crisis"—those facing death or a terminal illness of a family member; those dealing with drug and alcohol abuse, or physical, sexual abuse; those facing desertion or joblessness, etc. The predominant area of direct help is with individuals or families facing a terminal illness. CCC offers some health-care courses, hospice programs, and group interaction seminars that address both the emotional and physical needs of the client. CCC further works as a resource center for persons facing other crisis situations through direct counseling and indirect referral to the proper "specific service" agency. CCC maintains a checkout library—slides, films, video cassettes—available to individuals, families, or community service agencies; and CCC further offers a reasonably sized seminar room for community awareness programs and group interaction sessions.

The Hot Line Center is a separate agency funded in part by CCC. The Center will be housed in the new CCC facility and will offer a 24-hour telephone "hot line" for those persons in immediate danger or crisis. In addition to the office area, the Center will include an apartment for the supervisor—a position typically held by a graduate student in social work serving a three to six month community internship.

SPECIAL REQUIREMENTS

1. CCC wants to maintain a personal and non-institutional atmosphere throughout its facility. The interiors must be functional but also inviting and relaxing.
2. Particular attention must be given to the reception area and counseling offices in regard to the initial impression conveyed to those persons seeking help.

3. Window areas, and the natural light that they permit to enter, are very important features of the interior environment and must be used to full advantage.
4. As many clients are handicapped, all public spaces must be wheelchair accessible. (The HLC, both the office and apartment, are considered for private use and need not meet barrier-free codes.)
5. The private counseling offices should afford visual as well as acoustic privacy.
6. The HLC office and apartment must be a separate entity, with access to its spaces immediately entered from the reception area; and if possible, (building configuration permitting) with its own exterior entrance door.
7. Though personal or residential in appearance, furniture materials and finishes must be durable and practical and meet commercial standards.

PROGRAM REQUIREMENTS

A. Reception Area
1. Reception station to accommodate a client sign-in counter, 10 s.f. of clear work surface, a personal computer (22"w × 16"d × 12"h) to pull up current client records, a standard office typewriter to type forms and new client cards, a storage pedestal with two box drawers and one file drawer, a telephone, and a secretarial posture chair.
2. 18 l.f. of lateral filing.
3. A wall hung literature rack for information and educational brochures. This rack must be visible from the reception area and accessible to the public.
4. Secured storage for general office supplies (24 l.f. of shelving, 12" deep) and visual materials available for public check-out, i.e., slides, films, video cassettes, etc. (24 l.f. of shelving, 18"d).
5. Free-standing copier (30"w × 26"d × 38"h) and a table top computer printer (22"w × 16"d × 10"h), both accessible to the receptionist, but not visible to visitors.
6. Visitor seating for four to six.
7. Coat hanging space for ten visitors.

B. Counseling Offices (three)
1. Three private offices. Each requires a work area to accommodate 12 s.f. of work surface, 9 l.f. of filing and 6 l.f. of open shelving for books and artifacts. Work area should be separate, but not necessarily divided, from the actual counseling area. Each requires a managerial swivel-tilt chair.

    2. Counselor A prefers a casual conference table area—a round desk-height table and four chairs.

    3. Counselors B and C prefer a conversational arrangement—sofa and/or lounge chair seating for at least four.

C. CCC Director's Office

    1. A private office with both a work and a conference area.

    2. Double pedestal desk (18 s.f.) with full height box/file drawer pedestals.

    3. Credenza with a minimum of 6 l.f. of lateral filing.

    4. Swivel-tilt executive desk chair.

    5. Two guest pull-up chairs.

    6. 18 l.f. of open shelving for books and artifacts.

    7. Separate conference area for four using lounge chairs around a round coffee table (15"h).

D. Community Seminar Room

    1. Multipurpose room. Allow for varied and flexible seating arrangements—lecture style layout, i.e., classroom seating, for 40, or conference set-up, i.e., tables and chairs, for 20.

    2. Storage for folding tables, stacking chairs, and coat racks for 40 visitors.

    3. Coffee bar with undercounter refrigerator (60"w × 24"d × 36"h).

    4. One tackable wall, 8 l.f. min.

    5. One visual board (48"w × 48"h × 5"d closed, 96"w open). Includes writing surface, flipchart, and pull-down projection screen.

    6. TV monitor and VCR on a portable cart, 20" × 30" by 40" high.

    7. Storage for projectors, films, slides, and video cassettes (72"w × 18"d × full height).

E. Public Restrooms

    1. Men: two lavatories, one urinal, one toilet.

    2. Women: two lavatories, two toilets.

F. Kitchen/Lounge

Used by both clients and staff for lunches, breaks, and relaxing.

    1. Tables and chairs in flexible arrangement to seat at least 16.

    2. Work area: counter surface of at least 12 s.f., double sink, undercounter dishwasher, four burner range and oven (30" wide), microwave, standard refrigerator with icemaker (32" wide), and a full complement of base and wall cabinets.

G. Hot Line Center: Office

    1. Separate entry (from the exterior, if possible).

    2. Two work areas—semiprivate. Each to accommodate a 10 s.f. work surface, a telephone, a personal computer (22"w × 16"d × 12"h), a two-file drawer pedestal, and a managerial chair.

    3. 12 l.f. of lateral files, accessible to both workers.

    4. Storage closet or cabinet (36"w × 18"d × 78"h) for forms, manuals, supplies, etc.

H. Hot Line Center: Supervisor's Apartment

    1. Adjacent to the CCC office.

    2. Living area: conversational seating for four, reading chair, wall unit for TV, stereo, and books, 15 l.f. of shelving.

    3. Dining area: table and chairs for four; table will "double" as a writing/study work surface.

    4. Small kitchen: sink, refrigerator, range, microwave, counter, and cabinets; approx. 50 s.f. in size.

    5. Sleeping area (need not be a separate room): double bed, bedside table, drawer storage, clothes closet with 4 l.f. of hang rod.

    6. Bathroom: lavatory, toilet, shower, linen storage.

BUILDING SHELLS

1A, 1B, 1C,

2A, 2A-RC, 2B, 2C, 2C-RC,

2S, 3A, 3B, 3C, 3C-RC

BUILDING DESCRIPTION

SITUATED ON A HEAVILY TRAVELLED STREET, THIS TYPICAL WOOD FRAME "RANCHER" OF 1950's VINTAGE IS SITED ON AN OVERSIZED LOT WITH A DEEP AND WELL LANDSCAPED REAR YARD, MAKING IT APPROPRIATE FOR NON—RESIDENTIAL USES. EXTERIOR WALLS ARE OF LOAD BEARING WOOD STUD (16" O.C.) CONSTR-UCTION, WITH AN INSULATING SHEATHING BOARD AND PAINTED WOOD SIDING APPLIED TO THE EXTERIOR AND GYPSUM WALL BOARD APPLIED TO THE INTERIOR.
THE ROOF CONSTRUCTION IS OF CONVENTIONAL CLEAR-SPAN WOOD TRUSSES PLACED 24" O.C., WITH PLY-WOOD SHEATHING AND ASPHALT SHINGLES APPLIED. EXTERIOR DOORS ARE 7'—0" HIGH; WINDOWS ARE DOUBLE HUNG, WITH A 3'—0" SILL (A.F.F.) AND A 7'—0" HEAD (A.F.F.).

THE FIRST FLOOR IS OF WOOD JOIST CONSTRUCTION WITH A PLYWOOD SUB—FLOOR AND T&G OAK STRIP FINISH FLOORING. THE CEILING IS GYPSUM WALL BOARD, 8'—0" A.F.F. THE PARTITIONS SURROUNDING THE BASEMENT STAIR ARE OF WOOD STUD AND GYPSUM WALL BOARD CONSTRUCTION; THESE PARTITIONS HAVE A 6" HIGH WOOD CLAMSHELL BASEBOARD. THE DOOR TO THE STAIR IS A 7'—0" HIGH PAINTED FLUSH DOOR. THE HEATING SYSTEM IS A PERIMETER BASE-BOARD TYPE, 6" HIGH, PRESENTING A CONTINUOUS APPEARANCE ON ALL EXTERIOR WALLS. BECAUSE OF THE EXISTING WASTE LINE LOCATION IN THE BASEMENT, ALL OF THE PLUMBING FIXTURES MUST BE PLACED WITHIN 8'—0" OF THE NORTH WALL OF THE BUILDING. ALL INCOMING UTILITY LINES AND METER-ING EQUIPMENT ARE IN THE BASEMENT.

BECAUSE THIS STRUCTURE DOES NOT HAVE ARCHI-TECTURAL DISTINCTION OR HISTORIC SIGNIFICANCE, MODEST REVISIONS TO ITS EXTERIOR MAY BE MADE. THE BASIC PROVISIONS OF STANDARD REGIONAL BUILD-ING CODES, INCLUDING THOSE PROVISIONS RELATED TO BARRIER—FREE ACCESS AND DESIGN, SHALL BE COMPLIED WITH.

SITE PLAN

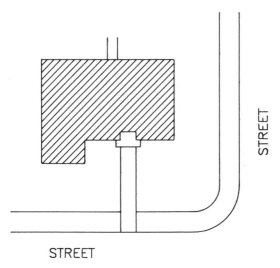

STREET

STREET

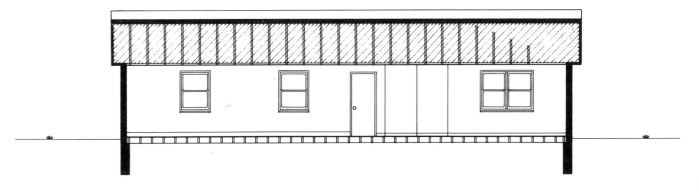

BUILDING SECTION

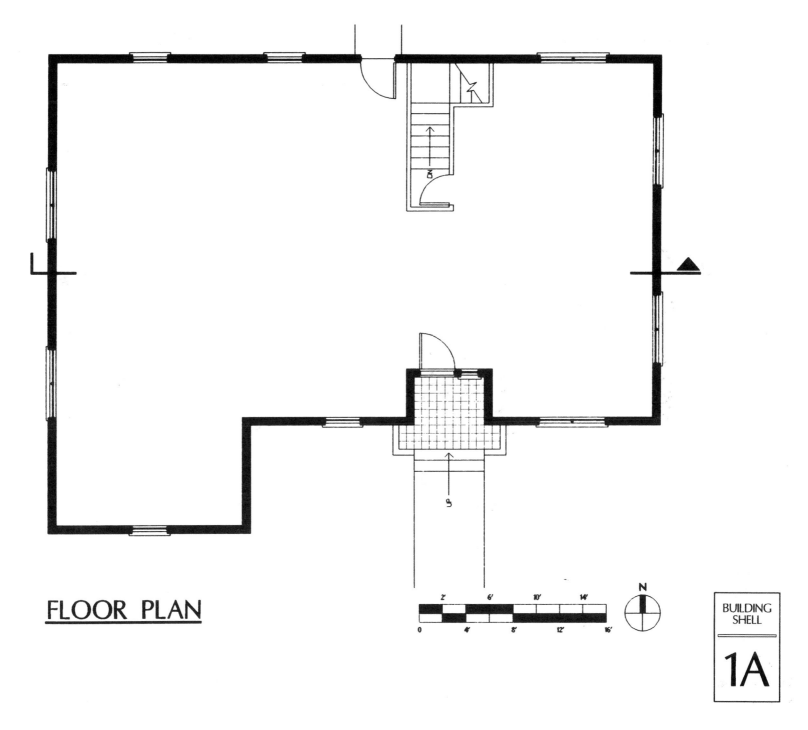

FLOOR PLAN

BUILDING DESCRIPTION

THIS TURN—OF—THE—CENTURY FIRE HOUSE HAS BEEN RETIRED FROM ACTIVE SERVICE AFTER MANY YEARS. IT IS PART OF A SMALL CLUSTER OF COMMERCIAL BUILDINGS WHICH ARE SEPARATED BY LOAD BEARING MASONRY FIRE WALLS IN ROW—HOUSE—LIKE MANNER. THE FRONT AND REAR WALLS ARE OF NON—BEARING MASONRY CONSTRUCTION. THE SECOND FLOOR AND ROOF STRUCTURES ARE OF TYPICAL WOOD JOIST CONSTRUCTION. THE GARAGE DOOR OPENINGS IN THE SOUTH WALL HAVE ARCHED LINETELS, 12'—0" AT THEIR MID—POINT. THE SIDE DOORS IN THE SOUTH WALL HAVE GLASS TRANSOMS ABOVE 7'—0" HIGH DOORS, WITH ARCHED LINTELS OVER THE TRANSOMS, 9'—0" HIGH AT THEIR MID—POINT. THE REAR SERVICE DOOR IS 7'—0" HIGH, AND THE WINDOWS IN THE NORTH AND EAST WALLS HAVE SILLS AT 3'—0" A.F.F. AND HEADS AT 9'—0" A.F.F. FOR THE PURPOSE OF THIS DESIGN PROBLEM, THE SECOND FLOOR WILL BE USED FOR FUTURE EXPANSION PURPOSES ONLY, WITH FUTURE ACCESS TO THE STAIR A BASIC PLANNING CONSIDERATION.

THE GROUND FLOOR IS A REINFORCED CONCRETE SLAB—ON—GRADE. THE INTERIOR FACE OF THE EXTERIOR WALLS AND THE PARTY WALL ARE EXPOSED BRICK. THE FREE—STANDING INTERIOR COLUMNS ARE 6" DIAMETER STEEL LALLY COLUMNS. THE FIRST FLOOR CEILING IS PLASTER, ON WOOD LATH ATTATCHED TO THE UNDERSIDE OF THE SECOND FLOOR JOISTS, AND IS AT 14'—0" A.F.F. A NEW HVAC SYSTEM IS PLANNED FOR ROOF TOP INSTALLATION, WITH SUPPLY AND RETURN DUCTS TO BE FED DOWN ADJACENT TO THE WEST PARTY WALL; NEW INTERIOR CONSTRUCTION ON THE FIRST FLOOR MAY EXPOSE NEW DUCTWORK, OR CONSTRUCT A NEW SUSPENDED CEILING TO CONCEAL THE NEW DUCTWORK. ALL PLUMBING FIX—TURES MUST BE PLACED WITHIN 8'—0" OF THE EAST PARTY WALL IN ORDER TO CONNECT WITH THE MAIN DRAIN LINE ALONG THAT WALL IN A TRENCH BELOW THE FINISHED FLOOR.

BECAUSE OF ITS CLEAR PERIOD CHARACTER, THE SOUTH WALL OF THE BUILDING MAY NOT BE ALTERED. BUT THE IN—FILL OF THE GARAGE DOOR OPENINGS MAY BE DESIGNED TO FIT THE NEEDS OF THE NEW INTERIOR USE. THE BASIC PROVISIONS OF STANDARD REGIONAL BUILDING CODES, INCLUDING THOSE PRO—VISIONS RELATED TO BARRIER—FREE ACCESS AND DESIGN, SHALL BE COMPLIED WITH.

SITE PLAN

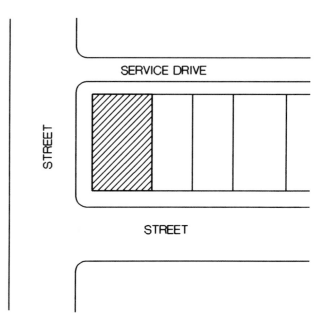

SERVICE DRIVE

STREET

STREET

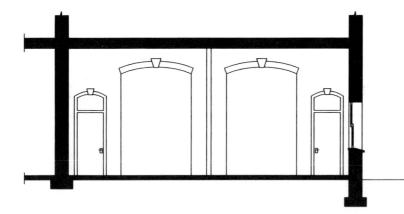

BUILDING SECTION

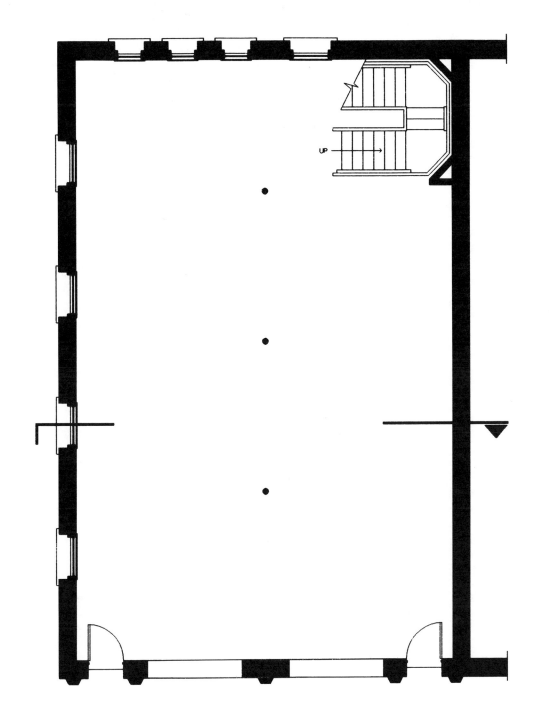

FLOOR PLAN

BUILDING DESCRIPTION

BUILT IN THE 1920's, THIS FORMER MUNICIPAL OFFICE BUILDING, DESIGNED WITH 'CLASSICAL' DETAIL AND SITUATED IN A PARK–LIKE SETTING, HAS BEEN MADE AVAILABLE FOR RENT FOR BOTH PROFESSIONAL OFFICES AND COMMUNITY AGENCY USE. THE SPECIFIC SPACE DESCRIBED HERE IS AT ONE END OF THE FIRST FLOOR OF THIS THREE–STORY–PLUS–BASEMENT BUILDING. THE BASIC STRUCTURE IS MASONRY BEARING WALL WITH REINFORCED CONCRETE FLOORS. THE EXTERIOR WALLS ARE BRICK WITH A PLASTER INTERIOR FINISH; THE INTERIOR BEARING WALL IS ALSO OF BRICK WITH A PLASTER FINISH. WINDOWS ARE DOUBLE HUNG, WITH THE SILL AT 3'–0" A.F.F., AND THE HEAD AT 8'–0" A.F.F., THE WINDOW TRIM IS 6" WIDE.

THE EXISTING FLOOR SURFACE IS TERRAZZO, IN SMOOTH BUT UNPRESENTABLE CONDITION. INTERIOR WALL SURFACES ARE PLASTER WITH AN 8" HIGH THREE–PIECE, WOOD BASEBOARD. THE INTERIOR BEARING

WALL MAY BE PENETRATED WITH AN ADDITIONAL OPENING UP TO 6'–0" WIDE, BUT THE LENGTH OF WALL AT EITHER END MUST BE AT LEAST 3'–6" LONG. THE ENTRY TO THE SPACE MUST BE CLOSED OFF WITH A DOOR. THE PLASTER CEILING IS JUST BELOW THE CONCRETE BEAMS OF THE FLOOR ABOVE, AND IS 10'–0" A.F.F. A NEW CENTRAL HVAC SYSTEM HAS BEEN INSTALLED; TO ACCOMMODATE SUPPLY DUCTWORK. A 1'–0" DEEP BY 2'–0" WIDE (MIN. DIMENSION) MUST BE PLACED ALONG THE EXTERIOR WALLS. PLUMBING FIXTURES MUST BE PLACED WITHIN 8'–0" OF THE DESIGNATED PIPE CHASES.

CHANGES TO THE EXTERIOR OF THE BUILDING ARE NOT PERMITTED. THE BASIC PROVISIONS OF STANDARD REGIONAL BUILDING CODES, INCLUDING THOSE PROVISIONS RELATED TO BARRIER–FREE ACCESS AND DESIGN, SHALL BE COMPLIED WITH.

KEY PLAN

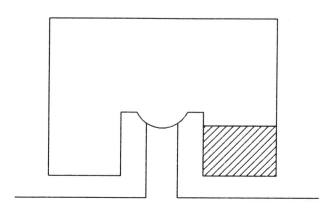

SECOND FLOOR

BASEMENT

BUILDING SECTION

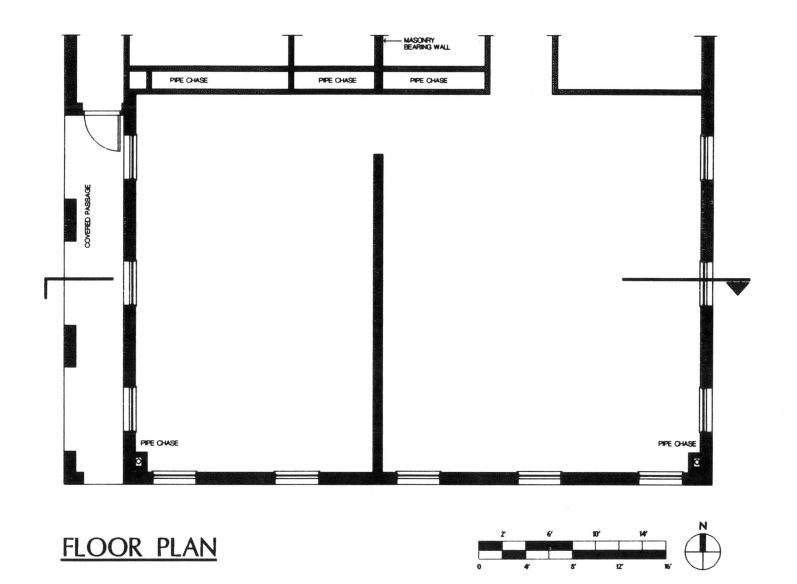

MASONRY
BEARING WALL

PIPE CHASE   PIPE CHASE   PIPE CHASE

COVERED PASSAGE

PIPE CHASE

PIPE CHASE

FLOOR PLAN

2'   6'   10'   14'

0   4'   8'   12'   16'

N

BUILDING
SHELL

1C

BUILDING DESCRIPTION

THIS TURN–OF–THE–CENTURY BOAT HOUSE IS SITED ON A RIVER DRIVE IN A PARK–LIKE SETTING. IT IS OF "ORDINARY" CONSTRUCTION. THE LOWER LEVEL WILL CONTINUE TO BE USED FOR ROWING SPORTS, AND WILL BE ENTERED ONLY FROM THE EXTERIOR, ON THE RIVER (EAST) SIDE OF THE BUILDING. THE COMBINATION HIP/GABLE ROOF IS SHINGLED WITH SLATE. ALL WINDOWS HAVE SILLS AT 3'–0" AFF, AND ALL DOORS AND WINDOWS HAVE HEADS AT 10'–0" AFF (DOORS AND RECENTLY INSTALLED SLIDING GLASS DOORS HAVE TRANSOMS OVER 7'–0" OPERATING DOORS). ALL OPERATING WINDOWS ARE DOUBLE HUNG; THE TWO PROJECTING BAY WINDOWS HAVE FIXED GLASS CENTER SECTIONS.

THE FLOOR IS THE ORIGINAL OAK PARQUET. THE WALL SURFACES ARE PLASTER WITH A 7" HIGH WOOD BASEBOARD. THE CEILING IS PLASTER, THE FLAT PART OF WHICH IS 12'–0" AFF; SEE THE REFLECTED CEILING PLAN FOR HEIGHT VARIATIONS IN THE CENTER BAY. A NEW HVAC SYSTEM WILL PROVIDE HEATING AND COOLING THROUGH FORCED AIR DUCTWORK ABOVE THE CEILING. PLUMBING WASTE AND SUPPLY LINES ARE CONTAINED IN THE DESIGNATED CHASES AND TIGHT AGAINST THE SOUTH WALL OF THE BUILDING, JUST BELOW THE FIRST FLOOR JOISTS. FLUSH FIXTURES (SUCH AS TOILETS AND URINALS) MUST BE PLACED WITHIN 7'–6" OF A PIPE CHASE OR THE SOUTH WALL OF THE BUILDING. ALL OTHER FIXTURES MUST BE PLACED WITHIN 10'–6" OF A PIPE CHASE OR THE SOUTH WALL OF THE BUILDING.

CHANGES TO THE EXTERIOR OF THE BUILDING ARE NOT PERMITTED. THE BASIC PROVISIONS OF STANDARD REGIONAL BUILDING CODES, INCLUDING THOSE PROVISIONS RELATED TO BARRIER–FREE ACCESS AND DESIGN, SHALL BE COMPLIED WITH.

SITE PLAN

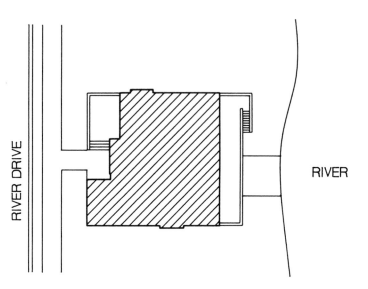

RIVER DRIVE

RIVER

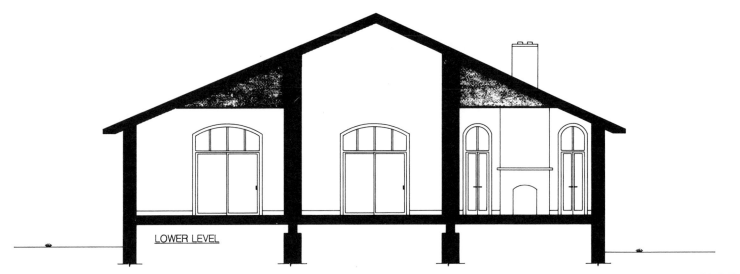

LOWER LEVEL

BUILDING SECTION

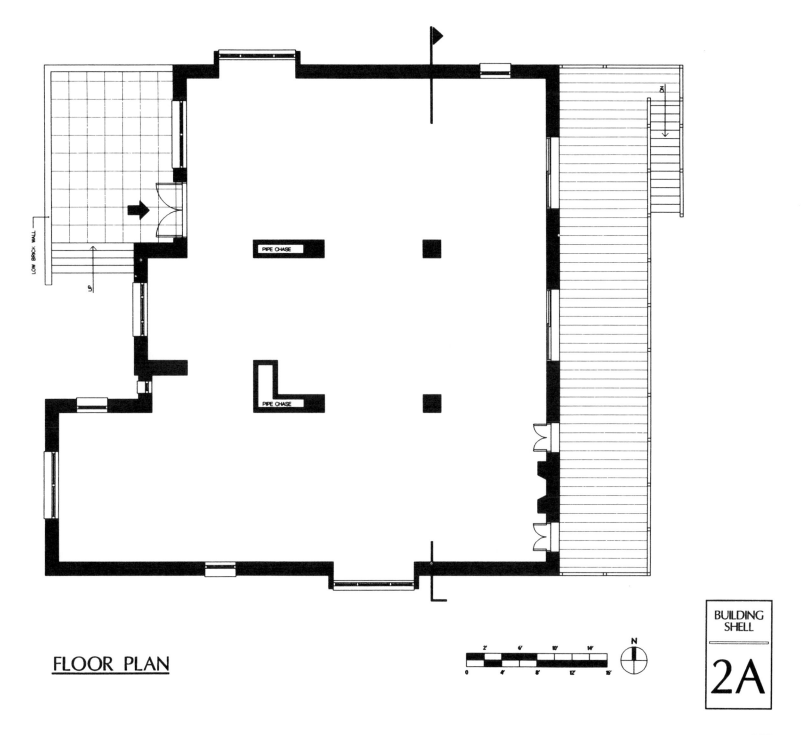

FLOOR PLAN

LOW BRICK WALL

PIPE CHASE

PIPE CHASE

BUILDING
SHELL

2A

N

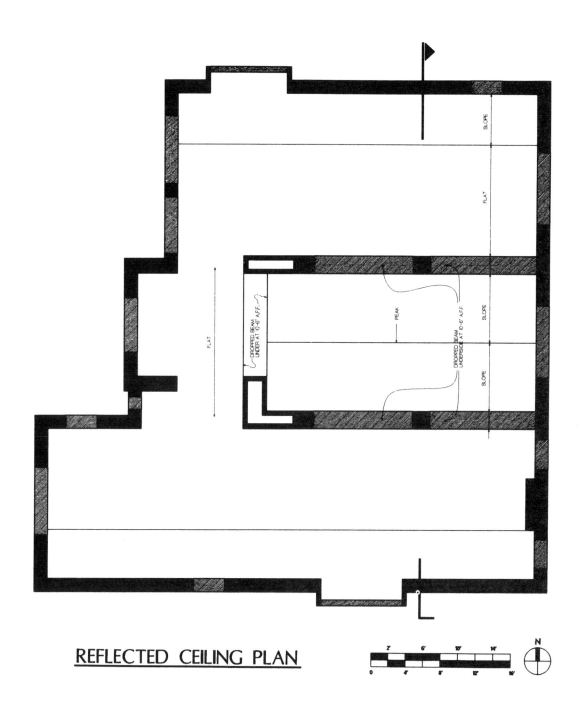

REFLECTED CEILING PLAN

REFLECTED
CEILING
PLAN

2A
RC

147

BUILDING DESCRIPTION

THIS 1980's BUILDING IS PART OF A SUBURBAN OFFICE PARK CONSISTING OF MANY SMALL AND MEDIUM SIZED ONE AND TWO STORY BUILDINGS IN A GREEN CAMPUS SETTING. THE BUILDINGS ARE OF LOAD BEARING STEEL STUD AND ROOF TRUSS CONSTRUCTION, WITH THE GROUND FLOORS OF SLAB-ON-GRADE CONCRETE, AND THE EXTERIOR WALLS SHEATHED AND SURFACED WITH BRICK VENEER. THIS PARTICULAR BUILDING IS A ONE STORY STRUCTURE WITH A SHINGLED, INTERSECTING CENTER RIDGE ROOF, AND A SUSPENDED 2' X 2' LAY-IN ACOUSTIC TILE CEILING SET AT 8'-6" A.F.F. THE 3'-0" WIDE (FIXED) AND THE 6'-0" WIDE (SLIDER) WINDOWS HAVE SILLS SET A 2'-6" A.F.F.; THE SLIDING GLASS DOOR (6'-0" WIDE), HINGED DOORS AND ALL WINDOWS HAVE HEAD AT 8'-0" A.F.F.

INTERIOR WALL SURFACES ARE PAINTED GYPSUM WALL BOARD WITH 4" HIGH STRAIGHT VINYL BASE. HVAC EQUIPMENT AND DUCTWORK ARE CONCEALED ABOVE THE CEILING. PLUMBING SUPPLY AND WASTE LINES ARE CONTAINED IN THE TWO IDENTIFIED PIPE CHASES AND IN THE TWO EXPOSED PIPE CLUSTERS IN THE WESTERN PORTION OF THE BUILDING (THESE CLUSTERS MUST BE ENCLOSED IN A CHASE OR INCORPORATED INTO PARTITION WORK). PLUMBING FIXTURES MUST BE PLACED WITHIN 9'-0" OF EXISTING SOIL STACKS.

IN CONSULTATION WITH AND THE CONCURRENCE OF THE DEVELOPER's ARCHITECT, VERY MODEST EXTERIOR CHANGES, SUCH AS DOOR AND WINDOW LOCATIONS, MAY BE MADE. THE BASIC PROVISIONS OF STANDARD REGIONAL BUILDING CODES, INCLUDING THOSE PROVISIONS RELATED TO BARRIER-FREE ACCESS AND DESIGN, SHALL BE COMPLIED WITH.

SITE PLAN

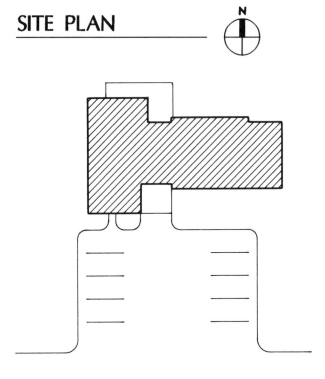

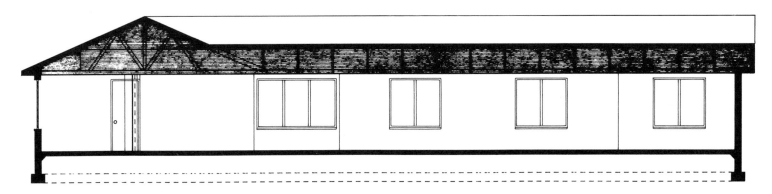

BUILDING SECTION

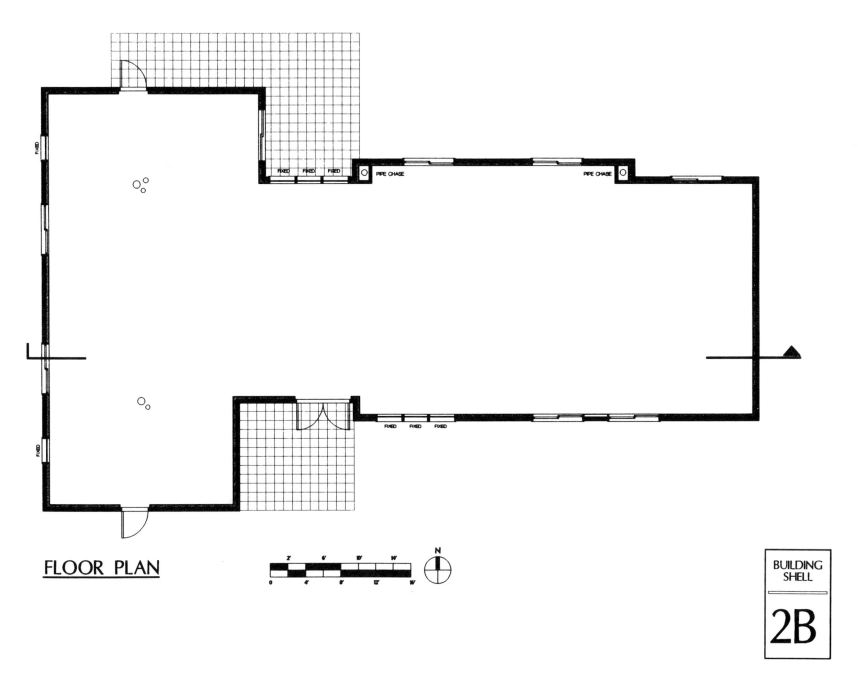

FLOOR PLAN

FIXED

FIXED   FIXED   FIXED

PIPE CHASE

PIPE CHASE

FIXED

FIXED   FIXED   FIXED

2'   6'   10'   14'

0   4'   8'   12'   16'

N

BUILDING
SHELL

2B

BUILDING DESCRIPTION

THIS SPACE IS AT THE END OF ONE WING OF A TYPICAL FLOOR OF A LARGE, URBAN CORE OFFICE BUILDING CONSTRUCTED DURING THE FIRST DECADE OF THE CENTURY IN THE GRAND MANNER OF THE BEAUX ARTS TRADITION. AS WAS TYPICAL OF THE PERIOD. IT IS OF STEEL FRAME CONSTRUCTION AND REINFORCED CONCRETE FLOORS, WITH UNUSUALLY HEAVY, LIMESTONE CLAD, MASONRY WALLS. ALL OF THE WINDOWS ARE DOUBLE HUNG, WITH SILLS AT 2'-6" A.F.F., AND HEADS AT 9'-6" A.F.F.

THE EXISTING FLOORS ARE BARE CONCRETE. THE INTERIOR WALLS ARE PLASTER WITH A 9" HIGH WOOD BASEBOARD. THE ORIGINAL CEILING HAS BEEN RE-MOVED, AND A NEW SUSPENDED LAY-IN TYPE ACOUSTIC TILE CEILING WILL BE INSTALLED AT 10'-0" A.F.F. THE DUCTWORK OF A RECENT VINTAGE, CENTRAL HVAC SYSTEM WILL BE CONCEALED ABOVE THE SUS-PENDED CEILING, EXCEPT FOR ONE MAJOR DUCT TRUNKLINE, SHOWN ON THE REFLECTED CEILING PLAN, WHICH WILL REQUIRE A CEILING HEIGHT OF NOT MORE THAN 8'-9" A.F.F.; PARTITIONS AND CEILING CONFIGURATION MUST ACCOMMODATE THE LOWER-THAN-NORMAL DUCT. ALL PLUMBING FIXTURES MUST BE PLACED WITHIN 8'-6" OF THE TWO PIPE CHASES ADJACENT TO THE FREE STANDING COLUMNS OR THE 3 "X 'D" OUT MECHANICAL SHAFTS BETWEEN THE EAST DEMISING WALL AND THE BUILDING's FIRE STAIR. THE DOTTED PARTITION SHOWN AT THE EAST EDGE OF THE SPACE INDICATES WHERE THE ACQUIRED SPACE ENDS; A DEMISING PARTITION MUST BE PLACED THERE, WITH AN ENTRANCE DOOR TO THE SPACE PLACED AS DESIRED WITHIN THAT PARTITION.

CHANGES TO THE EXTERIOR OF THE BUILDING ARE NOT PERMITTED. THE BASIC PROVISIONS OF STANDARD REGIONAL BUILDING CODES, INCLUDING THOSE PRO-VISIONS RELATED TO BARRIER-FREE ACCESS AND DESIGN, SHALL BE COMPLIED WITH.

SEE REFLECTED CEILING PLAN FOR ADDITIONAL INFOR-MATION.

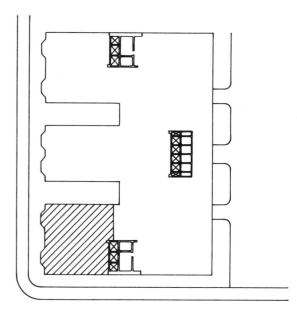

BUILDING SECTION

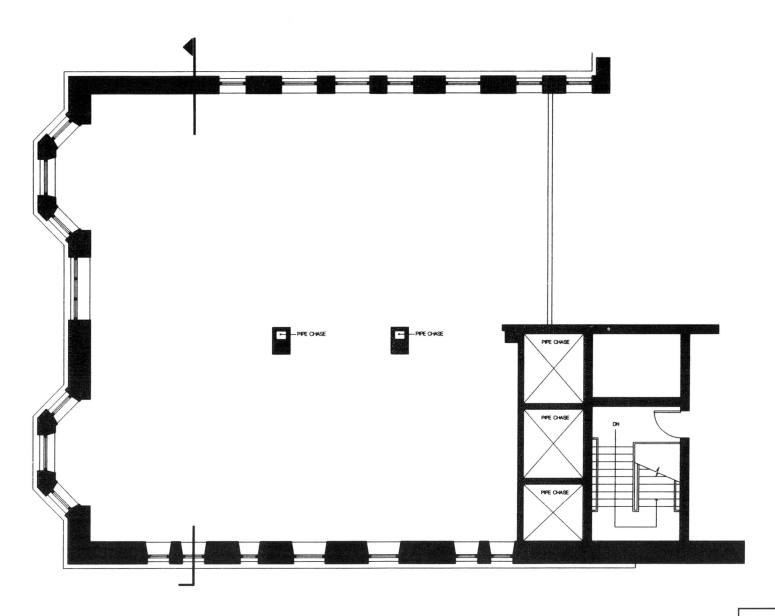

FLOOR PLAN

BUILDING
SHELL

2C

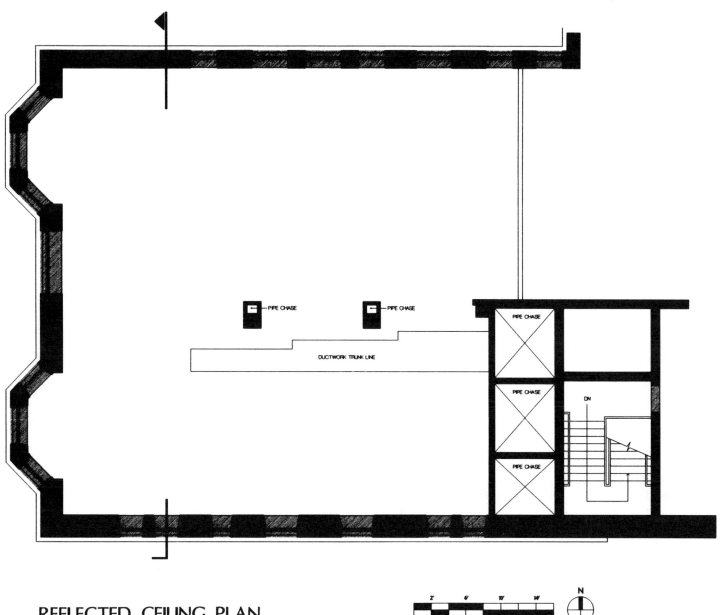

PIPE CHASE

PIPE CHASE

PIPE CHASE

PIPE CHASE

PIPE CHASE

DUCTWORK TRUNK LINE

DN

REFLECTED CEILING PLAN

N

BUILDING DESCRIPTION

THIS FORMER BRANCH BANK FACILITY IS OF LIGHT STEEL FRAME CONSTRUCTION, WITH LOAD BEARING STEEL STUD EXTERIOR WALLS FACED WITH 4" (NOMINAL) BRICK VENEER, WHICH PROJECTS ABOVE THE ESSENTIALLY FLAT ROOF, CREATING A CAPPED PARAPET WALL. DECORATIVE SQUARE COLUMN COVERS OCCUR AT 10'-0" INTERVALS WHERE THE GLAZING IS CONTINUOUS. THIS RECENTLY CONSTRUCTED BUILDING IS CONTEXTUALLY APPROPRIATE IN ITS COMMERCIAL SETTING AND IS ARCHITECTURALLY PLEASING, BUT HAS NO ARCHITECTURAL SIGNIFICANCE. THE BANK'S VAULT AND OTHER INTERIOR PARTITIONS HAVE BEEN REMOVED WITH THE EXCEPTION OF THE MECHANICAL ROOM, WHICH IS TO REMAIN. THE DRIVE-IN TELLER'S WINDOW ON THE NORTH WALL HAS BEEN REPLACED BY A BAY WINDOW, SIMILAR IN APPEARANCE TO THE OTHER COMMERCIAL ALUMINUM WINDOWS. WINDOW SILLS ARE 2'-6" A.F.F., AND HEADS ARE AT 8'-6" A.F.F.

THE FLOOR IS AN EXPOSED CONCRETE SLAB-ON-GRADE. THE INTERIOR WALL AND COLUMN SURFACES ARE PAINTED GYPSUM WALL BOARD, WITH 4" HIGH STRAIGHT VINYL BASE. THE ORIGINAL ACOUSTIC TILE CEILING HAS BEEN REMOVED AND SHALL BE REPLACED BY A SUSPENDED SYSTEM WITH ACOUSTIC TILE AND/OR GYPSUM WALL BOARD, TILE SIZE AND STYLE IS AT THE DESIGNER'S DISCRETION. THE MAXIMUM CEILING HEIGHT IS 9'-0" A.F.F. ALL HVAC DUCTWORK SHALL BE CONCEALED ABOVE THE CEILING. ALL PLUMBING FIXTURES MUST BE PLACED WITHIN 10'-0" OF THE NORTH WALL OF THE BUILDING, OR WITHIN 10'-0" OF EITHER OR BOTH OF THE FREE-STANDING INTERNAL COLUMNS. THE EXISTING ENTRANCE VESTIBULE SHALL REMAIN INTACT.

CHANGES TO THE EXTERIOR OF THE BUILDING ARE NOT PERMITTED. THE BASIC PROVISIONS OF STANDARD REGIONAL BUILDING CODES, INCLUDING THE PROVISIONS RELATED TO BARRIER-FREE ACCESS AND DESIGN SHALL BE COMPLIED WITH.

SITE PLAN

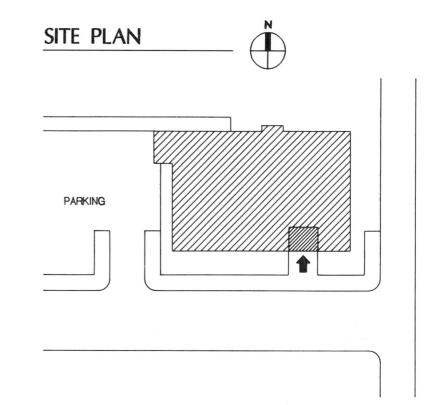

PARKING

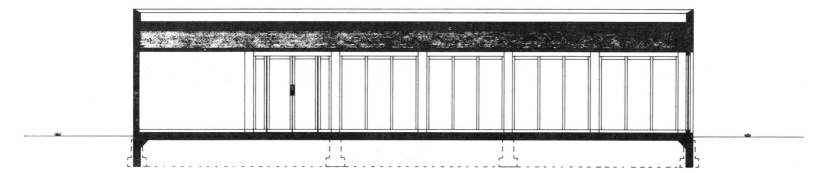

BUILDING SECTION

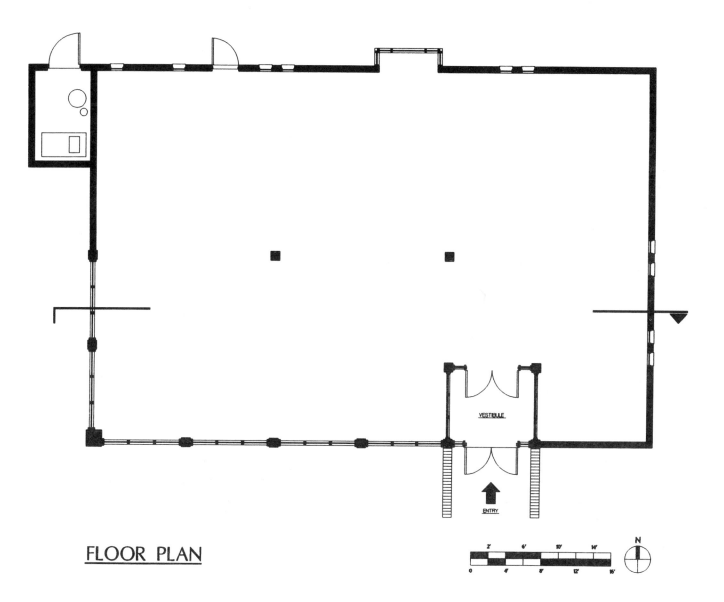

FLOOR PLAN

VESTIBULE

ENTRY

N

BUILDING
SHELL

2S

BUILDING DESCRIPTION

THIS ONE STORY SAVINGS BANK BUILDING OF CONTEM-PORARY DESIGN IN AN URBAN RESIDENTIAL SETTING, IS OF 1960's VINTAGE. ITS EXTERIOR BEARING WALLS ARE OF BRICK VENEERED STEEL STUDS, AND THE CLEAR SPAN ROOF IS FRAMED WITH LIGHT STEEL TRUSSES; THE FLOOR CONSTRUCTION IS SLAB-ON-GRADE. THE BUILDING SECTION INDICATES THE GENERAL CHARACTER OF THE SLOPED HIP ROOF WHICH COVERS THE BUILDING. THE SIDELIGHT WINDOWS ADJACENT TO THE MAIN ENTRANCE DOOR, AND THE WINDOWS ON THE WEST WALL OF THE PATIO, HAVE SILLS AT 6" A.F.F.; ALL OTHER WINDOW SILLS ARE 2'-8" A.F.F., ALL WINDOW HEADS AND DOOR HEADS, ARE AT 8'-0" A.F.F.

THE INTERIOR WALL SURFACES ARE PAINTED GYPSUM WALLBOARD WITH 4" HIGH STRAIGHT VINLY BASE. IT IS EXPECTED THAT A NEW SUSPENDED ACOUSTIC TILE CEILING WILL BE INSTALLED AT 9'-6" A.F.F. (MAXIMUM HEIGHT); THE SPECIFIC SIZE AND TYPE OF CEILING MATERIAL HAS NOT YET BEEN SELECTED.

HVAC EQUIPMENT IS HOUSED IN THE SMALL MECH-ANICAL ROOM WHICH IS ACCESSED FROM THE EXTERIOR ON THE NORTH WALL; ALL DUCTWORK SHALL BE CONCEALED ABOVE THE SUSPENDED CEILING. PLUMBING SUPPLY AND WASTE LINES ARE CONTAINED IN THE THREE EXPOSED PIPE CLUSTERS IN THE CENTER OF THE BUILDING (THESE CLUSTERS MUST BE ENCLOSED IN A CHASE OR INCORPORATED INTO PARTITION WORK). PLUMBING FIXTURES MUST BE PLACED WITHIN 10'-0" OF EXISTING SOIL STACKS. THE EXISTING ENTRANCE VESTIBULE MUST REMAIN INTACT.

CHANGES TO THE BUILDING'S EXTERIOR MAY ONLY BE MADE TO THE NORTH WALL OF THE BUILDING, ALTHOUGH THE LOCATION OF THE SECONDARY EXIT DOOR AND THE MECHANICAL ROOM MAY NOT BE CHANGED. THE BASIC PROVISIONS OF STANDARD REGIONAL BUILDING CODES, INCLUDING THOSE PRO-VISIONS RELATED TO BARRIER-FREE ACCESS AND DESIGN, SHALL BE COMPLIED WITH.

SITE PLAN

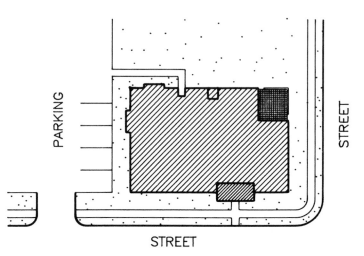

STREET

PARKING

STREET

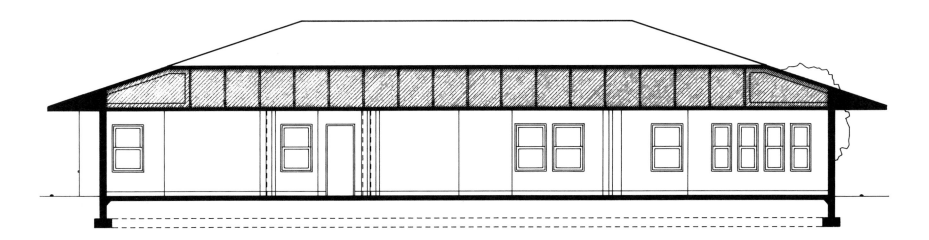

BUILDING SECTION

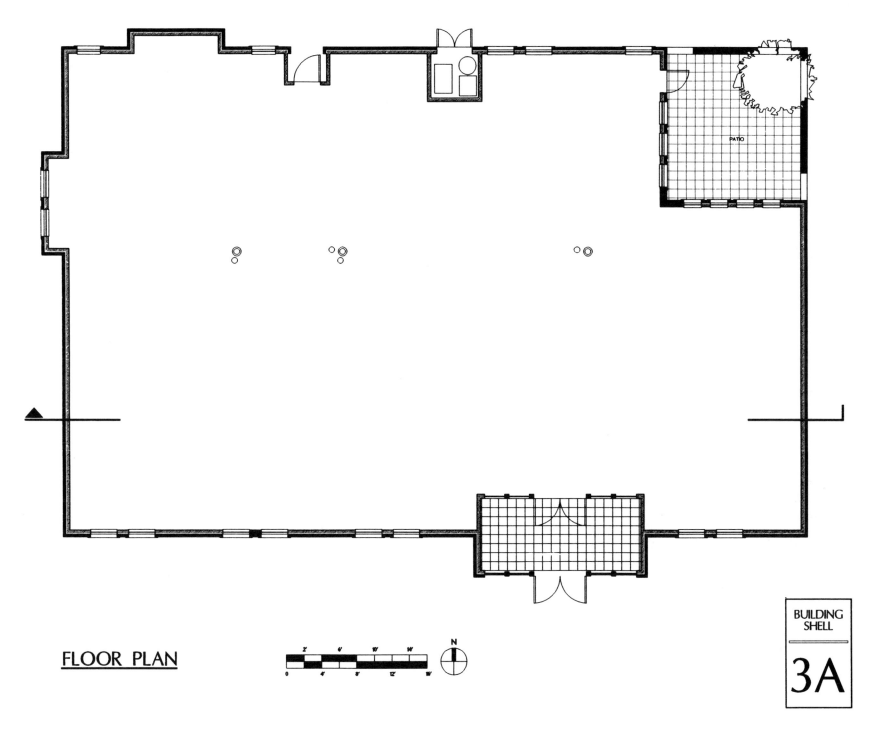

PATIO

<u>FLOOR PLAN</u>

N

BUILDING
SHELL

3A

157

BUILDING DESCRIPTION

THIS BARN STRUCTURE OF UNKNOWN VINTAGE IS IN A ONCE–RURAL, BUT NOW–SUBURBAN SETTING, FACING ON A HEAVILY TRAVELLED COMMERCIAL STREET. THE REMAINING ORIGINAL STONE PORTION FACES THE STREET, AND THE BACK PORTION, RECONSTRUCTED WITH WOOD FRAME, FACES A WOODED REAR YARD WITH A STREAM AT THE FAR END. THE FIELD STONE WALLS HAVE NEVER BEEN FINISHED ON THE INTERIOR, AND THE FRAME WALLS OF THE REAR HAVE A BOARD AND BATTEN EXTERIOR WITH RECENTLY INSULATED IN–FILL AND HARDBOARD FINISH ON THE INTERIOR. THE ROOF STRUCTURE, INTERIOR COLUMNS AND FLOOR/LOFT STRUCTURES ARE ALL OF HEAVY TIMBER CONSTRUCTION, NONE OF WHICH HAVE BEEN CLOSED–IN. THE ORIGINAL ROOF, A TRADITIONAL GABLE–END RIDGE ROOF, IS INTACT AND COVERS THE ENTIRE STRUCTURE. THE LOWER LEVEL CAN BE ENTERED ONLY FROM THE EXTERIOR (ON THE NORTH WALL), AND WILL BE USED EXCLUSIVELY FOR STORAGE AND UTILITY PURPOSES ONLY. THE UPPER LOFT LEVEL WILL BE RESERVED FOR FUTURE EXPANSION PURPOSES. WINDOWS IN THE ORIGINAL STRUCTURE ARE WOOD DOUBLE HUNG, WITH A 3'–0" SILL A.F.F. AND A 9'–0" HEAD A.F.F. IN THE SOUTH WALL, AND A 5'–0" SILL A.F.F. AND AN 8'–0" HEAD A.F.F. IN THE EAST AND WEST WALLS.

WINDOWS OF APPROPRIATE SIZE, STYLE AND PLACEMENT SHALL BE INSTALLED IN THE WOOD FRAME WALLS OF THE ADDITION. EXISTING DOOR OPENINGS SHALL BE RETAINED AS SUCH, OR CONVERTED TO WINDOW OPENINGS. THE TWO UNENCLOSED OPENINGS IN THE EXISTING MASONRY WALLS SHALL BECOME WINDOW OPENINGS, WITH SILL AND HEAD HEIGHTS TO BE DETERMINED BY INTERIOR USE.

THE EXISTING FLOOR IS ROUGH WOOD PLANK. THERE ARE NO FINISHED CEILINGS; THE HEIGHT TO THE UNDERSIDE OF THE LOFT BEAMS ABOVE IS 12'–0" A.F.F. FOR THIS FIRST PHASE OF RECONSTRUCTION, ALL HVAC EQUIPMENT AND DUCTWORK WILL BE CONTAINED IN THE BASEMENT. ALL PLUMBING FIXTURES MUST BE PLACED WITHIN 8'–0" OF THE MAIN EAST AND WEST WALLS.

EXCEPT AS NOTED ABOVE CONCERNING NEW WINDOW OPENINGS, CHANGES TO THE EXTERIOR OF THE BUILDING ARE NOT PERMITTED. THE BASIC PROVISIONS OF STANDARD REGIONAL BUILDING CODES, INCLUDING THOSE PROVISIONS RELATED TO BARRIER–FREE ACCESS AND DESIGN, SHALL BE COMPLIED WITH.

SITE PLAN

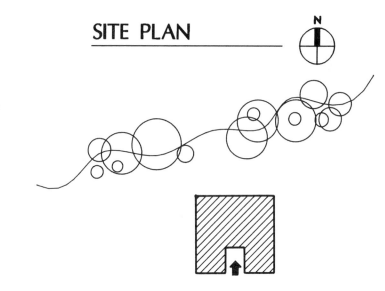

BUILDING SECTION

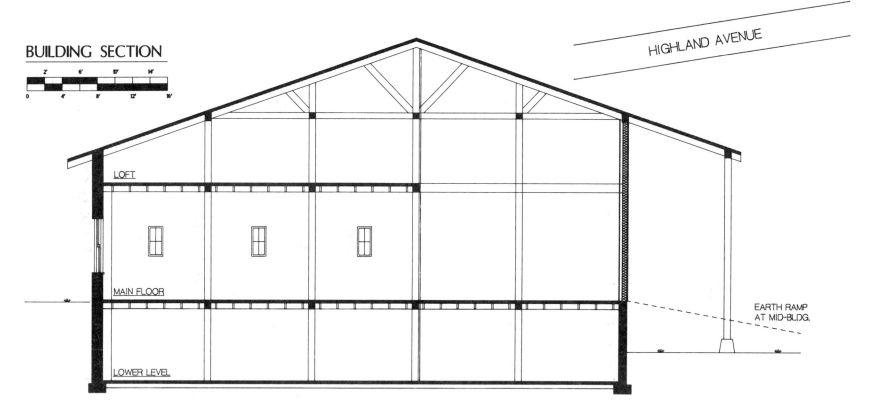

LOFT

MAIN FLOOR

LOWER LEVEL

HIGHLAND AVENUE

EARTH RAMP AT MID-BLDG.

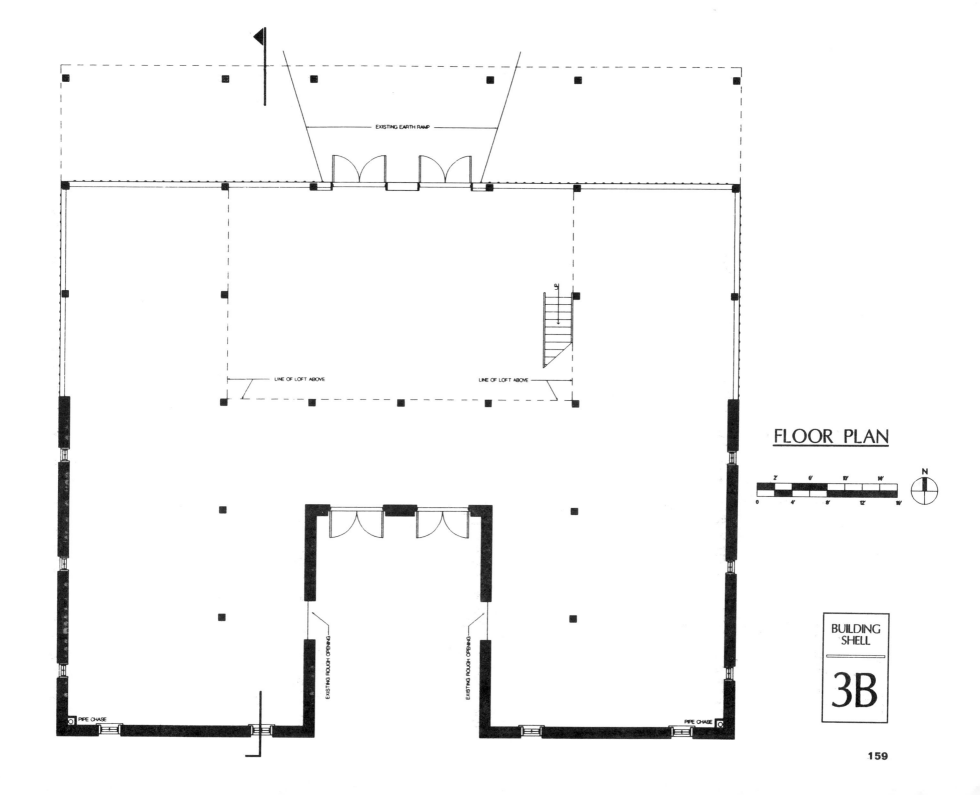

FLOOR PLAN

EXISTING EARTH RAMP

LINE OF LOFT ABOVE   LINE OF LOFT ABOVE

UP

EXISTING ROUGH OPENING

EXISTING ROUGH OPENING

PIPE CHASE   PIPE CHASE

BUILDING
SHELL

3B

159

BUILDING DESCRIPTION

THIS SPACE IS ON A TYPICAL FLOOR OF A RECENTLY BUILT, SUBURBAN HI-RISE OFFICE BUILDING. IT IS OF STEEL FRAME CONSTRUCTION, WITH A CENTRAL SERVICE CORE AND AN EXTERIOR WALL OF BRICK SPANDRELS AND NON-OPERATING ALUMINUM RIBBON WINDOWS WHICH ARE BROKEN BY BRICK PANELS AT THE BUILDING's CORNERS. THE WINDOW SILL IS AT 2'-6" A.F.F. AND THE HEAD IS AT 8'-0" A.F.F.

THE EXISTING FLOOR IS CONCRETE. THE INTERIOR WALL SURFACES ARE PAINTED GYPSUM WALL BOARD, WITH 4" HIGH STRAIGHT VINYL BASE. THE CEILING IS AN INTEGRATED 2' X 4' LAY-IN SUSPENDED ACOUSTIC TILE ASSEMBLAGE WITH LAY-IN FLUORESCENT LIGHTING FIXTURES WHICH ARE ALSO THE PRIMARY HVAC SUPPLY

SOURCE; THE CEILING IS SET AT 8'-6" A.F.F. ALL HVAC EQUIPMENT AND DUCTWORK IS CONCEALED ABOVE THE CEILING. ALL PLUMBING FIXTURES MUST BE PLACED WITHIN 10'-0" OF THE FREE-STANDING WET COLUMNS OR ANY OF THE 3 "X 'D" OUT MECHANICAL SHAFTS ADJACENT TO THE EAST DEMISING WALL.

CHANGES TO THE EXTERIOR OF THE BUILDING ARE NOT PERMITTED. THE BASIC PROVISIONS OF STANDARD REGIONAL BUILDING CODES, INCLUDING THOSE PRO-VISIONS RELATED TO BARRIER-FREE ACCESS AND DESIGN, SHALL BE COMPLIED WITH.

SEE REFLECTED CEILING PLAN FOR ADDITIONAL INFORMATION.

SITE PLAN

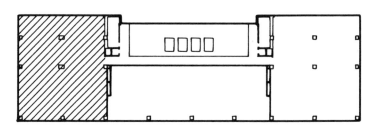

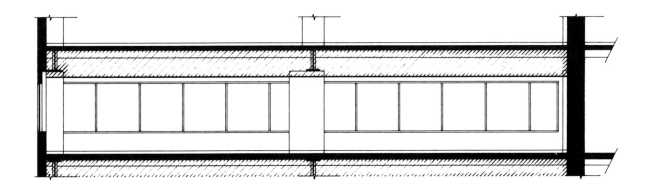

BUILDING SECTION

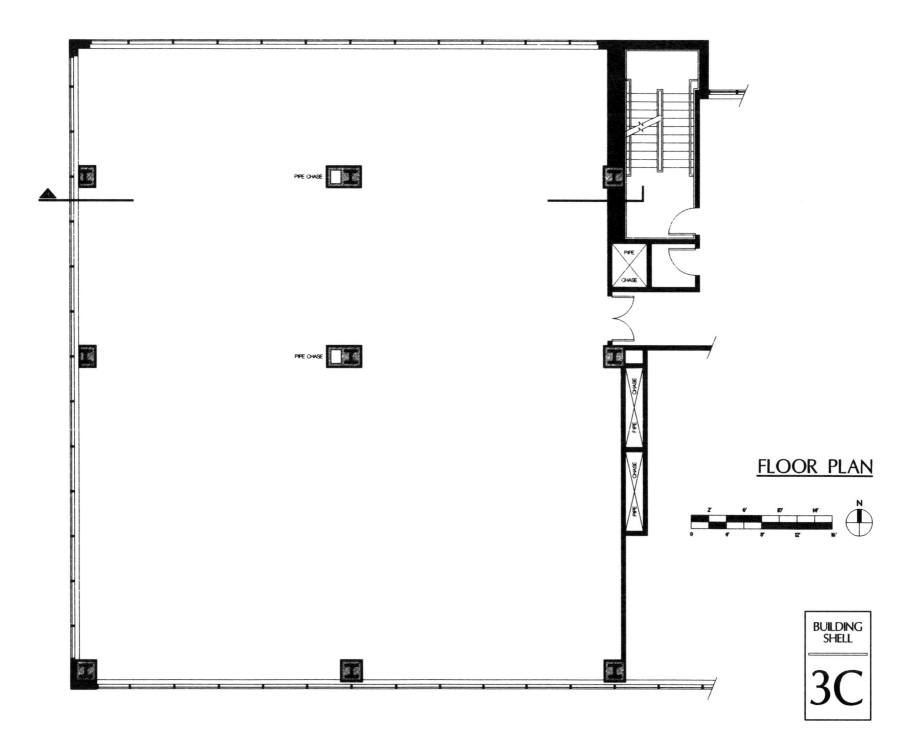

PIPE CHASE

PIPE CHASE

PIPE CHASE

PIPE CHASE

PIPE CHASE

FLOOR PLAN

N

2' 6' 10' 14'

0 4' 8' 12' 16'

BUILDING
SHELL

3C

161

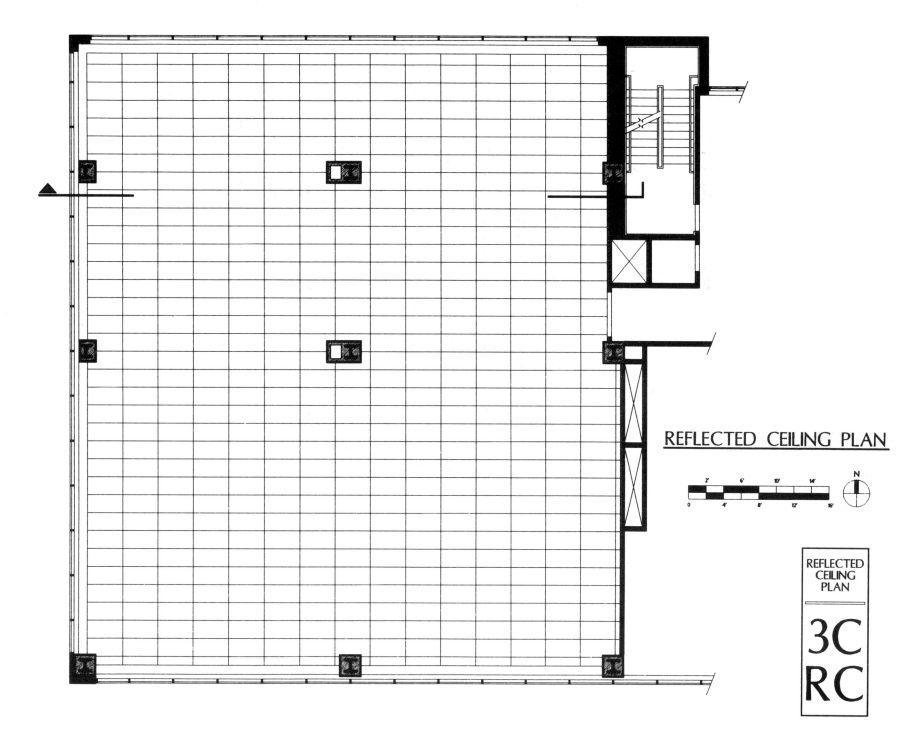

REFLECTED CEILING PLAN

2'   6'   10'   14'
0   4'   8'   12'   16'

N

REFLECTED
CEILING
PLAN

3C
RC

163

BIBLIOGRAPHY

This bibliography is a compilation of the recommended reading lists accompanying each chapter. It is separated into *reference* sources (denoted by an asterisk) and *reading* materials. The reference sources provide in-depth information related to basic and recurring planning and design issues and questions. The reading materials are intended to develop knowledge and skills in general planning and design areas and in some peripheral to space planning. One's personal selections in the reading areas will depend heavily upon previous background and experience.

A concerted effort has been made to keep this list to essential books only. It is suggested that one prioritize his/her planned reading efforts while using this book. More specifically, concentrate on the space planning issues and let the less critical "influencing factors," such as plumbing, acoustics, and interior construction, wait until later.

Many other worthwhile texts deal with space planning and related information and skills. An excellent source for locating additional reading related to space planning is the Interior Design Educators Council (IDEC) "Comprehensive Bibliography for Interior Design" available in many libraries; it can also be purchased directly from IDEC by writing to that organization at 14252 Culver Drive, Irvine, CA 92714.

1. Allen, Edward. *How Buildings Work: The Natural Order of Architecture.* New York: Oxford University Press, 1980.

*2. American National Standards Institute. *Specifications for Making Buildings and Facilities Accessible to and Usable by Physically Handicapped People.* American National Standards Institute, 1430 Broadway, New York, NY 10018, 1980. [Purchase directly]

3. Beranek, Leo L. and Stone, Geraldine, ed. *Acoustics and Architecture.* Melbourne, FL: R.E. Kreiger Publishing Co., Inc., 1979.

*4. Ching, Frank. *Architectural Graphics.* New York: Van Nostrand Reinhold, 1975.

*5. ———. *Building Construction Illustrated.* New York: Van Nostrand Reinhold, 1975.

*6. ———. *Interior Design Illustrated.* New York: Van Nostrand Reinhold, 1987.

7. Deasy, C.M. and Laswell, Thomas. *Designing Places for People.* New York: Watson-Guptill Publications, 1985.

*8. DiChiara, Joseph and Callender, John H., eds. *Time-Savers Standards for Building Types.* New York: McGraw Hill, 1990.

9. Egan, M. David. *Architectural Acoustics.* New York: McGraw Hill, 1988.

10. ———. *Concepts in Architectural Lighting.* New York: McGraw Hill, 1983.

*11. Groom, James N. and Harkness, Sarah. *Building Without Barriers for the Disabled.* New York: Watson-Guptill Publications, 1976.

12. Hall, Edward T. *Hidden Dimension.* New York: Doubleday & Co., 1966.

*13. Illuminating Engineering Society. *I.E.S. Lighting Handbook: Student Volume.* New York: Illuminating Engineering Society, 1980.

14. Kleeman, Walter. *The Challenge of Interior Design.* Boston: CBI Publishing, 1981.

15. Kira, Alexander. *The Bathroom.* New York: Viking Press, Inc., 1976.

16. Kirkpatrick, James M. *The AutoCAD Book.* New York: Macmillan, 1992.

17. Laseau, Paul. *Graphic Thinking for Architects and Designers.* New York: Van Nostrand Reinhold, 1980.

18. Lockard, William K. *Design Drawing.* Tucson: Pepper Publications, 1982.

19. Stein, Benjamin, Reynolds and McGuiness. *Mechanical and Electrical Equipment for Buildings.* New York: John Wiley & Sons, Inc., 1986.

*20. Panero, Julius and Zelnik, Martin. *Human Dimension and Interior Space.* New York: Watson-Guptill Publications, 1979.

21. Pena, William. *Problem Seeking.* Washington: CRSS/American Institute of Architects, 1987.

22. Pile, John F. *Interior Design.* New York: Harry N. Abrams, Inc., 1988.

*23. Ramsey, Charles G. and Sleeper, Harold R. *Architectural Graphic Standards.* New York: John Wiley and Sons, Inc., 1988.

*24. Reznikoff, S.C., *Specifications for Commercial Interiors.* New York: Watson-Guptill Publications, 1979.

*25. ———. *Interior Graphics and Design Standards,* Watson-Guptill Publications, 1986.

26. Smith, Fran K. and Bertolone, Fred J. *Bringing Interiors to Light.* New York: Watson-Guptill Publications, 1986.

27. Sommer, Robert, *Personal Space: The Behavioral Basis of Design.* New York: Prentice Hall, 1969.

28. Stonis, Richard E. and Pulgram, William L. *The Automated Office: A Guide for Architects and Interior Designers.* New York: Watson-Guptill Publications, 1984.

29. White, Edward. *Space Adjacency Analysis.* Tucson: Architectural Media Ltd., 1986.

30. ———. *Introduction to Architectural Programming.* Tucson: Architectural Media, Ltd., 1972.

31. Ziesel, Jon. *Inquiry by Design: Tools for Environment-Behavior Research.* Pacific Grove, CA: Brooks/Cole Publishing Co., 1981.

*32. Major Regional Building Codes:
BOCA—Building Officials and Code Administrators International
ICBO—International Conference of Building Officials
Life Safety Code of the National Fire Protection Association
National Building Code of Canada
National Fire Code of Canada
NBD—Basic/National Building Code
SBC—Standard Building Code
SBCCI—Southern Building Code Congress International
UBC—Uniform Building Code

Index